LifePlace

LifePlace

BIOREGIONAL THOUGHT AND PRACTICE

Robert L. Thayer, Jr.

University of California Press

Berkeley   Los Angeles   London

University of California Press
Berkeley and Los Angeles, California

University of California Press, Ltd.
London, England

Library of Congress Cataloging-in-Publication Data

Thayer, Robert L.
    LifePlace : bioregional thought and practice / Robert L. Thayer, Jr.
      p. cm.
    Includes bibliographical references and index.
    ISBN 0-520-21312-2 (alk. paper).—ISBN 0-520-23628-9 (pbk. :
  alk. paper)
    1. Bioregionalism. I. Title.
  GE43.T48   2003
  333.7'2—dc21   2002067880

Manufactured in the United States of America

12   11   10   09   08   07   06   05   04   03
10 9 8 7 6 5 4 3 2 1

The paper used in this publication meets the minimum requirements of
ANSI/NISO Z39.48–1992 (R 1997) *(Permanence of Paper).*⊛

For Lacey, Douglas, Stephanie, and Neal,
and for the life-place that has nurtured us.

Contents

Illustrations

Table

Preface

In the summer of 1973, I left Boulder, Colorado, to become an assistant professor at the University of California in Davis, an agricultural town in California's Great Central Valley. I had abandoned a place well known for its quality of life, scenic beauty, and network of stream corridors and trails. Boulder in 1973 was a healthy, outdoor-oriented community with a refreshingly changeable but sunny climate, where people wore hiking boots into restaurants. It was a place where glacial meltwater literally flowed from the tap.

I was leaving to become a "professor" (the word itself sounded exciting at age twenty-six). Following a trajectory similar to that of many college-educated young men and women before me, I was to forsake the obvious physiographic and cultural attractions of a popular city and region to follow the call of my profession—landscape architecture, particularly the academic variety—wherever it might take me. At the time, it seemed the natural thing to do. Wasn't this what was expected of me—to ignore what attachment I had developed to Boulder and, following the needs of my "career," to move to a flat, hot agricultural town in a region looking more like Oklahoma or Kansas than like mountains, coasts, golden-gated bridges, or wine country? But the University of California, Davis, was where the professional challenge and opportunity were, or so I thought. I was leaving the confines of private practice for the wide intellectual territory of academia. The idealized mental landscape of possibility glowed beyond the horizon and seemed to eclipse the beauty of the Boulder region as it receded in my rearview mirror.

Perhaps it was meant to be. Had I stayed in Boulder, I would not have written this book. But if Boulder was an affair with a flashy fashion model, the flat agricultural landscape near Davis was a mail-order spouse whom I would grow to appreciate, then love, over a long time. Love at first sight, however, it was not. I might have known it would be a rough transition when, on the day the van loaded my furniture in Boulder, my cat was hit and killed by a car in front of the house amid the frenzy of moving. Shortly after my arrival in Davis, a similar disaster struck when my dog, trying to follow me as I left for a Yosemite vacation, was hit and killed on the nearby four-lane highway. I could hardly bear such tragic symmetry on both sides of a major life move. As I questioned my own transient judgment and grieved for these lost companions, I paced the rows in the nearby agricultural field, nervously rehearsing my first lecture, perversely watching a distant fire advance toward town and secretly wishing that it were my new "academic job" that was burning up so that I could be released from this emotional hell and return to Boulder.

A short time later, exhausted by the terrors and delights of jump-starting a faculty career, I took a walk with friends out by the U.C. Davis airport. There ran Putah Creek, hemmed in by agricultural fields planed laser-flat by heavy machinery, deprived of all but the tiniest summer trickle of water by an upstream diversion dam, and invaded by weedy exotic species from other continents. Was this what I received in trade for the Rocky Mountains? Poor, bedraggled Putah Creek was the only "nearby nature" for ten miles all around me, and I could easily throw a stone across it.

I have now lived in this region—Putah Creek country and the community of Davis—for thirty years, much longer than I have lived anywhere else on earth. This is my life-place, my bioregion. This, I have concluded, is what Wes Jackson refers to as "becoming native to one's place."[1] In the past five years, this awareness has grown stronger and moved outward from the depths of my subconscious to become the central organizing principle of my work as a land planner and educator, and a rudimentary personal cosmology as well. Perhaps I have merely experienced a middle-age "passage"; we all must eventually settle down and accept life's imperfections. But I have discovered that this transformation is not unique to me. It is taking place in the hearts of millions of people nationwide, in hundreds of local groups, each focused on a watershed, a stream corridor, or some other natural feature worth defending. It is a fundamental and growing movement of considerable social importance, as groups strive to become one with the nature of a place. Gary Snyder calls it "reinhabitation"; Jerry Mander refers to it as the process of "relocalization." Some label it the "bioregional movement"; philosopher Albert Borgmann explains it as a necessary task of communal celebration in which we must finally settle down in the land, stop searching for a hyperreal elsewhere, and come to terms with nature and tradition.

Gradually, I have come to know and appreciate the significance of Putah Creek. In May 1980, I sat creekside in the sun by a tiny rapids and wrote my wedding vows. Years later, my wife and I often towed our three children in a bicycle trailer out past the sheep barns to the creek for picnics. In the past decade I have made numerous solo excursions up and down the creek, launching my small thirty-two-pound canoe near the spot where I first received such a poor impression in 1973. On the waterline, Putah Creek is a different world. It is not glacier meltwater; the hot temperatures, high nitrate loads, and low flows bring clumps of algae to the surface. But Putah Creek has shown me a biodiversity I have never experienced elsewhere. On the first few trips, I would paddle, drag over a beaver dam, or skid through a shallow gravel bar, stopping to identify the mammals, fish, or birds I saw and to record the sightings in a soggy field notebook. Soon I tired of stopping so frequently to write and just looked deeply instead. On each occasion, Putah Creek was a biotic profusion: great blue herons, green herons, and black-crowned night-herons; beaver; muskrat; otter; innumerable frogs; Swainson's, red-tailed, and various other hawks, an eagle or osprey on rare occasions; many species of fish, most of which were unfamiliar; intricate spiderwebs spanning the creek; vermilion dragonflies; strange crustaceans and crayfish crawling the creek bottom; once a coyote; several times a fox. During the drought years I imagined the mountain lion that had been sighted in the creek vicinity far from the mountains twenty miles upstream, but never actually saw her. There were pond turtles, lizards, snakes, and amphibians but always very few humans other than myself and perhaps a sole human companion to appreciate it all. In sum, an intricately complex community of life was hidden in the vestigial riparian corridor of Putah Creek as it transected the agricultural landscape of the Sacramento Valley bioregion.

On the days when I return from these local canoe pilgrimages, I revel in the fruits of experience that I have been able to harvest from what looked at first like such impoverished surroundings. I have worked with a group called the Putah Creek Council to increase the flow releases from the upstream diversion dam. Water purveyors and environmentalists have settled their differences to form the Lower Putah Creek Coordinating Committee. The Putah Creek Cafe is doing a brisk business in Winters, a local town west of here. There are the Putah Creek Crawdads, a group of gents who play acoustic music at the local fairs. Is a "Putah Creek" wine label or microbrewery next? I doubt it, but the escalating reverence on the part of our local community for this small, formerly degraded creek is intoxicating enough to the spirit. It is also representative of the hundreds, if not

Figure 0.1 Aerial photograph of Lower Putah Creek, by Mark Francis.

thousands, of similar grassroots watershed movements springing up all over the country. Like the floodwaters of many river basins, the increasing care and concern for our broader region have first flowed in the stream corridors and then overflowed to revitalize other dimensions of our sense of place.

Good things are happening here in this bioregion and out there in other bioregions as well. This book examines the implications of the bioregional movement from two viewpoints at once: from my personal immersion in the Putah and Cache Creek watersheds in the Sacramento Valley bioregion and also from the best academic scrutiny I can muster. In essence, I have written a book in which the concepts and promise of the bioregional idea are interbraided with a "tributary" of personal experience that originates from my life in this place. Or, to use a less pretentious metaphor, perhaps the book is like lacing a shoe, where subject and object cross back and forth, hopefully tying together securely at the end. After twenty-eight years as an academic, I can no longer feign the objectivity and detachment once so vehemently demanded of my genre; I am, indeed, deeply and personally immersed in my subject. The life-place concept in general and my own relationship to my bioregion in particular have fused, and I could not do justice to the reader without admitting this up front. With this approach to writing a book, I invest hope that readers are also ready to admit that we must all live in the world subjectively and that true knowledge can be gained only by a combined experience of inner and outer realities.

Ultimately, in addition to a desire to communicate the nature and potential of the bioregional idea, I have two very subjective goals for readers: to share with you my deepening attachment to my own bioregion—and to encourage you to explore and deeply attach yourself to yours.

Acknowledgments

I owe the body, mind, heart, and soul of this book in great part to others whose work preceded, paralleled, or assisted my own. Without the patient and persistent efforts of Doris Kretschmer, Laura Harger, Anne Canright, and other editors and affiliates of U.C. Press, readers would not be holding this book in their hands. From the two most pivotal figures of the bioregional movement, Gary Snyder and Peter Berg (whose term "life-place" I appreciatively borrowed for the title of this book), followed by the works of other thinkers and practitioners, came the intellectual foundation upon which I have tried to build. In nearly a decade of association with my colleagues and friends in U.C. Davis's Putah-Cache Bioregion Project—particularly David Robertson, Joyce Gutstein, Dennis Pendleton, Peter Moyle, Jake Mann, Jan Goggans, Amy Boyer, Dan Leroy, and Laurie Glover—I found ample inspiration and encouragement to complete this volume. And, finally, in the many volunteer bioregional groups active throughout the Putah and Cache Creek watersheds, the Sacramento Valley, and elsewhere, I discovered the true purpose for writing this book. To all of these individuals, groups, and others too numerous to mention here, I offer my sincere gratitude.

Introduction

BIOREGIONAL THINKING

Living-in-place means following the necessities and pleasures
of life as they are uniquely presented by a particular site, and
evolving ways to ensure long-term occupancy of that site. . . .
It is not, however, to be thought of as antagonistic to civilization,
in the more human sense of that word, but may be the only way
in which a truly civilized existence can be maintained.

PETER BERG AND RAYMOND DASMANN, 1978

Somewhere in the swirl of life, each of us ponders three essential questions: "Who am I?" "Where am I?" and "What am I supposed to do?" We
often consider the first question in isolation, as if it were the true key to
our existence—as if the matter of who we are could be resolved independ-
ently of the two remaining questions. But all three of these questions must
be answered in consort, as together they articulate the totality of the human condition. We do different things with varying degrees of understanding and purpose. We are born, live, feel, think, act, move, settle, and die. Questions of our existence and action are separable neither from each other nor
from place—but it is place that we have most often ignored.

(With this book, I wish to argue that without a fundamental realization
of the question "Where are we?" human meaning is not stable, and the
logic of our own being collapses.)Each of the three essential questions is
connected to the other two; to deeply comprehend *where* one is is also to
know *who* one is and to understand *what* needs to be done. As members
of *Homo sapiens* var. *"technoeconomicus,"* we live in a dominating culture that mistakenly expects us to resolve the puzzle of our own existence
through compartmentalizing our lives and separately examining each existential question. This approach has failed; many of us are more alienated
than ever before. Just past the turn of the millennium, we have all become,
in certain fundamental ways, homeless.

A number of factors have contributed to this "homeless" condition: the
Cartesian assumption of separation of mind from body; the evolution from
ecosystem-based to globally based economies; the drug trip of fossil fuel;
the substitution of mechanism for organicism; the dissolution of space and
time by electronic communication; and the erasure of uniquely placed cul-

ture by all of the above. We wander the postmodern landscape like hunter-gatherers, searching for bits and pieces of meaning, unconsciously emulating the atomized consumers of economists' elaborate models. Governments and transnational corporations expect us to substitute a shallow awareness of the entire globe for whatever deep wisdom and affection we might have had for a specific place. In the process of becoming postmodern, we have abandoned the notion of "home," and like innocent natives presented with beads and trinkets of shining luster and unfamiliar purpose, we have surrendered our former homelands to the new gods of consumerism, transience, shallow information, global communication, and ever-expanding technology. We are trained in schools and universities to "become" before we "locate." The ends of these hopeless wanderings, in terms of both purpose and place, very often elude us.

The question "Where are we?" has a deep, sustaining ring to it. It is a simple question with a deceptively complex answer. To some readers, we are where our address is—our street, city, county, state, and nation. To a few others, we are in some division of territory on earth, perhaps marked by a particular topography and climate. Many others might find the question absurd: How are we to answer? We are at many locations at different times. Planners, landscape architects, geographers, and others occupied with mapping, planning, or designing places are supposedly more aware of "where they are" than most—yet how deeply do any of us really know where we are?

The third question—"What am I supposed to do?"—is even less easily dismissed or trivially answered. When considered in relationship to the other two questions, it calls forth a host of corollary concerns about *how* we currently live and how we might live *best* in relation to the land we occupy. Do we live deeply within the land or shallowly upon it? In community with other living things or at their peril? Do we live in a manner that presumes permanence or broadcasts transitory detachment?

I have been a resident of the hot, fertile Sacramento Valley of California for about thirty years, yet I am still learning the crops that are grown on the prime agricultural fields one quarter-mile from my house, and the sophisticated mechanical, hydraulic, and chemical methods by which those crops are mostly produced. Conversely, my agricultural neighbors still have much to learn of the adjacent academic world I "inhabit"; my reality is another space to them, and vice versa, and our respective interpretations of life's purpose are apt to be greatly divergent. In North America we are confused by caricatures of each other while we share common landscapes—in my case the urbanizing agricultural fringe in a low-elevation former seabed, then grassland, now agricultural quilt in the Mediterranean climate region at the center of a territory now politically known as California. In spite of my quarter-century of residence, there is much I do not know about the place and about my neighbors, human and nonhuman, living and inanimate. (After a decade of self-conscious investigation, I have discovered that the more I know, the more there is to be known.)

Much has been written about contemporary severance from nature and the loss of community, identity, purpose, and sense of place. Our places and communities have been usurped by machines, sprawled out by the automobile, homogenized by consumer culture, seduced by the globalizing economy, trivialized by television, and disconnected from deep wisdom by the shallow superficiality of the "electronic superhighway." The evolutionary tendency of humans to attach themselves to place and to one another has been co-opted by a culture that feigns such an attachment through advertising but seems only to demand that we consume more, communicate frivolously and electronically, and care less. The academic world has compartmentalized knowledge and occupation while the corporate world has globalized the "location" of business and commerce.

However, social trends are most often accompanied by their opposites. A number of simultaneous movements toward "relocalization" are now converging that challenge many of the basic and most dis-placed assumptions of postmodern culture: grassroots watershed conservancies, "Friends of . . ." groups for particular natural features, holistic ecosystem management efforts, coordinated resource management plans (CRiMPs), community-supported agricultural establishments, alternative local currencies, farmers' markets—even microbreweries that produce beer with proudly local labels. In particular, a body of theory and technique with great significance to the nature of community life, public citizenship, personal lifestyle, regional planning, ecosystem management, and education is coalescing around the term *bioregion.*

A *bioregion* is literally and etymologically a "life-place"[1]—(a unique region definable by natural (rather than political) boundaries with a geographic, climatic, hydrological, and ecological character capable of supporting unique human and nonhuman living communities) Bioregions can be variously defined by the geography of watersheds, similar plant and animal ecosystems, and related, identifiable landforms (e.g., particular mountain ranges, prairies, or coastal zones) and by the unique human cultures that grow from natural limits and potentials of the region. Most importantly, the bioregion is emerging as the most logical locus and scale for a sustainable, regenerative community to take root and to *take place.* In reaction to a globally shallow, consumer-driven, technologically saturated world where humans are alienated from nature and offered simulations of it instead, a bioregion offers an appropriate venue for the natural predisposition toward graceful human life on earth. The bioregional or "life-place" concept suggests the efflorescence and emplacement of *biophilia,* our innate affection for the totality of life in all its forms. Although by no means a unified philosophy, theory, or method, (the bioregional approach suggests a means of living by deep understanding of, respect for, and, ultimately, care of a naturally bounded region or territory.)

Words ending in *-ism* are conceptually dangerous and immediately raise red flags. Bioregionalism is no exception, coming under criticism as utopian, idealistic, oversimplified, or just plain fallacious. To minimize needless risk to the efficacy of the concept, I hereafter try to minimize use of the suffix *-ism* in the remainder of this writing. (Instead, I use the words *bioregion* and *life-place* interchangeably to evoke either a particular place on earth or the general concept of such places) *Life-place* is perhaps the better of the two synonyms; it is lighter and more flexible on the tongue and in the mind.

But like the word/concept *sustainability* before it, *bioregion* has become too prevalent, powerful, and useful to ignore. *Bioregion* and its related terms have entered the lexicons of planning, design, geography, and ecosystem management and now appear in academic journals, popular magazines, and planning reports. Geographer Hartwell Welsh lists sixteen California bioregions; the *Jepson Manual,* ten "floristic provinces"; the California Biodiversity Council, eleven bioregions; journalist/author Phillip Fradkin, seven eco-cultural "states" within the greater state of California.[2] In defining twenty-one North American ecoregions, the Sierra Club wrote: "Nature has messy boundaries, and systems that blend into each other— so do our ecoregions."[3]

The notion of life-place is informed by various disciplines. From ecosystem geography comes a fuzzy natural way for humans to partition the earth's territories. From ecology comes an understanding of the role of abiotic conditions, disturbance, inter- and intraspecies competition, predation, and symbiosis that results in spatially distributed natural assemblages or associations, if not communities. From ecosystem management comes a pressing need to holistically manage land, habitat, resources, and species in reasonably sized, scientifically defensible chunks. From regional theory, planning, and landscape architecture comes a battery of methods and techniques for analyzing, planning, and managing land on the regional scale. From architecture and sustainable development comes the possibility of tuning the built environment to the conditions of the natural region. From alternative economics come the rudimentary means of emphasizing and strengthening local and regional economies. From sustainable agriculture come specific means to link local food producers and consumers in reasonably scaled, regenerative relationships. From social and political theory comes a resurgence of participatory democracy and civic responsibility focused on place and capable of solving regional environmental problems. Finally, from artists, poets, painters, and writers emerges a sense of the true nature of culture and an inkling of *why* we might want to do all this in the first place.

If this were all, however, bioregional thinking could still be dismissed as merely another utopian byproduct of a culture obsessed with buzzwords, shallow information, and surface imagery. However, all across the United States, North America, and elsewhere, groups of people of widely disparate backgrounds within common, naturally definable regions are sitting down, discussing issues, reaching compromises, and making plans for areas of land and resolving resource and environmental issues in what can only be called *bioregional actions*. Judith Plant reports that this "naming of something that is already going on is the power of bioregionalism."[4] What is going on is the *widespread occurrence of grassroots, on-the-ground action toward resolution of environmental and social issues by voluntary, nonprofit groups that strongly identify with naturally bounded regions and local communities.*

This book simply presupposes that the various regional relocalization movements are better off together than apart. Might not a focus on the potential regional "foodshed" relate to the protection of biodiversity? Could the geography of energy production, distribution, and use relate to the viability of a regional or local economy? Would an enhanced local art and literature contribute to a more civic, participatory democracy? The symbiosis made possible by considering these dimensions together is too potent to resist.

The ultimate measure of a convergent bioregional approach, if it is to influence the mainstream, will be its contribution toward regenerating local cultures, ecosystems, and resources into the indefinite future. A life-place framework will be judged not on how "warm and cuddly" it makes people feel but on whether it contributes in a physical sense to the fulfillment of needs of life on earth: clean water and air; sufficient food, shelter, and clothing; peace from violence; a sense of meaning in life and a motivation for continuing to live; and enough of all of this to sustain life for other living systems as well as for our own species. When I look beyond the pragmatic requirements of a life-place approach, I see a simple set of axioms: People who stay in place may come to know that place more deeply. People who know a place may come to care about it more deeply. People who care *about* a place are more likely to *take better care of it.* And people who take care of places, one place at a time, are the key to the future of humanity and all living creatures. At first glance, these axioms might imply a linearity of logic, but many of the effects are also causes. In essence, the idea of a life-place or bioregion connects natural place, awareness, knowledge, wisdom, affection, stewardship, sustainability, and, most important, *action,* as a "fuzzy set" of nested and covariant concepts. Embedded in the bioregional idea, therefore, is a very general hypothesis: that a mutually sustainable future for humans, other life-forms, and earthly systems can best be achieved by means of a spatial framework in which people live as rooted, active, participating members of a reasonably scaled, naturally bounded, ecologically defined territory, or *life-place.*

I work in an office and live in the other rooms of a house in a subdivision in a city in the state of California in a political nation called the United States of America. I have an official address, and I am a census data point. I reside in a city and within a county. I live in a fire district, a school district, a water and flood control district, an air pollution control district, a hospital and ambulance district, a senatorial district, a congressional district, an assembly district, a state senatorial district, and a county supervisorial district. I also live in a voting precinct and will die in a cemetery district. I am within a water quality control board district, a highway maintenance district, a landscape and lighting assessment district, and a cellular phone communication cell. I'm in a zip code and an area code. I live along an electric utility branch, a cable television line, and a natural gas network. I live within a sewage treatment service area and a solid waste management district. Virtually none of these spatial zones coincide.

There is, however, another way in which I may consider where I am. I also live on Yolo clay loam soil at an elevation about fifty feet above mean sea level, two miles north of Putah Creek and two miles south of Willow Slough, eight miles west of the Sacramento River at latitude 38.8' N near the West Coast of the North American continent. I live in a mild temperate, interior, Mediterranean climate zone on quaternary alluvium several tens of thousands of feet deep. On average, about eighteen inches of rain fall in my area each year. I live on a former sedimentary outwash plain that became first grassland/savanna, then cattle pasture, then orchard, and then tomato and row crop field, and that now is a housing subdivision. Near my house, one to two miles to the north and south, are lands that were once riparian forests, and three miles east are former seasonal and permanent marshlands. Most of this land is now prime agricultural row crop, field crop, pasture, and orchard land. Groundwater lies sixty feet beneath my house. Blue oak savanna and oak woodland hills lie ten miles upstream; chaparral, riparian forests, and mixed oak woodlands, twenty miles up. Twenty miles south of me is a river delta and farther west a freshwater estuary where that river meets the coastal tides. Fifty miles southwest is an ocean. I live along the migratory routes of hundreds of bird species. I share my immediate surroundings with crows, magpies, jays, mockingbirds, flickers, possums, dogs, cats, goldfish, and turtles. There are snails, ants, sow bugs, earthworms, mealybugs, tomato worms, spiders, flies, bees, fleas, wasps, cockroaches, moths, crickets, and literally hundreds of insects and arachnid species I could not possibly name. Also sharing the immediate areas near my home are innumerable exotic and a few native species of trees, grasses, shrubs, vines, annuals, and perennials. A half-mile to two miles or so away are foxes and raccoons; hawks, egrets, herons, kites, ducks, geese, swans, stilts, avocets, willets, killdeer, and pigeons; lizards; and blackfish, carp, bass, suckers, and other fish. Countless hundreds of thousands of small and microscopic organisms crowd the entire region around me.

If my species vanished tomorrow, the land would gradually assume a new equilibrium, with many new exotic species, but with many others similar to those of its condition several hundred years ago: scattered grassland and valley oak trees here, marsh and riparian forest nearby, with blue oak savanna, woodland, and mixed coniferous/deciduous forest a bit farther up the watershed. Floods would readjust the river and stream profiles (after they succeeded in wearing away or breaking through the concrete dams and removing the earthen levees) and would eventually rejuvenate the soil. Groundwater tables would rise. This new human-less equilibrium would be dynamic and changing, as always, but with a periodicity far less than in the current era during which my species occupies the land. Browsing and grazing animals would return (many of which might be feral forms of contemporary, domesticated grazers), and carnivorous predators would prey upon them. Migratory waterfowl would again flock here by the hundreds of thousands, even millions. The land I live on has natural tendencies toward certain kinds of ecosystems and species, even though they change over time. The land mosaic and species mix following humans, however, will not replicate the ones preceding us.

However, mine is a species of animal with a particularly elaborate and highly symbolic, self-reflective culture. For years, my particular continental group of our species has "located" itself mostly by means of zones, districts, and networks that have weak, nearly invisible, or incongruent relationships to the latent character and potential of the lands and waters that these districts overlie. The zones of heaviest human use of water are far removed from their sources. Energy is generated by fuels obtained thousands of miles from where they are converted into electricity, and the subsequently generated electrical power is further spatially distributed so that no real relationship can be shown between the source of power and its end use. City, county, state, and national boundaries ignore natural features. Transportation corridors for humans connect our own species, yet they disconnect and fragment countless other species. A majority of my food items travel an average of over one thousand miles before I consume them.

The incongruity between our culturally constructed districts, zones, and networks and the natural abiotic and biotic tendencies of the lands upon which we live can be traced to the ways in which we understand where we are. To a great extent, we have forgotten where we live because we have ignored the natural dimension of the land. This incongruity is one of perception, scale, and time. We perceive ourselves to be principally residents of human compartments. The scale of these compartments is far too large or too unrelated to the essential structure and function of the natural living systems upon which we ultimately depend. The rates at which we alter ecosystems exceed the rates by which those systems can regenerate. And finally, the locations of origin of our material necessities, like the ultimate locations of the deposits of our wastes, are often far away from where we live. To presume to live only in human districts unrelated to local natural conditions leads directly to the exaggeration of the scale of human infrastructure and to the extraction of resources at rates far in excess of rates of natural regeneration.

I am pursuing a simple, implicit premise here. Unless we humans can find ways to consider ourselves residents of natural regions and to clearly identify with endemic dimensions, limitations, and potentials of land, water, and other life-forms, we will not be able to live sustainably, and we will continue to overestimate the carrying capacity of the regions we inhabit. It makes little sense to discuss "sustainable development" at the global level if no thought is given to the local places and scales where human life actually takes place. The first step toward a regenerative future for humans is to reassess where we are.

This book stalks its topic from several sides simultaneously, drawing on personal experience, objective theory, and the voices of other inhabitants. Chapters are hierarchical. The first two can be considered a foundation of sorts. I begin with "Grounding"—in the physical, geographic sense as well as the sense of locating oneself in place on the earth. I follow with "Living," discussing the nonhuman life of a place and the awakening of humans to that shared life. The next three chapters, "Reinhabiting," "Fulfilling," and "Imagining," deal with successively deeper notions of the human culture of place: associating, celebrating, and interpreting what it means to share a life-place. The remaining five chapters, "Trading," "Planning," Building," "Learning," and "Acting," form the operating manual for a life-place; here the bioregional notion is manifest in *action*, and the idea of a life-place returns, full circle, to the ground.

1 Grounding

FINDING THE PHYSICAL PLACE

Ecosystems and their components are naturally integrated. They existed before mankind and would continue to exist if mankind disappeared. In other words, we do not integrate anything; it is already integrated.

ROBERT BAILEY, 1996

Bioregions are natural assemblages of plants and animals with discernible but dynamic boundaries existing simultaneously along both spatial and temporal trajectories.

HARTWELL WELSH, 1994

Landing

It is a clear day in September, and I am sitting by a window in a sparsely filled airliner en route from Portland to Sacramento. Our course takes us southward along the Cascades; peak after volcanic peak pokes up out of expanses of coniferous forest tied together by rivers glinting sunlight and reflecting occasional clouds. As we fly over the Klamath Plateau the land changes: large patches of open grazing land appear, then a broad high-desert announces the arrival on this scenic stage of a major actor: Mount Shasta. An immense cone of forest, cinders, snow, and ice thrusting upward, Shasta is hard to ignore, so massive that the airplane seems to fly by it at half-speed.

I feel a slight tingle, then crane my neck downward to look as nearly vertically out the window as possible. I recall the August day in 1968 when, driving south from Alaska to California, I first came upon Shasta. I was struck by how well this mountain held its own, even compared to the massive Alaskan peaks I had seen close up that summer. But my overwhelming memory is of contrasting heat and cold. On that automobile trip, shortly after passing the mountain, while its snowy-summit afterimage was still in my mind, we descended into the valley, gaining heat rapidly. Conifers changed to mixed oak forest, then to oak grassland, then farmland. I had entered the river valley of the Sacramento: an entirely different world.

Now, in the airplane, I squint to discern the first tributaries of the Sacramento River on the flanks of Shasta and its westward neighbor, Mount Eddy. Soon Shasta Lake passes underneath us, an immense reservoir, its drawdown "bathtub ring" revealing it as a human artifact.)Behind Shasta Dam, winter storm runoff is stored and metered out during the intense dry summer heat for agricultural uses in the fertile alluvial soils of the southerly valley. The forest trails off rapidly. We cross over the city of Redding, framed by Mount Lassen to the east and the Trinity Alps to the west. These snow-capped peaks mark respective walls of mountains diverging east and west to accommodate the expanding Sacramento Valley. A few golden, rolling foothills, then a high plateau of grazing land, and the vast farmland begins: rich, brown corduroy earth, rectangles of bright-green alfalfa, textures of almond, olive, walnut, and citrus orchards. The plane's southward-streaking shadow races across irrigated pastures, tan fallow fields, yellow wheat, and the sensuous, sinuous check dams of rice paddies so uniquely striking that they could have been created by artists. Perhaps, in some way, they were.

Westward, the mountains recede in the distance, turning from tan to light green to dark green to gray with increasing distance. They are lower in altitude than their eastern Sierran counterparts but more mysterious. We know those Sierra characters, but who are the Coast Range peaks?

The valley of the Sacramento is here sixty miles wide, flat as Kansas or Iowa, but the farm patterns are different: no tidy, farm-barn-and-house complex on each 160-acre section but an odd, hybrid collection of aluminum buildings, dilapidated barns, occasional farmhouses, equipment yards, and a trailer park here or there. Only the grain elevators could be Midwestern. Even from the airplane, one can sense the immense productivity of the place, imagine the hum of machinery, "feel" the heat on the remote ground, and marvel at the persistence of those who plant, plow, irrigate, harvest, store, and ship the land's bounty. This bioregion is a hybrid of a different sort, a vast, productive watershed with its outflow in the fast-moving California culture, its headwaters touching the moist, coniferous Northwest, its main valleys a cornucopia of grains, fruits, and vegetables, and its foothills in the beef business. Parts of the Sacramento Valley, to an outsider, might induce vague memories of the Midwest or Wyoming, but only vague ones. This bioregion is suspended between family and corporate agriculture, caught up in the ironies of growing rice in a semiarid area, and bordered at the edges of the valley by genuine cattle country—complete with all the associated imagery: crystal-clear skies, chaparral, foothill scenery worthy of the best Marlboro billboard, remote ranches at the ends of dirt roads, Indian reservations and casinos, miles of barbed wire and range, cattle pens and chutes, isolated watering troughs fed by classic windmills, and characteristic double-pitched, metal-roofed red barns. Judging from most visual indicators, the Sacramento Valley is truly Western, but the lines of minivans, BMWs, and Acuras zipping along I-5 between the Bay Area and Seattle might disqualify the place for deep consideration by the *High Country News.*

The riparian vegetation along the Sacramento River is a mere line of trees, interrupted occasionally by stretches of bare trapezoidal flood levee. As one's perception acclimatizes to this flat mosaic, a ring of jagged tan hills, miles from any confining mountain range, juts into its midst. These are the Sutter Buttes, eroded intrusions of andesite and rhyolite, islands in the vast surrounding alluvium. The tingle of homecoming returns as I recall another grounded experience. Many years before, my wife, Lacey, and I explored Sutter Buttes on foot with a guide, seeing golden eagles, feral pigs, a buck deer with his harem. We marveled at the fact that no gray pine, the dominant low-elevation conifer of the foothills immediately east or west, ever made it across the valley to this ecological island.

South of the buttes, the airplane descends in its approach to the Sacramento Airport. We move closer to ground, the airplane physically and I emotionally. The lay of the land and the line of the river are familiar: Gray's Bend, the Fremont Weir, the Yolo Bypass. To the distant horizon westward is the Putah "notch," where the Blue Ridge is penetrated by the creek. Cache Creek's ungainly settling basin, dry and rectangular, is visible below. As the airplane rushes to touch the land, a unique landscape composition is framed by the window: straight brown, green, and tan fields and a curved swatch of blue water lined by tall trees, now seen from a nearly level perspective. Wheels chirp as they touch the runway pavement, and the airplane jolts me into the inevitable conclusion: this is my region, my home.

Physiography

One look at an aerial photograph of the Great Central Valley startles the viewer with the geographic uniqueness of this heartland of California. As landforms go, few regions of North America are so immediately set apart by topographic form alone. Consider, for a moment, an ancient porcelain bathtub, only one with faucets at both ends. Now take a sledgehammer and bang a notch out of the left side as a sort of tub drain, and you have a reasonable physical model of the Central Valley. The Sierra forms one side of the tub, the Coast Range the other; the Siskiyous form the north end, matched by the Tehachapis at the south. San Francisco Bay drains the valley-tub sideways into the Pacific Ocean.

Strangely, the uniqueness of the valley's geomorphology seems matched only by the degree to which California residents and tourists alike deny that

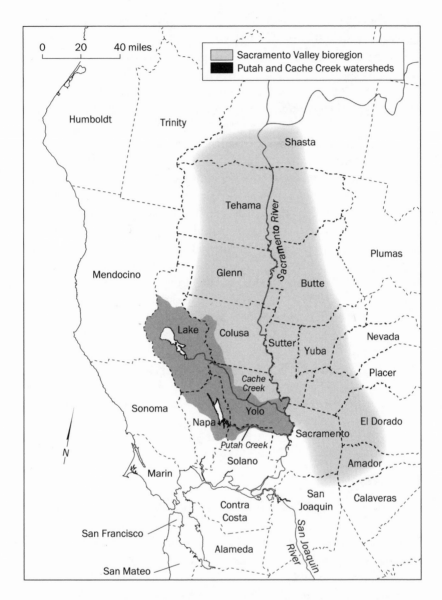

Figure 1.1 The Sacramento Valley bioregion, with the Putah Creek and Cache Creek watersheds highlighted. Map based on original by Jacob Mann, based on Hartwell H. Welsh, Jr., "Bioregions: An Ecological and Evolutionary Perspective and a Proposal for California," *California Fish and Game* 80, no. 3 (1994).

this region contains anything memorable. Go to any bookstore in California: you will find picturesquely illustrated tour guides to Big Sur, the Bay Area, Lake Tahoe, the Sierras, Gold Country, Wine Country, North Coast, and the redwoods. You will find little about touring the Central Valley—in fact, hardly anything about the valley at all.

Yet despite this lack of attention, a rich nature exists, atop tens of thousands of vertical feet of alluvial soil, on the valley floor. It is what might be called an "ecocline," where the annual rainfall grades from a high of seventy-five inches at Mount Shasta to a desertlike six inches in the Kern Basin. The result is one geomorphic province occupied by two bioregions, the Sacramento and the San Joaquin. I reside in the moister and smaller of the two: the Sacramento Valley bioregion (figure 1.1). Through experience and study, I have attempted to discover the essence of this life-place, beginning with its physiography, the basic earthly dimensions of land, water, and atmosphere. In the course of this book, I posit several bioregional "hypotheses," and here is the first one, the Physiographic Hypothesis: *A bioregion is a physiographically unique place, a geographically legitimate concept, an identifiable region, and an operative spatial unit.*

Bailey's Map

Robert Bailey wears a white shirt, a tie, and gold wire-rim glasses. Although not a professor, he looks much like what the public expects an academic to be. In a darkened, chalk-dusty lecture room in a 1950s-vintage building just off the center of the U.C. Davis campus, Bailey begins an impeccably illustrated slide presentation on his thirty years of work as a U.S. Forest Service geographer mapping the ecological regions of, first, the United States and, later, the entire globe, including all of its continents and even its oceans. A "maverick" biogeographer, Bailey tells our audience of one hundred or so students and faculty that his work has come in and out of favor over the decades more than once as the environmentalism of government agencies has ebbed and flowed with the changing tides of Washington politics. Throughout all this, as we soon note from his lecture, threads a continuous passion for identifying the natural regions of the world.

Bailey begins: Essential to the differentiation of life-places on the surface of the earth, he says, are the factors most of us learned in our earliest experience with the globe in geography classes. Sunlight warms the earth differentially between equatorial and polar latitudes; water bodies cover most of the earth, buffering extremes in temperature and producing ocean currents fundamental to the global and local climate; land masses have vastly differing shapes and areas; continental climates are influenced in ways relating to their total land mass, mountain ranges, and position relative to prevailing winds and ocean currents; climates are colder in polar latitudes and higher altitudes, warmer in lower and in more equatorial areas. Bailey has illustrated some of these generalizable relationships and their interactions by diagramming a "theoretical" continent.

Because the geographies of individual land masses vary greatly, however, these generalizable principles, when taken in real-world context, produce a complex mosaic of different physiographic and climatological domains. Building on a climate-driven system of differentiation of the earth's surface first articulated by Wladimir Köppen and later graphically articulated by L. R. Holdridge, Bailey identifies four major large-scale ecoregions, or domains: _polar, humid-temperate, humid-tropical, and dry._ Within these large ecoregions, smaller _divisions_ can be identified, based on finer distinctions of temperature and moisture: for example, the humid-temperate domain includes "Mediterranean," "subtropical," "prairie," "marine," "hot continental," and "warm continental" divisions (figure 1.2). Each of Bailey's divisions is further divided into _provinces,_ where the controlling factors are altitude and vegetation. For example, in North America, the Mediterranean division, which includes much of what we know as central California, includes lowlands once dominated by grassland and mountains dominated by drier, sclerophyllic ("hard-leafed") forest and scrublands. At this intermediate scale, Bailey's ecoregional provinces follow closely the designation of biomes (dominant vegetation in relation to mesoclimate) originally articulated by Frederick Clements and Victor Shelford, the "biotic provinces" of Dice, the "biogeographical provinces" of Udvardy, and the "biotic regions" described by Raymond Dasmann.[1]

Bailey's hierarchical categories of domain, division, and province define a nested set of territories that he generally refers to as "ecoregions." Technically, _ecoregion_ is perhaps a more accurate term for a bioregion, since it recognizes the significant role for abiotic influences, such as climate and landform. However, I continue to use the term _bioregion_ and the more comfortable term _life-place_ interchangeably; both have strong implications for the forms life might take in a particular place.

A critical contribution Bailey and his predecessors have made to the fundamental notion of life-places is the idea of controlling, or causal, factors. Layered spatial analysis techniques like those pioneered by Ian McHarg (described in his _Design with Nature_) and expanded upon by contemporary geographic information systems work well empirically or statistically

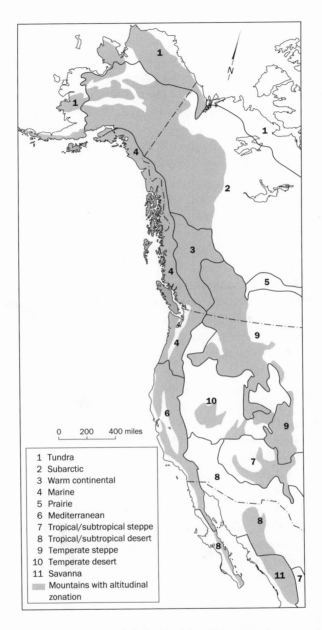

Figure 1.2 Detail of Bailey's North American ecoregions map. Ecoregion maps divide territory by changes in natural conditions, offering inhabitants and visitors a new geographic perspective. Map based on work by Robert Bailey, *Ecosystem Geography* (New York: Springer, 1996).

to describe the nature of a place. They do little, however, to explain *why* it is so: they are largely acausal. In contrast, because Bailey's hierarchical system of ecoregions is based upon the abiotic factors most critically influencing subsequent, spatially distributed expressions of life, his ecoregions are expressions of cause and effect. In other words, Bailey tells us *why* bioregions are different, not merely *that* they are. In Bailey's system, macroregional differences create large geographical domains through varying manifestations of latitude, position with respect to oceans, and shapes of continents; mesoregional differences reflect responses to altitude, landform, aspect, and topography; and microregional differences relate to microclimate, geology, soil characteristics, and major vegetation zones. At the fundamental physiographic/abiotic level, the largest scales of territory relate to those characteristics that change least over time (geology, climate), while the smallest scales are those that change most over time (animal populations, plant succession after disturbance). The theory of ecoregions that Bailey espouses is a complex combination of abiotic factors, scientifically supportable causes, resultant spatial distributions, and ultimate biological responses. It is simultaneously both analytic and synthetic.

In essence, Bailey has skillfully and scientifically derived a "top-down," almost "fractal-like" arrangement of ecoregional scales, from large continental domains to small areas of landscape. His methods have been officially adopted by the U.S. Forest Service, whose regional mapping staffs have produced finer subregions, or, in official USFS designation, *sections* and *subsections.* In Bailey's system, I live in the "Yolo alluvial fan" subsection of the "Great Valley" section of the "California dry steppe" province of the "Mediterranean" division of the "humid temperate" domain of Planet Earth. If I had started that sentence with my "landscape" location at elevation fifty feet above sea level, two miles south of Willow Slough, it would complete my "bioregional" address without using any politically determined differentiation of territory whatsoever. (In the case of the California dry steppe province, "California" is a strictly natural description, with no reference to the political state.) — *Dry and overly Informational* [handwritten]

The Region

Gazing upon Bailey's ecoregion map of North America is a lesson in creative intellectual endeavor in which the question "What if?" strongly arises. What if the political world were arranged in divisions that followed the scientifically defensible regions Bailey has outlined? Would our interventions on the land be any more regenerative or sustainable? Would the people of today find these regions logical or natural? Or would they feel as though Bailey, the scientist, were coaxing out structure and pattern for the earth's regions without consulting its most dominant inhabitants, the people themselves?)

One way to answer these questions is by appealing to direct experience: What does an ecological region or bioregion *feel* like to a person inhabiting it? How do we know or sense what natural region we live in? Even though our existence is dominated by sociopolitical demarcations, residents often describe their regions in natural terms. Midwesterners may feel a kinship to states in the short- or long-grass prairie agricultural heartland region, while Southwesterners may relate to the aridity of sagebrush, creosote bush, Joshua tree, or piñon-pine country. Appalachian-mountain dwellers may relate to similar mixed hardwood/softwood forest terrain, whether in Georgia, the Carolinas, Virginia, Tennessee, or Pennsylvania. North Americans have always related to natural dimensions of their home territories.

From our immediate perception, we are aware of the apparent holism of areas of similar topography (mountains, plains, canyon lands, coastline) and climate zones (temperature, winds, aridity/humidity). Each of us lives somewhere within a watershed or hydrological region (although we are only now coming to that realization), and these watersheds are relatively distinct and do not always correspond with city, county, state, or national boundaries. We simultaneously perceive both the homogeneity and the heterogeneity between chunks of territory at a number of different scales, from the simple immediate changes in patchy local landscapes to the regional differences we encounter over longer periods of dwelling.

The critical geographical assumption behind the concept of bioregion, then, is that these definable, natural, physiographic "boundaries," although soft, hierarchical, and sometimes difficult to define, have as much or more legitimacy than political ones and perhaps much more long-term utility. As environmental issues intensify, naturally defined territories will become more central to the future of human existence. As globalizing economic, technological, and political relationships render arbitrary national boundaries less relevant, we will increasingly deal with the physical realities of environmental, resource, and biodiversity issues by focusing upon natural divisions within physiographic regions. In this strange condition of localization within globalization, it may even become necessary to formalize bioregions (as the world has formerly done with political boundaries). The bioregion, then, although a human construct, is a construct whose time has come.

Serpentine

Ray Krauss is not a geologist, but he might as well be, working as he has for over fifteen years as the environmental manager for the enormous, state-of-the-art McLaughlin gold mine at the upper Putah Creek headwaters. The McLaughlin sits alongside some of the most complex geology known to humanity: within a ten-mile radius are the late Jurassic sandstones, shales, and graywackes of the sedimentary Franciscan complex, deposited off-shore in marine trenches by erosion of former volcanic areas; Cretaceous Great Valley mudstones and siltstones laid down as a former shoreline of a great Mesozoic ocean; volcanic andesites, rhyolites, and basaltic rock forced upward as igneous intrusions at the intersection of tectonic grinding between Pacific and continental plates; (and serpentine, the shiny, gray-green state mineral of California, formed when thermal hot springs of ancient, trapped seawater intruded into the fissures in surrounding sedimentary rock. Serpentine is loaded with magnesium, chromium, and iron but is deficient in sodium, calcium, and potassium; geologists speak of it as an "ultramafic" rock, the suffix -*mafic* referring to the unusually high magnesium-to-calcium ratio) Krauss's domain of concern lies in the heart of the highest concentrations of serpentine anywhere, and he knows well the unique adaptations of plant and animal life to serpentine soils. Among the variety of plant associations Krauss has managed on the mine's land is the dense, fire-prone chamise chaparral often found in serpentine conditions.

The geologic complexity of the immediate region produces other by-products. One is geothermal steam, and not too far from the McLaughlin Mine is the Geysers geothermal plant, where energy is harvested from ancient water heated by magma eight thousand feet below the surface. Another is mercury, often found in geological association with entrapped seawater and active volcanism. But the reason Krauss has had to work his environmental magic is a simple four-letter word: *gold.*

"How did the gold come to be at the mine?" asks my colleague, as we sit over sandwiches after a local stakeholders' meeting. Krauss easily explains the complex process whereby former hot-spring vents brought gold in solution from parent rock into the cracks in the surrounding rock matrix, and then both gold and mercury precipitated out in sulfide deposits beneath the earth's surface. The McLaughlin Mine uses a very complex extractive process involving recycling cyanide and other compounds to carry and later release the gold. The site of the mine overlaps sites of several former mercury mines that leaked toxic tailings into the watershed, but the effluent now coming off the modern McLaughlin Mine is clean—far better than the mercury-laden runoff before the gold mine was established. "*Nothing* bad gets away from us and off that land," Krauss proudly and emphatically points out. The McLaughlin mine has set the new standard for excellence in the mining industry in containment of potentially toxic runoff and the restoration and mitigation of environmental impact. All of the gold extracted during the entire life of the huge McLaughlin Mine, however, would fit into a large-sized passenger van. It is true that the mine has altered the topography to a significant degree. But lest we jump to conclusions about the unfortunate "consumption" of the landscape by modern gold mines, we must ask ourselves how many of us do not possess some items made of gold: fillings in our teeth, our electronic equipment, our wedding rings. We are all "principal responsible parties"; we are all materialistic moderns to varying degrees, and, as the bumper sticker says, "If it can't be grown, it's gotta be mined," even though much of it should be recycled *after* it has been unearthed.

Upper Putah Creek and a number of Cache Creek tributaries therefore emerge from a tumultuous alchemy of earth, air, fire, and water. Mercury, geothermal steam, serpentine, and conglomerations of all ages and types of rock join traces of gold in a uniquely crazed geological slow dance that defines the place, marked on the surface by a mélange of various exposed rocks and minerals and by a dense chaparral of chamise, buckbrush, manzanita, and a host of other fire-adapted shrubs. It is a strangely beautiful synergy unlike that of any other place. Study and live with this landscape for a few years, and you'd swear you could taste its uniqueness in the fine wines of the nearby Guenoc Valley, a hunch confirmed to me (after I indulged in repeated, informal tests of this hypothesis) by Patrick Reuter, a U.C. Davis graduate student who wrote a thesis on the French concept of *terroir*—the sense of place embodied in wine.[2]

Earthquake Country

Eldridge Moores is a geologist, and somewhat of a celebrity at that, having been featured in John McPhee's *Assembling California*.[3] Professor Moores is my colleague at U.C. Davis, and his enthusiasm for his subject is both obvious and infectious as he lectures to both academic and lay au-

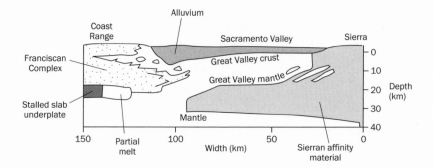

Figure 1.3 Cross section of the Sacramento Valley, showing major geological features in relative scale. The valley is one of the deepest deposits of alluvium in the world. Based on N. J. Godfrey, B. G. Beaudoin, and S. L. Klemperer, "Ophiolitic Basement to the Great Valley Forearc Basin, California, from Seismic and Gravity Data: Implications for Crustal Growth at the North American Continental Margin," *Geological Society of America Bulletin* 109 (1997): 1536–62, figure 11.

diences. This time he is speaking to the Putah Creek Council, our fledgling watershed group. The subject is the geology of the Sacramento Valley, particularly our own southwest corner of it. His eyes twinkle behind gold-rimmed glasses, and his white-shirted arms gesture emphatically at his slides and maps. A seismic specialist, Moores calmly informs us that although we live near the center of the broad, alluvial Sacramento Valley, we are not immune to earthquakes. The major San Andreas "action" is moving eastward through a series of related faults, one of which, he informs us, is a few miles west of tonight's lecture site. The Plainfield Ridge, a subtle swelling in the local, flat landscape, is actually overlying an active fault system. Here on the west side of the Sacramento Valley, the alluvium is some thirty thousand feet deep. The Sierran batholith dives beneath the valley, extending westward and descending deeper as it approaches the foundations of the Coast Range on the valley's west side (figure 1.3). The Coast Range, tectonically speaking, is mere fragmentary detritus that was broken off from the diving Pacific plate and is now riding up and over the valley as the continental plate moves westward. The town of Winters, a mere ten miles away, experienced an earthquake a century ago, and, Moores tells us, we should look suspiciously at the humps in our flat valley floor. Our smooth, rolling Dunnigan Hills, he says, are suspect territory disguising a growing geologic substructure of folds and faults. Interestingly enough, the Dunnigan Hills constitute an officially designated grape-growing region and envelop our other fine winery, R. H. Phillips. Is a taste for latent seismic activity hidden in the body of our wines?

Valley Soil

David Kelley is a soil scientist in private practice, and he has agreed to educate my friends and colleagues David Robertson and Gary Snyder and me on the complex subtleties of our valley soil. We meet him at the Russell Ranch, a Putah Creek floodplain agricultural research station recently acquired by U.C. Davis. Kelley immediately takes us on a soil-testing transect starting near the creek channel itself. Over the millennia, Kelley says, when flooding creeks have hit flat valleys, they have dispersed their water through various channels and dropped their sediment load in "fans"—the inverse of the pattern found in the steeper valleys, where tributaries flow into the main stream. The Putah Creek fan is obvious in the deposition of surrounding soils; the stream builds adjacent, natural flood levees, but the land slopes away from the streambed beyond these, and farmers' fields adjacent to the creek actually tilt away from the stream corridor unless graded in the opposite direction.

Kelley is another professional vigorously in love with his subject matter. He digs his soil test holes with a rare enthusiasm, working up a sweat, lecturing all the while, marveling at every new soil stratum he uncovers. "Landscapes," he affectionately calls these layers, although they have not been exposed to atmosphere or eye in thousands of years. "The most important ingredient in soil is *time*." I scramble for my notebook to record this obvious but deep bit of wisdom. Older soils have more oxidized minerals, such as iron oxide (common rust). Some soils go through reduction-oxidation cycles, alternating blue and orange casts respectively. The size of the aggregate relates to the speed of the water depositing it; larger aggregates mean moving water, while the manifold clays of the region are deposited by nearly still water. Some clay particles alluviate, or move down through the soil profile, after deposition, as if to find a resting place after eons of activity.

David Kelley could dig his test holes downward for weeks in most local places and never hit solid rock; the Sacramento Valley region is a vast basin of sediment layered upon the deep Sierran basement far below. Here the soil rules, and the farmers (or "growers," a corporate euphemism) have expropriated from the native grass ecosystems all but the least productive lands. We have them to thank, however, for our full bellies. To them, indirectly, I owe my job, for I work at a land grant university at the behest of the State of California Agricultural Experiment Station, which pays 40 percent of my salary as I write this book. In my immediate downstream watershed region, we export far more food than we could possibly eat: specifically, tomatoes, rice, wheat, alfalfa, corn, safflower, and sugar beets, in roughly that order of importance. We are, for better and sometimes worse, a breadbasket to the world via the vast network of international agricultural commodity markets. We are also vulnerable to many threats to this vital global food supply. The most serious of these is development. The typical pattern of urbanization in the Sacramento Valley bioregion makes it one of the least dense regions in the world, yet 17 percent of our best farmland will be threatened by development as the valley population grows in the next forty years. As the old saw goes, the last (and the longest-lasting) "crop" in the rotation is too often housing.

The sun dips; Gary and I both find polite words to suggest departure, and David Kelley still digs, this time uncovering a terraced soil where Pleistocene aggregates laid down by ancient landscape events rest on the top strata. "Look at this guy," Kelley says, picking up a tiny piece of gravel from several feet down in the hole. "It's never seen a human before!"

Several days later, David Kelley phones me, excited. He has discovered a rare 1913 county soils map, done in the glory days of exacting field research, elaborate color, and exquisite cartography. Upon seeing it, I share his enthusiasm, for as a map lover, I find it a candidate for the most beautiful map I have ever seen—this is the kind of cartography that seduces the mind completely. There, amid the descriptions of variously colored soils, is pure graphic evidence of the lesson of Putah Creek fan dispersal that David Kelley had so enthusiastically shared in the field. Our immediate region—the valley plain—is the domain of soil, particulate remembrances of former, greater rock formations rendered fine and distributed broadly by eons of flooding water. Extending across the valley are pathways of fine sediment, marked as colored patches on Kelley's antique map—territories once ruled by native perennial grasses and now invaded and occupied by the precise furrows of grains, row crops, tomatoes, and alfalfa. For me, after all of this, our valley soils will never be the same; they have come alive; they are beings.

Building on the Land

It is 1989, and I am standing with a group of architects, planners, engineers, and specialists on a low terrace just off the valley floor. The land is a mosaic of old mudflows and consolidated ash from ancient volcanic eruptions. Peppering the site are numerous red, brown, black, and beige boulders once carried downslope like so much flotsam on a moving sea of liquid earth. Below our site, the rich prime agricultural lands in the middle of the Sacramento Valley, Butte Creek watershed, spread out to the Sacramento River. We are here with Andres Duany, an architect and planner well known for his neo-traditional, compact new-town plans. As landscape architects, my partners and I are hired to advise him in site analysis, landscape ecology, and resource conservation issues, but the major accomplishment was already achieved before we set pen to paper. The new town we are planning, a few miles from the growing university town of Chico, is *off* the best soils, which lie one mile downhill, and *on* the least agriculturally valuable land beneath our feet.

The site we plan is nearly ten square miles in extent, yet most of it is to be dedicated to open space, and the remaining 1,600 housing units will be clustered in six tight, dense, Mediterranean-style villages on the mesa tops, conserving the sensitive stream corridors as wild matrix for animals, birds, microorganisms, and limited human use. We are painstakingly working up a master plan for the best possible response to the thorny issue of accommodating growth while saving the valuable agricultural soils of the Sacramento Valley region. Our solution is to build compact villages on poor upland soils in close proximity to existing cities and known mass-transit corridors, leaving the most productive agricultural lands and delicate biodiversity networks alone. Were we to repeatedly adopt this relatively sustainable bioregional development pattern, a major dilemma of human occupation in the Sacramento Valley would be resolved.

For now, we are facing a more pleasant challenge in the completion of our planning process: what to establish as the color palette for the village architecture. Andres and I discuss a unique idea. We visit the site, selecting samples of eight or ten major rock and soil types from the volcanic landscape—beige, deep purple-reds, dark browns, and gray-taupe colors. We also gather leaves, berries, and bark. Back at the design studio, we crush these various rocks, soils, and other natural substances to powder and mix them with water, and Andres, an experienced watercolorist, paints solutions of the earthy slurries onto a matrix of predesignated swatches of paper. After they dry, we are presented with a wide range of surprisingly colorful options, and we pick various choices for walls, roofs, or accents. It is an inspiring moment.

Although we do not know it at the time, the project will never be built because of the coming California recession of the early 1990s. But as I drive home with my office partners after an exhausting week of the most intense design and planning I have ever experienced, I am exhilarated with an awakening of possibilities to anchor human development in a regional context.

Weather

On a college hitchhiking trip across the west in 1966, I stood on a Sacramento side street in the 105-degree heat of August and wondered how anyone could ever survive these sweltering summer temperatures. Little did I know that thirty years later this heat would have seeped into my being to such an extent that, upon my arrival back at Sacramento Airport in the dead of summer, the heat-induced odor from the surrounding agricultural soils would be a familiar and welcome sensation. Temperatures in the Sacramento Valley region break the hundred-degree mark about twenty days or so per year, even more in Redding, our northernmost city. In the southern bioregion, where cool breezes from the San Francisco Bay–San Joaquin Delta pass through the Carquinez Straits and up the river, nighttime temperatures can drop down well below seventy, making possible the operation of natural house cooling by "dumping" of heat built up during the day. Folks in the upper Sacramento watershed aren't so lucky: Redding holds the heat, with little cooling breeze in the evenings. Much of that city's livability is owed to the hydroelectric power from nearby Shasta Dam that runs the ubiquitous summer air conditioners. But residents are paid well for their endurance of summer heat: an embracing snowy-mountain backdrop rewards them each winter.

Here in the south valley, unless one is a farmer, one soon learns to dress like an Aussie: always short pants in the summer, no matter what one's age or gender; sandals; and a wide-brimmed hat to keep the sun off (especially for a baldy like me). Our local farm foremen and crop pickers, exposed to bright sun all day, opt to shield every inch of skin with long jeans, jury-rigged caps with cloth napes, or the handsome straw Western hats of the *campesinos*. The sun seems cruel around six o'clock on those long summer days, and when the delta breeze finally kicks in, smiles come to the people's faces. The fresh southwest breeze blowing cool and moist after a day of dry heat in the hundreds is a joy only local inhabitants can really know. Evenings become enchanted, sometimes even shivery if the temperature drops into the lower sixties—a forty-degree gross diurnal differential.

The lower Sacramento Valley is characterized by "tule fog" in winter. This is the famous San Francisco fog's opposite; that city sees fog in summer, when warm continental air crashes against the cool ocean air along the coastal land belt. We get rapid night-sky radiant heat loss on still, clear winter evenings. A layer of still, cold air is suppressed by warmer air some five hundred feet up, producing the densest fog known to humanity. These ground fogs are thick and persistent, occasionally lingering for weeks at a time. Although the tule fog drives some folks stir-crazy, there are two means of coping. The first is escape: to head up to the five-hundred-foot contour on either foothill side at midday to greet the sun, which is inevitably shining there. Tule fogs in the valley mean shirtsleeves in the nearby foothills and a rare opportunity for winter picnics or hikes. The second is coming to terms, or acceptance. Fog is the valley's *koan*—like the ironic word puzzles used by Zen monks, tule fog forces us to practice just living, with no expectation of enlightenment. Like life's impermanence and imperfection, fog is not what I would choose, but it is a part of the place, and each home place has its quirks. I have not resolved my tule fog koan—only accepted it.

It is in the nature of this region, too, to be alternatively parched and flooded, sometimes to extremes. In the winter of 1862–1863, the valley was a lake sixty miles wide, and steamboats plied the waters rescuing farmers from the roofs of their barns. The first Yolo County seat, Fremont, abandoned its town site after three consecutive years of flooding wore down the people's will to stay. Now Fremont is only the name of the flood weir that spills Sacramento River water into the Yolo Bypass. During the past several years, while this book was being prepared, we have had more than the normal winter rainfall. As I write this chapter on May 28, 1998, it is cold, rainy, and fifty degrees, and it is snowing in the Sierra. Floodwaters have made national news; calls for more levees and dams have accelerated. The circular, drainlike "Glory Hole" spillway at Lake Berryessa has overflowed each year for three years running, providing a minor tourist attraction for locals. Ten years ago we had three years of drought, with every-other-day lawn watering encouraged by impoverished suburban water districts.

Water and Earth

Indeed, the subject of water deserves its own discussion: this natural resource is the lifeblood of an agricultural region such as ours. The Sacramento Valley, from roughly Mount Shasta, or a bit southward, on down, receives ten to thirty inches of rain in the winter and is dry as a bone in summer; on its west side lies a thirty-thousand-foot depth of alluvial soil. It is a former grassland savanna with vast seasonal marshland, now drained, and riparian forests long since cut down to fuel commerce and propel the steamships that once plied the river from San Francisco to the northern valley. Of those former riparian lands, less than 10 percent remain. Today, too, the land is almost entirely private; it supports a few more "family" farmers than its southern landform counterpart, the San Joaquin Valley, but still it is not the Midwestern, democratically gridded farm mosaic of Iowa, Nebraska, or Kansas. The land patterns here, in fact, speak of multiple cultural influences, from the Spanish and Mexican land grants to the homesteads of early American settlers to the patterns of twentieth-century irrigation technology. The valley is ringed by water impoundments uphill on its major streams and rivers and laced with water supply and drainage canals. It is the most significantly altered of all California's diverse landscapes, and it provides a substantial chunk of not only the American but the global food supply.

The transformation of this region has not been without problems. Foremost among these is the loss of prime farmland to development. Since most valley towns originated as farming centers, they occupy some of the best arable soils in the world. (For years after the houses were built, volunteer tomatoes came up in the backyards of my own neighborhood in Davis.) According to estimates by the California Department of Finance, the population of the Great Central Valley (Sacramento and San Joaquin Valleys combined) will double in the next twenty years, a rate more than twice as fast as the already steep statewide growth rate. Existing urbanization has already taken 17 percent of the prime agricultural land out of production. Another 17 percent will be removed if each incorporated town or city grows merely to its existing general plan boundaries within the next two or three decades. Furthermore, the overall residential density of the Sacramento Valley is only 1.5 dwelling units per gross acre—much lower than that of coastal communities in the state. New development caters to a demand for low-density, single-family residences and thus gobbles up farmland voraciously at the cities' edges. I should remind readers that two of what were once California's most productive agricultural valleys are now paved: Los Angeles and Santa Clara. Without some combination of avoidance of development on prime agricultural lands, greater density for new housing projects, and reduced growth rates, the Sacramento Valley bioregion risks losing its productive farming future to development.[6]

Along with the loss of agricultural soils, water tops the list of concerns in the Sacramento Valley. Most tributary creeks from mountain regions to the immediate east and west are impounded for summer water supplies, often denying downstream valley reaches adequate flows to keep ecosystems viable but enabling agriculture and, in so doing, defining the bioregion. Southerly regions covet our water, and northern, up-valley farmers and ranchers far from the middle-state Sacramento–San Joaquin Delta system (and the state capital in Sacramento) do not look kindly upon southward water transfers. Agriculture uses over 80 percent of the water supply in the region,[7] and losses of water to any other use or to any other region are deemed by the agricultural sector to be an erosion of local agricultural capacity. Farming, wildlife, and cities all compete for water here. Local runs of Chinook salmon and steelhead are now listed as endangered species. Listing of these fish runs has been a wake-up call for all parties, as nearly every tributary in the valley now has some form of nonprofit conservancy aimed at watershed protection and restoration. Money to accomplish these tasks was not forthcoming until a referendum aimed at solving ecological problems in California's bay-delta estuary (Proposition 204) passed a statewide popular vote in 1996.

In the bay-delta, an area often defined as its own bioregion and the hinge point for delivery of northern California water to southern California farms and cities, streams are forced to run backward as the vast statewide canal system sucks the freshwater southward—and the fish smolts with it, through the intake turbine blades. Saltwater intrusion backwashes into the formerly freshwater channels of the delta as well, causing increasing salinity in the water supply intakes of several delta cities.

A vast quasi-governmental superstructure funded by state voter initiative, Cal-Fed, has been established to restore riparian habitat, improve water quality, and ensure the proper ecological function of the bay-delta. Conservative Sacramento Valley agricultural groups suspect government collusion to deprive them of their water; liberal environmentalists worry that they are being bought off with restoration money to pave the way for another attempt to build a "peripheral" canal around the delta. The first such effort, in 1976, prompted the creation of the original West Coast bioregional group, Planet Drum. As I write this, public suspicion on both right and left over Cal-Fed policies and programs and their possible impact on southward water transfers is high, yet the lure of easy money for restoration has everyone's attention.

In the foothills surrounding the valley floor, all is not well either. Exotic tamarisk and false bamboo choke the riparian corridors and impoverish streamside ecosystems. Cattle prices (as of this writing) are among the lowest ever in real dollars. Star thistle, an ecologically useless exotic weed injurious to cattle, has by some scientific accounts usurped more land area in California than urban development itself. Cattle ranchers, who have been relatively free of interference by federal statutes, will soon be brought within the purview of the Clean Water Act, which seeks to eliminate nonpoint

sources of pollution, and will be under increasing scrutiny for those management practices that affect water quality. As protective riparian vegetation that filters surface inflow into streams is removed, eaten, or trampled
by cattle, sediment and nitrate loads increase in tributaries, and other ecological functions are lost. But grazing allows less-than-prime agricultural
land to contribute to the economy and regional food supply, and in defense
of the ranchers, most residents of the bioregion eat beef. What is needed is
much more two-way communication between beef growers and beef eaters
so that the former are paid by the latter to protect the water quality, which
is a resource for all.

As farming becomes increasingly mechanized on the flat valley floor, agricultural jobs are lost to technology and to foreign producers. Away from
urbanizing suburbs and growth cities, rural economies in the bioregion are
hurting, and unemployment approaches 20 percent in more remote areas.
Mining brings some revenue, as do agricultural processing, shipping, and some
manufacturing. The Sacramento Valley bioregion has little timber, and forest industry activities in the adjacent North Coast, Klamath, Cascade, and
Northern Sierra bioregions have been hampered by their own problems.
Also, the Sacramento Valley has very little public land or topography on
which to base a recreation and tourism industry. Traditionally, nonresidents
have considered the valley a "negative" space: a hot, boring, flat region to
pass through on the way to somewhere else. With populations expanding
due to inexpensive land for development, pressures for outdoor recreation
are growing, and fear of loss of private property rights and potential liability prevails among rural landowners. This situation has led to a serious lack
of mutual understanding, to declining trust, and to an eroding quality of
life for the traditional agricultural and growing urban communities alike.

Yet there is considerable hope. The Sacramento Valley, like the San
Joaquin to the south, has of late become regionally self-aware. A think tank
of sorts, the Great Valley Center, has been established in Modesto; painters,
poets, writers, photographers, and museum curators have begun to turn to
the valley as their subject; and restoration ecologists and wildlife managers
have rediscovered the immense potential to regenerate the valley's endemic
wetlands, riparian corridors, grasslands, and faunal populations. As in other
regions, the many volunteer organizations that have emerged on behalf of
the tributaries, streams, rivers, and recently constructed or existing wetlands
would fill a map of the valley with color. There is, as yet, no ecotourism to
speak of, and few travel guides have been written, but perhaps these await
the arrival of agro-tourists desiring to learn where their food *really* comes
from. Where *does* it come from? From irrigation water, applied on top of

soil originally deposited over eons by floodwaters; an ancient duet of water and earth.

Grounding

(Perhaps the first and foremost comprehension of where we are emerges through the simple, direct experience of geographic space, geological land-form, and a tactile perception of the dirt beneath our feet. *Grounding,* both physically and emotionally, is just what it implies: a sense of the ground— and of the space defining and defined by it) How often have we suddenly become aware of terra firma—that familiar, atavistic feeling of resting our feet on the surface of the earth while sensing the structural form of the land around us? I vividly recall the ancient stone Druid circle my wife and I vis-ited in the Lake District of England on our honeymoon and the kinship we felt with those humans who preceded us by several thousand years to that site with its remarkable 360-degree command of the local landscape. No words were necessary; their grounding was also ours, although, unlike them, we were merely visitors.

Yet this quality of experience is available to us in our home places. The bones of a life-place can be experienced anywhere. Some science is helpful, but it need not be a straitjacket. (Visit a familiar open space in your home region, stand in its center, turn around very slowly, and perceive the en-veloping earth and its landforms. This is where you live. Start from there. Equipped with such awareness, it is then an easy step to the subject of the next chapter: the life of the place itself.)

2 Living

AWAKENING TO A LIVE REGION

The Great Central Plain of California, during the months of March, April, and May, was one smooth, continuous bed of honey-bloom, so marvelously rich that, in walking from one end of it to the other, a distance of more than 400 miles, your foot would press about a hundred flowers at every step.
JOHN MUIR, 1894

Hyperbole or not, John Muir's description above has kindled the imagination of valley residents for over a century. Living here, now, we find it hard to imagine duplicating or matching his experience of life in this region. Yet the picture his words paint serves as a measure of biotic potential: given the correct conditions, this land just might reach a similar efflorescence again. Life-places produce specific flora and fauna partly because of their fundamental conditions and partly in response to human disturbances. We are but another species of animal pushing on the equilibrium. Since Muir, we humans have converted a vast majority of the "Central Plain" to agriculture, as we have converted arable regions the world over, simply because it held the potential for cultivation. Muir's "honey-bloom" is now our breadbasket.

This chapter brings to the forefront two very important notions. First, any bioregion has the inherent potential for specific, unique kinds of life, human and otherwise. Second, and most important (although we rarely realize it), the life-place enveloping us is truly and completely *alive*. The second notion—of a live region—should be simple and obvious. It is not. Like anything else in life, awakening to it takes concentration, practice, and an open mind. On occasion, if we are primed for the possibility, life-places emphatically assert their living dimensions when we least expect it, and not always in the visual or olfactory conditions Muir relates above.

The year is 1986, and I am seeking places to recapture the superlative fishing conditions I once experienced in the far Northwest when, for one brief summer between college years, I was a deputy warden for the Alaska Department of Fish and Game and became accustomed to the presence of vast migrations of salmon and the ease with which they were enticed to the line and net. Today, with fly rods and waders, a friend and I explore the Feather River Wildlife Area, just below Oroville. It is a fall run, with the big fish reaching the spawning gravels just as the cottonwood leaves are showing the rust spots of autumn. I am exhilarated as I wade into the stream and experience the familiar, slightly sweetish but mildly foul odor of decaying fish. Huge carcasses lie on the gravel edge, while the riffles are frequently broken by salmon breaching to shake off sea lice. Out in the water, I barely pay attention to the fly line as it drifts, being far more pleasantly distracted by the antics of the male and female salmon, which are darting about en route upstream in their terminal dance. I haven't seen fish populations like this since Alaska, and for a time, I wonder where I really am. Same huge fish, same odor, but different trees and climate. The capstone of this very significant moment in my bioregional education comes without warning. Drifting my wet fly line while facing downstream, I am suddenly knocked off my feet and into the water by what I presume is either a person stumbling upon me or a log hitting the backs of my knees. I turn to see the half-decayed carcass of the most enormous salmon I have ever spotted float past me to some unknown downstream destination.

The Biotic Hypothesis

The notion that we all live in places shared by thousands of other species of organisms—that we truly live in a world that is *alive*—leads us to another fundamental bioregional hypothesis, the Biotic Hypothesis: *Bioregions can be defined in terms of distinct communities of life, both human and non-human, where implicit conditions suggest particular ecological adaptations.*

A pivotal but controversial word in the above axiom is *communities*. We share our world with countless other organisms, but are these organisms merely individual objects of our natural perception or our structured, scientific inquiry? Or do they form true, interdependent "communities" or delicate webs of interacting feedback loops? Or are they, perhaps, somewhere in between?

These questions are now being vigorously examined by academic ecologists and practicing resource managers, upon whose shoulders the job of protecting biodiversity now falls. With recent and growing critique of the Endangered Species Act as being too highly focused on single species, political pressure is building and consensus is slowly swinging toward protecting endangered ecosystems and landscapes that support unique associations of species, some of which may be legally listed as endangered. "Habitat conservation plans" have emerged as a favored means of comprehensively resolving the resource impacts of development. This multispecies, multiresource ecosystem management approach has been endorsed and formalized by the California Biodiversity Council, a group of federal, state, local, and private agencies that signed a memorandum of understanding in 1991 to work together to produce a bioregional framework for managing the state's biodiversity and natural resources.[1]

Community versus Continuum

The year is 1994. I arrive early for the presentation and take a seat facing outward in the small seminar room on the ninth floor of Sproul Hall, the tallest building in Davis. While awaiting the speaker, I look out the floor-to-ceiling picture windows across the tops of the urban forest canopy that now covers Davis and glance toward the distant foothills. I see imported oaks, sycamores, elms, and hackberries in the foreground, black walnut rows along middle-distance agricultural fields, and the faintest traces of blue oaks and chaparral on the distant ridges. It seems, from my high vantage point, a natural transition: exotic vegetation close in, natural vegetation farther out. Soon, Michael Barbour enters the room. Broad-shouldered and bespectacled, Barbour is perhaps the preeminent field biologist in California, with a publication record both long and influential. He and I are Humanities Institute Fellows this year, and he will now give our small gathering a presentation on a most pivotal scientific question, one pertinent not only to the "bioregional" movement and the biotic hypothesis but to the very way humanity sees itself in the natural world.

Barbour tells us of an old and continuing debate originating in the early twentieth century between two plant ecologists, Frederic Clements and Henry Gleason. He begins by drawing graphs of the frequency distributions of plants over some hypothetical distance, each plant achieving its highest population density at a different place on the horizontal axis, like a group of hills whose profiles overlap. Biologist Frederic Clements, Barbour tells us, argued that vegetation occurred naturally in "communities," each of which could be considered a near organism unto itself, in which at least some of the members had an essential role in the interaction of the entire plant community. In other words, Clements would have seen in Barbour's graph a purposeful clustering of species whose distribution "hills" combined to make up a singular "mountain range" on the chalkboard. Henry Gleason, in contrast, argued that each plant species was located along its own continuum of opportunity and "associated" with other plants only when its own specific ecological conditions were met. In Gleason's argument, three conditions determined whether a plant species existed or failed to exist in a particular location: *colonization* ("arrival" at the site), *extinction* ("departure" of plants from a particular location), and the *changing environmental conditions* of that location. Gleason's view of plants as existing along independent continua according to individual needs was a reductionist conclusion in direct opposition to Clements's holistic assumption that plants existed in mutually interacting and interdependent communities. In Barbour's crude chalkboard plant distribution graph, Gleason would have seen only the individual "hills" of each plant's unique spatial distribution independent of the distributions of others.[2]

There has never been an adequate "scientific" resolution to the community-continuum debate. Sawyer and Keeler-Wolf, in their *Manual of California Vegetation*, mention the community-unit versus continuum view of vegetation and discuss the risks of calling anything a vegetation "community" at this particular moment in the evolution of science. Instead they classify California vegetation groups as "series," "alliances," or "associations," basing their groupings on dominance of the most obvious genus or species by means of visual assessment or, less frequently, quantitative sampling. Unfortunately, they stop short of mapping the various series.[3]

Despite the scientific debate, a "bioregion" may depend more on human perception, use, and conservation of particular assemblages of vegetation than on whether that vegetation itself, exclusive of humans, is scientifically labeled a community or merely an association. We humans *perceive* vegetation in terms of patterns of dominant species, and these groupings have fuzzy boundaries. In the Sacramento Valley bioregion, one senses the difference between a blue oak woodland, a valley oak savanna, and a mixed coniferous/black oak forest. The important questions are how humans have related to these plant associations and sustainably extracted their living from them and how they might do so in the future. There is ample evidence that human evolution necessitated development of the ability to both "lump" and "split": to differentiate between plants and "reduce" information about each one and to recognize patterns of association among numerous species and various categories of landscape. It seems reasonable to assume that a functional dependency of certain peoples on certain associations of plants (e.g., the indigenous acorn-eating peoples in central Cali-

fornia or the salmon eaters of the Pacific Northwest) resulted in a distribution in space and time that can be interpreted only as "bioregional," or
"life-place," dependent.**)**

Of course, animals, to highly varying degrees, move about and migrate
more easily than plants do. Therefore, identifying a "biological" region may
depend a great deal on which species are spatially recorded or mapped. However, Forest Service scientist Hartwell Welsh draws conclusions about the
relative uniqueness of bioregions by examination of the spatial distributions
of less vagile (far-ranging) species such as amphibians, which are likely to
have evolved over greater periods of time within more finitely constrained
spaces than other species have. Salamanders, for example, reveal a strong
relationship between watershed boundaries and speciation and therefore
serve as a kind of "indicator" species for bioregional uniqueness.[4]

It is possible to extend this line of thinking to ridiculous conclusions: to
manage territories of land for human affairs based upon the distribution of
salamanders would be patently absurd! Yet there is some worth in investi-
gating where logical "biotic shifts" occur—where a substantial number of
species change as one moves between territories.

Holism Returns

To some extent, views about the ecological legitimacy of bioregions may follow general cultural attitudes toward structuralist versus deconstructivist
paradigms. In the past several decades, Gleasonian continuum distribution
has dominated biogeography, a trend matched by a more general reductionism in science, where individual species have often been studied without concern for their relation to other species. In this scientific climate, few
holistic patterns are likely to be developed, and arguments against "natural regions" carry more weight.

Lately, however, a modest swing back toward holism has been taking place.
While scientists still focus primarily on one species at a time through academic research or protection plans for individual species (under the Endangered Species Act), field managers of natural areas struggle to integrate their
tasks of managing for the whole environment in terms of multiple objec-
tives, resources, and species. Buttressed by the other integrative disciplines
of landscape ecology and conservation biology, the relatively new field of
"ecosystem management" is more likely to be inclusive than exclusive and
may begin to successfully incorporate social and cultural variables as well
as abiotic and biotic factors. But beyond these relatively narrow academic

debates, the general public itself has grown tired of a world seemingly splintered by science and technology.(The bioregion has emerged as a potent conceptual idea simply because people are now intently striving to see overall pattern and purpose in life once again.)

To deliberately oversimplify, academic and experimental biologists focus on the parts; field managers and, to some extent, the public focus on the whole. The piecemeal approach has accomplished little in the way of actual progress toward the sustainable and mutual maintenance of water quality and quantity, species diversity, forest structure, soil fertility, flood management, or wildlife abundance.(To some extent, the life-place concept is about *applied* science rather than basic science. Just as physics and chemistry gave birth to engineering, which structured the industrial era, biology and ecology are now faced with siring an adequate applied field (a synthesis of ecosystem management, conservation biology, landscape ecology, and environmental ethics, perhaps) to provide society with a practical way to reconstruct a more regenerative future for life on earth.)

Living Indicators of Place

Human perception is a magnificent patterning and recognition tool. Just as ecologists have come up with key indicator species whose presence or absence marks the existence or condition of ecosystems, one might also speak of *perceptual* indicator species—particular plants or animals that so dominate their surroundings by their ubiquitous presence that whole regions are identified with them. Consider the importance of the ponderosa pine to the mountainous western regions, the long- and short-grass prairies to the Midwest, the Douglas fir to the Northwest, the birch to the far north, and the mangrove to the Florida Keys. Picture the "buffalo plains," caribou on the tundra, ducks and geese in the great flyway wetlands, white-tail deer in eastern deciduous forests. Societies from primitive to modern have recognized these straightforward biological indicators of place. Plants and especially animals have helped to define regions, as totems, animist spirits, team mascots, and official "state" emblems, from the beginnings of civilization through today.

TREES

The vegetative patriarch of the Sacramento Valley bioregion is *Quercus lobata*, the valley oak (figure 2.1). Look in any western tree field guide with

Figure 2.1 *Quercus lobata*, the valley oak, icon of the Sacramento Valley bioregion. Photograph by Robert Thayer.

range distribution maps, and you will find that the valley oak is the most prominent and characteristic tree species of the Central Valley. An isolated valley oak at maturity has a massive, stout trunk, heavy scaffold limbs, and countless smaller branches that seem to change direction at every old node, making it a caricature of a Halloween tree against the skyline. This is the emblematic tree of California, and a large specimen may practically constitute an ecosystem unto itself: acorn woodpeckers and ground squirrels (and formerly humans) depend on its acorns; hawks and owls feed on the ground squirrel population. Mistletoe, a parasite, survives by rooting in the branches to steal the sap; bluebirds and phainopeplas, in turn, feed on the mistletoe and spread the seeds to other branches and other trees through their fecal droppings. Countless insects eat or nest in all of the oak's various parts, while wood rats eat the leaves. Valley oaks have evolved as a food and shelter source for so many organisms that to preserve them is literally to preserve an entire way of life.[5]

Valley communities each have their special, identifiable old valley oaks, many of which have anchored past parkland preservation efforts. Chico had its "Hooker oak" tree, which drew British botanist Sir John Hooker halfway around the world to examine it, and Chico still boasts some of the world's largest valley oaks in its Bidwell Park. Davis's current specimen, called merely "the Oak Tree," sits in the middle of the city's Community Park. It provides a nexus for soccer referees during frequent tournaments, and whole teams seek refuge under its canopy during spring downpours or intense summer sun.(Anderson Marsh State Historic Park, near Clear Lake, has a valley oak whose trunk takes six people with arms outstretched, hand to hand, to encircle.)Set off against the gold hues of the late-summer dry season, or isolated amid surrounding crop fields or pasture, the majestic valley oak is the quintessential natural icon of central California.

Gray pine *(Pinus sabiniana)* is the unsung hero forming part of the vegetative fringe of the bioregion (figure 2.2). It grows in rocky, alkaline, thin soils and endures extreme temperatures and long summer drought. Its light gray-green foliage and long, graceful needles diffuse the bright sunlight and reduce the heat load, creating a feathery, ghostlike silhouette (some prefer to call it the "ghost pine"). Deadly-sharp spikes on the cones have evolved to pierce the duff to find mineral soil upon contact with the ground. Gray pine cones are opened by fire, a requisite for the species' ecological dispersal and regeneration. Its pine nuts were used by natives when acorn crops were poor. The trunks of the gray pine bifurcate in adolescence, giving it a scraggly, asymmetrical character that seems to befit the rugged low foothills of its domain. The wood is brittle, making it nearly useless as a lumber tree.(Ranging in elevation from about five hundred feet up to about three thousand feet, the gray pines signal an important transition: if you've left the gray pines behind on the way uphill, you've left the Sacramento Valley bioregion.)

Blue oaks *(Quercus douglasii)* are the gray pine's frequent companions. Smaller and less spreading than the valley oak, blue oaks also have slightly grayer foliage, again an adaptation to the foothill heat and drought. Blue oak often grades into gray pine on upper slopes and into valley oak lower down in broad valleys or riparian corridors. Often occurring in pure stands in oak woodland or savanna, blue oaks are the last oaks on the lowest ridges as one makes the transition downward and onto the agricultural mosaic of the valley floor. Blue oaks are suffering a lack of regeneration, however, and the precise cause is still being debated. Non-native grasses, overgrazing, inadequate predation of acorn-eating ground squirrels, fuel wood harvesting, lack of the evolutionary fire regimes to which the trees are adapted, and overpopulation of browsing deer have all been suggested by ecologists and botanists as possible factors contributing to the declining populations of blue oaks.

Other trees help define the region: black walnut *(Juglans californica* var. *hindsii)*, sycamore *(Platanus racemosa)*, and cottonwood *(Populus fre-*

Figure 2.2 Gray pine, *Pinus sabiniana* (sometimes called "foothill" or "ghost" pine), seen in the right foreground, often accompanies blue oaks *(Quercus douglasii)*, which dot the distant foothills. Trees such as Fremont cottonwood *(Populus fremontii)*, white alder *(Alnus rhombifolia)*, and red willow *(Salix laevigata)* populate the riparian edge of Solano Lake, an impoundment of lower Putah Creek. Photograph by Robert Thayer.

montii) along valley streams; redbud *(Cercis occidentalis)* in the lower side canyons, black oak *(Quercus kelloggii)*, madrone *(Arbutus menziesii)*, and yellow pine *(Pinus ponderosa)* in the extreme upper elevations. Then there is the much-maligned eucalyptus, imported from Australia and Tasmania as a fuel wood, windbreak, and pulp tree. Rectangular groves of blue gums *(Eucalyptus globulis)* amid the mosaic of farm fields are a characteristic sign of central California, so much so that first-time visitors mistake them for indigenous trees. One reason I now live in California is that on approach to my interview for graduate school at Stanford University, I passed through pleasantly scented eucalyptus groves along Palm Drive and concluded that any place with such balmy climate and aromatic vegetation must be quite special and worthy of future time spent there.

Eucalyptus is a *biome* tree—its native territory is an area of the world climatically similar to California but not necessarily ecologically similar. Hence, few of the eucalyptus's native compatriot organisms accompanied it here, and its role in enriching our own ecosystems is minimal, which prompts the consternation of many a native-plant purist. However, eucalyptus is part of California now and brings with it a history of cultural association with our region in paintings, in flower arrangements, and, in the northern Sacramento Valley, as a source of fiber for high-quality paper.

FLOWERS

Although in the Sierra John Muir likely saw—and maybe even named—a few Bear Valleys (given the ubiquity of the name), it is doubtful that he ever saw *our* Bear Valley.[6] Ours is a flat, remote wildflower heaven just west of the Sacramento Valley and up over the first ridges into the Coast Range, and it is known mainly to local ranchers and a few people of an intense botanical bent.

Bear Valley apparently receives its English name from *tsukui*, the "bear-place village," a name in turn derived from the Hill Patwin word for grizzly bear *(Ursus chelan)*.[7] Homesteaded for at least four generations, Bear Creek was modified to drain a formerly marshy area for cattle grazing; hence the world-class wildflower display each spring, a by-product of the interventions of human nature. Even the most avid wildflower buffs understand the necessity of cattle grazing to the perpetuation of this display. Today, this place, with its four hundred species of plants, has a much higher chance of survival than it did in the past because it recently has received a conservation easement to allow ranching and wildflowers to coexist in perpetuity. Native plant specialist Craig Thomsen has set up a number of small test plots to determine the best ways to protect and enhance the native grasses, forbs, and wildflowers. The valley's current protector, the American Land Conservancy, has published a pocket-size guidebook featuring fifty Bear Valley wildflowers, neatly arranged according to color. It tells us that the rare, elegant snowdrop bush *(Styrax officinalis)* hides in moist canyons edging the valley and reveals its white, fuchsialike flowers only to the seeker. In April, huge yellow carpets of tidytips *(Layia chrysanthemoides, L. platyglossa)* show no such timidity, covering the valley floor. Distinctive Ithuriel's spear *(Triteleia laxa)* paints small patches of violet, while orange California poppies *(Eschscholzia californica)* and purple owl's clover *(Lupinus bicolor)* compete for center stage. Yet the officially threatened adobe lily *(Fritillaria pluriflora)* is the botanical star of this annual performance, occupying western-edge fields in the valley as bulbs in the clay soil until the right combination of rainfall, sunlight, and temperature coaxes them out in vast sweeps of rose-pink. Bear Valley provides such a concentration of adobe lilies that the very future of the flower depends on the place and, perhaps, vice versa.[8]

FISH

If asked where "salmon country" is on the continent, most folks would probably point to the northwest coastal regions of the United States, Canada, and Alaska. It is little known that the Sacramento River drainages once produced one of the largest Chinook salmon populations in North America. Prior to the turn of century, enormous schools of *Oncorhyncus tshawytscha* migrated up the main stem and into the various tributaries in three different runs: a fall run, a winter run, and a spring run enticed by cold snowmelt from Sierra streams draining the east side of the valley. Native River Patwin peoples depended heavily on this plentiful source of food and, in so doing, became plentiful themselves. At the time of European contact, River Patwin people numbered over 10,000, living in large permanent villages of up to 1,200 people each—easily the largest concentration of natives in what was later to become the state of California.[9] The size and stability of these Patwin groups were evidence of the size and stability of the salmon runs and acorn crops, which together provided a rich and balanced food economy. The Patwin, unlike their far northern counterparts, often dried and pulverized the salmon into a powder, which they added to various foods. After whites settled the region, early canneries and overfishing, plus rapid agricultural development, upstream logging and ranching, water impoundment, urbanization, and loss of spawning habitat, left the fishery at only a fraction of its former strength. There are a few runs, however, where Chinook are still plentiful, and at specific times and places on the Feather River, the state of California allows an open season with a two-fish limit.

Peter Moyle lives, breathes, and even smiles fish. He is a collaborator in our university's student-staff-faculty-initiated Putah-Cache Bioregion Group and is regarded as the foremost fish biologist in California. Moyle

Figure 2.3 Spawned-out Feather River salmon lodge in the shallow gravel of the Oroville Wildlife Area. Photograph by Robert Thayer.

has written books for managerial, scientific, and lay audiences and has been threatened anonymously with violence for his role in listing the delta smelt as an endangered species. Most importantly and most recently, he was the key expert witness in the litigation to require the Solano Irrigation District and Solano Water Agency to release sufficient summer water from the upstream Monticello Dam on Putah Creek to keep the lower creek's stock of native fishes alive. Moyle's research finds that since impoundment of the stream in 1956, the anadromous, or migratory, fish runs have been declining, other native species have been disappearing, and non-native species have been expanding in the lower creek.

Putah and Cache Creeks do not flow directly into the Sacramento year round; they are rather tenuously connected to the Sacramento–San Joaquin Delta and the San Francisco Bay via irrigation drainage canals in summer or by flood events in winter. Anadromous fish must find their way up through a maze of marsh, sloughs, ditches, drains, and check dams into the Yolo Bypass, where both creeks ended in a seasonal wetlands prior to the establishment of modern flood control and irrigation structures.

The winters of 1995, 1996, and 1997 have been unusually rainy. In fact, it is raining when, on a day in January 1998, I check my e-mail to find a message from Peter: "Salmon in Putah Creek!" On December 31, 1997, Marilyn Whitney and her husband, who live about eight miles upstream along the creek, observed a strange, large, brassy-colored fish vigorously preparing a "redd," or spawning area, in the gravel, and shortly thereafter they saw two males accompanying her. They videotaped the fish for several minutes. A few days later they found the female spawned out, dead, a short distance downstream, and they hauled her carcass out for more video footage and a measurement, later notifying Peter, who observed the footage, confirmed the fish as Chinook salmon, and sent the e-mail. Some of us suggest a press release (well aware that our successful litigation for "environmental" summer water downstream is being appealed by the Solano County water agencies), and Channel 3 TV in Sacramento runs a story. To both our local citizen-based Putah Creek Council and our university Putah-Cache Bioregion Group, this event is both fortuitous and deeply gratifying.

A day in April, four months later, we receive a second e-mail from Peter: his students have found juvenile salmon fingerlings in Putah Creek, most likely from the New Year's spawner or her cohorts. This time, a press release goes out right away, and the spawning success of the salmon is toasted among the various watershed groups.

We have been assembling our own anecdotal evidence of the viability of Chinook in these minor, intermittent westside tributaries to the Sacramento. From oral evidence, we hear that just after the turn of the twentieth century, farmers routinely (and probably illegally) pitchforked salmon into their wagons from the small sloughs between Putah and Cache Creeks. Dreams of restoring this kind of habitat potency keep us enthusiastic about such meager evidence as we now witness in our own backyard. Cal-Fed, the multi-agency umbrella organization charged with spending millions in publicly approved bond money to restore habitat and water quality to the bay-delta and Sacramento River system, may very well be interested in looking more closely at Putah Creek, once thought to be only a minor contributor to saving the salmon. For decades, there has been no significant salmon population in Putah Creek; Monticello Dam and the near-complete diversion of summer water downstream have seen to that. But Peter Moyle says the Sacramento Valley Chinook have a "rove gene," allowing them to try a new tributary now and then just to broaden their survival chances and recolonize new territory. I like to think that the salmon have waited until our own human attitudes and behaviors were adequately proven before they attempted to recolonize; perhaps now we will give them a better welcome home.[10]

BIRDS

In the fall of 1996, we are introducing ourselves at the main meeting table at the local Indian college, Deganawidah-Quetzalcoatl University (a name so hard to pronounce that it is officially known, even to the natives, as "DQU"). It is my first time inside the academic buildings, which have been salvaged from leftover federal property. The general topic for the day is a master plan for the square mile or so of agricultural land that surrounds the modest buildings and facilities. Dwayne Chamberlain, also in attendance, is the farmer to whom DQU leases the land: his lease provides a large fraction of the college's meager operating budget. Today, we are discussing the possibility of some federal matching funds and cooperation from the local resource conservation district. Also, a number of traditional native basket makers and a crafts instructor at the college would like to have some of the small, naturally occurring wetlands on the college's property dedicated to the growing of native wetland basketry plants, which have been disappearing in recent decades. The only problem is that basket makers hold the reeds in their mouths to keep their hands free to weave; they therefore ingest orally the toxins that have been absorbed by the plants.

Dwayne carefully explains about each of the four or five major pests that invade his alfalfa fields during the year, and the three or four pesticides he must spray if there is to be any crop at all to pay DQU's bills. "I'll use whatever low-input or organic control will work; just tell me what it is, and I'll use it," says Dwayne, half pleading, yet rationally demonstrating the dilemma: no pesticides, no crop—no budget for basketry classes, no marsh restoration, and no baskets made from native wetland plants. The meeting ends with both sides agreeing to consider creative solutions and meet each other halfway, and a master plan for wetland restoration is begun by the Yolo County Resource Conservation District, with active participation by both Chamberlain and the Indians.

About one year later, I am riding a bicycle one late spring day in the afternoon; it has rained unusually hard the past several days, and many of the fields are partially flooded. I make the turn around DQU and stop for a water break at my traditional spot, with a view of the Blue Ridge to the west. There, in Dwayne's DQU alfalfa field, which is about half covered with water, are thirty or more Swainson's hawks, a bird officially classified as threatened by the state of California. The hawks appear to be eating insects, probably crickets or grasshoppers, flushed out by the advance of water across the field. Whatever Dwayne has or has not been spraying on his alfalfa has allowed this raptor feast to occur.

Swainson's hawks migrate annually in spring from South and Central America to California, nesting in riparian trees and foraging in agricultural fields. Ironically, Swainson's hawks may end up as one of the region's best farmland preservation allies. Once native to the California lowland prairie and marsh environments, Swainson's hawks have adapted to foraging in low-growing field and row crops, and nesting in nearby riparian—or even suburban—trees. Pressure to mitigate the loss of Swainson's hawk habitat has led a number of valley counties to establish or propose conservation easements on agricultural land, a move beneficial to the preservation of hawk and farmland alike.

The next trip I make to DQU, nearly another year later, is with the staff of the Yolo Resource Conservation District. We are inspecting a small grassland restoration project on college land that is included in a "model farms" grant project aimed at bolstering biodiversity and conserving water, soil, and energy. Ground squirrels dart in and out of their holes as we walk up a slight rise in the otherwise low-lying irrigated fields surrounding the campus buildings. Soon we approach what is obviously a storage yard for the ejecta of agriculture; various rusted implements, fence parts, and farm equipment remnants lie scattered about. To our great surprise, hopping and flitting among the various forgotten items are two burrowing owls, another formerly prevalent bird now rapidly declining in population in the region. We treat this sighting as a positive sign of environmental health, quite contrary to the first impression given by the scatter of agricultural relics.

As we are about to enter the truck for the ride home, there, circling high overhead and slightly southward of the DQU campus buildings, is a golden eagle. Normally upland and mountainous hunters, golden eagles rarely make forays down so low in our valley. Paul, a former student and resource conservation district staffer, and I take turns with the binoculars: it is flying, as eagles commonly do, in the company of turkey vultures, rising on the thermals of this late September afternoon.

[More than once I have marveled at the interesting combinations of endangered birds and other wildlife I have seen at or near this homely-looking, remote Indian college. Why is it such an avian mecca? It is tempting to presume a more mystical connection between the vulnerability of both native peoples and native birds, but I am convinced that these raptors may be drawn to the area simply because DQU does not load the land with agricultural toxins or replace native or naturalized grasses with expensive, prestige-driven, manicured, irrigated landscapes. Fields are plowed, planted, and harvested not only with the crop in mind but with respect for a long-standing tradition of giving nature enough time and space to operate. Low landscape maintenance budgets at DQU translate to whole upland areas left fallow. The lesson may be simply this: if you leave it alone, they will come.]

Near sunset on a brisk, sunny November day in 1987, Lacey and I follow a caravan of cars through the gates and into Gray Lodge State Wildlife Refuge, near Colusa in the wet, marshy, lowland heart of the Sacramento Valley. We have been attending a two-day field course on the natural history of the Sutter Buttes and surroundings for my fortieth birthday. This is to be our last stop, and the naturalist has packed folding tables and coolers full of wine, cheese, and bread. It is duck-hunting season, and as we proceed inward toward the center of the refuge, the occasional, distant thumping of shotguns grows less frequent as the sun sinks toward the ridge of the Cortina Hills. At sunset, according to the regulations, the hunting must stop. "Give the ducks about twenty minutes," says the naturalist. "Have a glass of wine, some cheese and bread, and just watch." The sky turns a most iridescent orange, like the flesh of a golden trout. We talk quietly and sip Chardonnay in the still, cooling air. Slowly, toward the west and from the interior section of the refuge—always off limits to hunting—small clouds of ducks rise from the water, their distant, dark silhouettes no larger than the mosquitoes we now swat immediately around us. First one group, then three more; now many clusters, and soon, in the distance, the mandarin-orange-glowing wetland seems to be boiling off thousands of ducks, all clouding the pink-and-azure-tinged sky. Some groups get larger; a squadron whistles directly overhead, their cyclically hissing wing beats taking them beyond our picnic site to the marshlands from which the hunters have excluded them for the entire day. Then, squadron after squadron passes us, fanning outward, four or five species in as many directions. The sky is filled

Figure 2.4 Ducks, geese, and other migratory waterfowl blacken the skies over the Sacramento Valley. Photograph from the Yolo Basin Foundation.

with more birds than I have ever seen at one time in my life, and for a brief moment, the words of the writers encountering the valley's vast wetlands in the nineteenth century are animated in my immediate vision. The event itself lasts only as long as the sunset; the memory will last a lifetime.)

MAMMALS

Formerly, the charismatic megafauna of the Sacramento Valley and the Putah-Cache watersheds were the tule elk, grizzly bear, mountain lion, and pronghorn, as well as black bear and deer. Unfortunately, the grizzly bear has long since been extirpated by overzealous guns, and it now exists here only as a symbol on the state flag.(No one ate grizzlies, not even the natives, who, in fact, left them alone, thinking it bad medicine to consume grizzly bear flesh.)

Hiking the upper Putah Creek watershed on the east side of the Palisades with my two sons, I am alerted by our border collie, who stops dead in his tracks on the gravel road, staring down one of the largest black bears I have ever seen. This one is a reddish-golden brown—a cinnamon phase—though still a black bear, and it easily weighs four hundred pounds. The bear stares back momentarily, then lumbers off, leaving the four of us (dog included) breathless with excitement. Walking up to the spot where the bear had been feeding, we find chunks of enormous gray pine cones torn apart.

At water level in the valley streams that course through vastly altered agricultural lands, a canoeist or kayaker may see considerable wildlife without much evidence of humanity. Impounded creeks (especially Putah) are often deeply incised into the valley floor, their sediment budgets deprived of replacement gravels by upstream dams and reservoirs. This has two serendipitous benefits. First, it places the paddler well below the valley grade, hiding surrounding fields and human infrastructure from view. Second, by concentrating riparian cover in a narrow channel, it creates a secretive wild corridor of essential habitat for many species driven out of cultivated lands. Thus, the small creeks and sloughs of the lower Sacramento Valley create a connective web of riparian and aquatic life, much of it secluded from view.

On my frequent excursions to such places, I occasionally paddle into groups of river otter, who inquisitively tumble and dive around my canoe, then swim off, leaving only a trail of bubbles on the surface. At other times, rounding bends in the creek, I hear the slap of beaver tails—a sound taking me back to days in Algonquin Park in Canada's north woods, where I was once a canoe guide. Otter and beaver are indicators of a healthy stream system. (By damming tributaries, beaver allow nutrients and sediment to be captured and to nurture edge vegetation, which further protects water quality and provides habitat for multiple species, yet their dams allow large flows to pass.)

However, beaver in the narrow valley riparian corridors are not without their detractors. Restoration ecologists lament the loss of newly planted willow and cottonwood to the beaver's voracious appetite for food and building materials. Beaver can easily outgrow their own food supplies. On one bike trip along Putah Creek, I find a very large beaver carcass, obviously killed by a car, but still intact and robust in death. He most likely had run out of riparian vegetation in the slim stream channel and had perished while heading across the road into a young almond orchard in search of new forage.

In 1992, the mountain lion population in California is suffering, having been saved from hunting in 1986 only to endure six continuous years of drought. Word comes one day that a mountain lion has been sighted in the western extremities of the U.C. Davis campus. Two deer from the fenced-off experimental ecosystem are killed by the lion. Another sighting places the mountain lion even closer to campus, among the research grape vineyards.

Both vineyard and experimental ecosystem lie directly north of the Putah Creek corridor but at least a dozen miles from even the most meager foothill, to say nothing of mountains. Evidence soon surfaces of just how hungry and desperate the lion or lions are: a friend tells of a horse carcass that has been discovered three miles west of town, only partly consumed, as if the predator had been too exhausted or weak to drag it to a concealed place to eat. While on a walk, another friend and his wife encounter a fox carcass, completely bitten in half, out by the creek. Later, expert interpretation of the paw prints reveals a female puma and her cub, and the female is underweight.

A week later, we attend an evening fire circle at "Camp Putah" on the creek near the university, where our three children are participating in a summer night camp-out. At one point in the singing, games, and skits, a counselor playfully leads all the children out of earshot, while the camp director tells the remaining adults that a mountain lion was sighted in the area several days ago and that any parents who feel sufficiently concerned are free to take their children home but should do so in a manner that does not alarm those kids wishing to remain. The director adds that the counselors will sleep in a perimeter line around the children for added protection and that the best wildlife biologists have been consulted and feel the risk is not that great. Our children stay, and we later tell them of the comments.

Mountain lions? Perimeter lines of camp counselors to "protect" our children from becoming food for large carnivores? Is this *really* Davis, California? Putah Creek would change us all that year, as if telling us to pay attention. The lion would return the next year, killing another "experimental" deer, and a black bear would be found roaming the neighborhoods in northwest Woodland, having followed the mined-out gravel beds of Cache Creek down from the mountains to the west. Much later, another mountain lion and, two months later, another black bear were sighted near the Road 98 bridge over Putah Creek, a scant two miles from town. These events signal expansion of populations beyond habitat carrying capacity, forcing animals to forage and hunt in territory formerly unknown to them. People are of two minds about this. One argument follows the traditional American tendency to open up mountain lion hunting again (an initiative to do so failed again in 1996, with twice as many "no" votes as "yes" votes). The other argument, however, rejects this idea, preferring to develop other solutions in which we improve habitat and share our bioregions with other animals.

Putah Creek, Cache Creek, and the whole lower Sacramento Valley have somehow changed for me now. Although the mountain lion remains elusive, I fully notice the smaller creatures: beaver, otter, muskrat, numerous fish species, countless birds, aquatic organisms, and amphibians. And there is a living thread weaving them all together, tying the insects to the valley oaks and the valley oaks to the blue oaks, the gray pine to the chaparral, the geese to the eagles, the burrowing owls to the Swainson's hawks—and all of them to me and to this place.

3 Reinhabiting

RECOVERING A BIOREGIONAL CULTURE

No real public life is possible except among people who are engaged
in the project of inhabiting a place.

DANIEL KEMMIS, 1990

There is no such thing as a citizen of the world.

MANUEL CASTELLS, 1997

The Politics of Place

The year is 1999. When I arrive slightly tardily to the Regional California
Fish and Game Headquarters in Yountville, Napa watershed, the meeting
is standing-room only: at least twenty people are in chairs squeezed together arm to arm around the table and an equal number are seated or
standing at the perimeter. Incongruously, a stuffed polar bear, moose, and
caribou peer upon the assembled crowd from outside the glass-walled entrance of the room, adding irony to this most regional assemblage of voluntary participants—the newly forged Blue Ridge–Berryessa Natural Area
Conservation Partnership. Our common bond this Friday, like that of a dozen
or more monthly Fridays before it, is four hundred thousand acres of mountainous terrain covered by oak woodland, grassland, chaparral, serpentine
outcrop, and creekside riparian lands. The "BRBNA" (Blue Ridge–Berryessa
Natural Area) is the awkward moniker arrived at by committee as a label
for the wild, interior Coast Range lands extending southward from the Men-
docino National Forest nearly to Interstate 80 between San Francisco Bay
and Sacramento. Stretched between the upper watersheds of Putah and
Cache Creeks, BRBNA is an extraordinary mosaic of spectacular cattle
ranches, nationally significant wildflower displays, rugged whitewater creek
canyons, two water supply reservoirs (one ringed with double-wide trail-
ers and dotted with jet-skis and fishing boats), an enormous open-pit gold
mine, a university wildlands research center, a secluded, clothing-optional
hot springs resort, a federally designated wilderness study area home to bald
eagle and tule elk, and vast expanses of scrubby chamise chaparral so dense
that a human could not penetrate more than a foot into its midst. In spite
of its location in the California "Coast" Range (a misnomer), this is true,

Figure 3.1 Bioregional culture begins when volunteers identify with the natural features of the places they live. Blue Ridge–Berryessa Natural Area (BRBNA) T-shirt design by Robert Thayer; Cache Creek Conservancy hat logo by Julian Inchaurregui; Putah Creek Council logo by Yan Nascimbene.

nearly arid, remote, wild, *western* land that Zane Gray or Louis L'Amour would have loved. There is something for everyone in the BRBNA, and nearly everyone has come to this meeting, including the politicians.

The meeting agenda is full and proceeds with a report of the Bureau of Reclamation's concession services plan for the resorts around Lake Berryessa; news of the acquisition of the twelve-thousand-acre Payne Ranch by the Bureau of Land Management; talk of the possibility of a six-million-dollar congressional budget line item request to the House Interior Subcommittee for conservation land acquisitions; and vocal concerns over threats to biodiversity from a proposed "Moonie" (Unification Church) community on the BRBNA periphery. The agenda closes with a progress report on the transfer of Homestake Mine land to the university's McLaughlin Ecological Reserve. As items are discussed, the eyes of the local politicians widen; it seems they have rarely seen private ranchers, environmentalists, agency folk, professors, and game wardens around a table free of dispute or conflict. We leave the meeting with a heady, optimistic feeling.

The BRBNA, which is the brainchild of Ray Krauss, Homestake's former environmental manager, is one of several "bioregional" groups that have

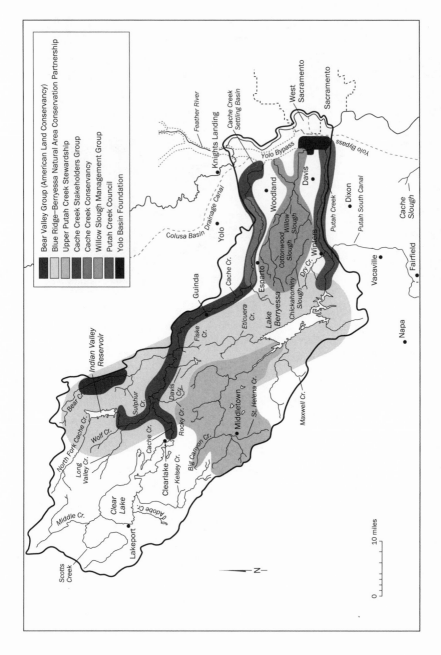

Figure 3.2 Territories addressed by some of the environmental groups in the Putah Creek and Cache Creek watershed area. Map based on original by Jacob Mann.

emerged in the Putah and Cache watersheds. Yet the extensive map of volunteer domains of concern here (figure 3.2) shows but a fragment of a growing phenomenon: all over North America people have begun to assemble on behalf of various watersheds, coastlines, mountain ranges, prairies, and lake regions. It is as if some long-lost ingredient of the national character has suddenly been rediscovered, a vital puzzle piece of democratic community in the midst of the myth of American individualism. Whatever the reason, people are now forming shared "communities" of mutual concern and action around the "tables" of natural regions. As the author and progressive politician Dan Kemmis might say, community is forming around the politics of place.[1]

What drives the human predisposition to gather in small groups that identify strongly with naturally definable regions, and to consider and participate in the best ways to guide those regions' futures? I cannot be certain, but I suggest a hypothesis: the newly globalized and highly specialized society in which we now find ourselves embedded is not the evolutionary norm; rather, what sustains us are finite natural territories inhabited by small bands of humans. We establish groups working on behalf of river basins or mountain ranges simply because it feels quite natural for us to do so. This chapter builds a bridge between those first people who originally inhabited a life-place and today's residents who seek to "reinhabit" theirs in a manner befitting the place.

Life-Place and Human Evolution

For most of our existence on earth, *Homo sapiens* banded together cooperatively to sustainably harvest the natural potentials of finite territories. Perception of the extent of the world and the size of its communities matched the ability of a particular group to derive livelihood from its world. Thus, the evolutionary survival of humanity has depended largely upon *social cooperation in place*. As late as 1981, economist Hazel Henderson pointed out that most of the world's people were still sustained by "growing their own food, tending their own animals in rural areas, and living in small, cooperatively run villages and settlements or as nomads following herds, harvesting wild crops, fishing, and hunting in economies based on barter, reciprocity, and redistribution of surpluses according to customs."[2]

The story of humanity, of course, is not finished; and in its latest chapters it has begun to diverge from this theme. While humans have flourished as economics and technology have allowed a certain transcendence of time and place, the fate of many other characters in the story—our companion species—is less certain.

Raymond Dasmann differentiates between *ecosystem people* and *biosphere people*, the former being those who live within the ecological limitations of their home area in order to survive and the latter being those tied into the global economy, whose livelihood is not necessarily dependent on the resources of any one particular region.[3] As tool use, long-distance trading, communication, and technical dependency evolved, human existence turned away from regional ecosystems toward the modern "biosphere-based" condition. In the process many regions became highly dependent upon imports from remote places, and to pay for those imports, particular commodities were harvested far in excess of regional carrying capacities and exported out of home regions in exchange for needed currencies. This extended the geographic range of human impact well beyond the limits of immediate human perception. In recent history, the main preventatives for the collapse of modern biosphere-based cultures have been the widespread utilization of military force, the accelerated creation of new technologies, and the exploitation of nonrenewable fossil fuels. To those three characteristics of modernity, technophiles now add a fourth: information, which some advocates suggest is an equivalent partner to matter and energy among essential qualities of the universe. Information and the technologies that store and transmit it seem to have become emblematic of our modern biosphere-based society. Yet ecosystem people dealt with matter, energy, and information in ways that were equally powerful and that allowed them to thrive in their regions for thousands of years.

Place, Language, and Culture

Language is one good indicator of life-place boundaries. By the time of European settlement, the Putah-Cache Creek region and its human inhabitants were a small subsection of what some anthropologists have called the "central California cultural climax"—a presumed territory and quality of existence where human habitation was in sufficient balance with its surroundings to achieve a significant population density with little apparent detriment to the carrying capacity of the enveloping region.[4] The Sacramento Valley contained a culture with a common linguistic heritage (Penutian) and widely shared ritual practice yet marked by very localized dialects. These dialects are a consequence of California's unique geography, in which the "warp" of its main ecosystems is transected by the "weft" of its streams and rivers. The major ecoregions of California are primarily determined by latitude, elevation above sea level, landform, and distance from the ocean and its prevailing winds and currents. California bioregions are more lush at higher elevations, higher latitudes, and locations closer to the ocean, while lower elevations, lower latitudes, and areas remote from maritime influences are more arid. Vegetation zonation in California stratifies according to altitude bands, moving from low-elevation desert and grassland in the interior to semiarid oak savanna foothills, then to mixed forests at middle elevations, and then to more moist coniferous forests at high elevations. As they descend rapidly from mountains to the ocean, California streams and rivers cut across these ecosystems. Watersheds in California, therefore, are not necessarily coincident with bioregions.[5]

Indigenous peoples developed distinct languages (figure 3.3) often roughly corresponding to watershed boundaries (e.g., Wintun-speakers in western tributaries of the Sacramento River, Maidu-speakers in the southeastern tributaries), as well as uphill versus downstream conditions (Hill Patwin in upper Putah and Cache Creeks; River Patwin in the lower reaches). All owed their language to the Penutian linguistic root stock, but settlement over eons in the various specific valleys and basins allowed local dialects to evolve to the point where a group from the next watershed north could barely be understood by those living just southward.

What spiritual glue held these cultures together? There were the dances— Hesi, Bole Maru, Kuksu—where spirits were impersonated, young men and women were initiated into secret societies, supposed calamitous events featuring evil spirits were staged and then dramatically resolved, and in the process, the world was renewed and made whole again. The mythology of these cultures centered on *Sede-Tsiak* (Old Man Coyote), *Ketit* (Peregrine Falcon), and other anthropomorphized animals, including Condor, Grizzly Bear, Elk, Antelope, and Rattlesnake. Several excavations dated to the Late Emergent period have revealed whole tule elk carcasses buried together with human remains, a sign of human reverence for this animal. Interestingly, of the above animals, only rattlesnake and coyote are still abundant in the bioregion; the others are extinct, extirpated, endangered, or threatened.

The River Patwin tribes who lived adjacent to the Sacramento River and its seasonal floodwaters had access to vast schools of salmon, steelhead, and other anadromous fish, and these harvests provided a considerable portion of their diet. People on tributaries such as Putah and Cache Creeks, which prior to upstream impoundment and twentieth-century flood control structures merged with the Sacramento floodplain marshes mainly during high

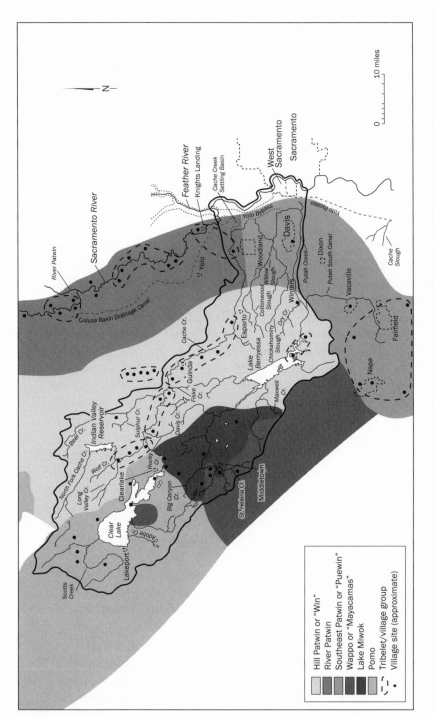

Figure 3.3 Home territories of the people of the Putah Creek and Cache Creek watersheds, circa 1830. Map based on original by Robert Thayer and Jacob Mann, based on Alfred Kroeber, *The Patwin and Their Neighbors*, University of California Publications in American Archaeology and Ethnology, vol. 29 (Berkeley: University of California, 1932), and Robert Heizer, ed., *Handbook of North American Indians*, vol. 8, *California* (Washington, D.C.: Smithsonian Institution, 1978).

water, found at least enough salmon and sturgeon to provide auxiliary food. For these groups, a favorite way to prepare and preserve salmon was to dry the meat and pulverize it into a flourlike powder, which then could be easily carried, stored, or mixed with other foods.

For the Sacramento Valley bioregion as a whole, including the lands extending up low foothill tributary streams both east and west, the major food source by far, and the single most important bio-indicator of culture, was the acorn. Starting about two thousand years ago, the flat stone *metates* and *manos* of the inhabitants of this bioregion, used to process grass seed, were gradually and almost entirely replaced by the round, stubby pestles and bedrock mortars more appropriate for releasing the many calories available in the oilier acorns. Acorns figure significantly in the geography of native Californians; there is a modest congruity among oak distribution, regional boundaries of the Penutian languages, the drainage basins of the Sacramento and San Joaquin Rivers, and the territorial extent of the central California "climax" cultures characterized by semisubterranean dance lodges, spirit impersonation, and secret societies. These four extents do not precisely coincide, but there is sufficient overlap to suggest a general life-place relationship among landform, watershed, dominant foods, major linguistic patterns, and spiritual and cultural practices (figure 3.4).[6]

The Cultural Hypothesis

(As distinctly unique associations of plants and animals defined general biological regions and as these regions were further dissected by watershed corridors, original human cultures adapted to these patterns in close relation to natural boundaries.)Although the cultural ecology of acorn-eating peoples varies considerably, the California acorn-dependent cultures are far less distinct from one another than they are from the northwestern salmon-based cultures, the southwestern cultivators, or the Great Basin hunter-gatherers.

(The spatial relation of indigenous peoples to the regions they occupied suggests a possible "cultural hypothesis" about bioregions. In contemporary terms, bioregions, or life-places, are an alternative geography for humans that recognizes the limitations and potentials of the immediate regions in which people live and localizes the affections and actions of inhabitants in a manner that is socially inclusive, ecologically regenerative, and spiritually fulfilling. In short, an overall Cultural Life-Place Hypothesis might be summed up as follows: *Human culture is best suited to*

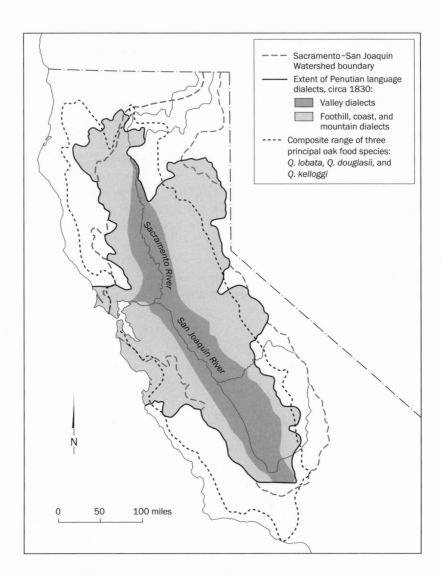

Figure 3.4 A composite map of the range of distribution for the three most important food-producing oaks *(Q. lobata, Q. douglasii,* and *Q. kelloggii),* the boundaries of the Sacramento and San Joaquin River Basins, and the extent of the precontact Penutian language family. Map based on original by Robert Thayer, based on Alfred Kroeber, *Handbook of the Indians of California* (1925; reprint, New York: Dover, 1976), and J. R. Griffin and W. D. Critchfield, *The Distribution of Forest Trees in California,* U.S. Forest Service Research Paper PSW 82 (Berkeley, Calif.: Pacific Southwest Forest and Range Experiment Station, 1972).

naturally defined regions and reasonably sized communities. Bioregions,
or life-places, are the evolutionary norm, not the exception.)

I now live within the memory-space of a formerly bioregional culture. I
reflect upon these first peoples with an eye to understanding their response
to our region and hold forth the hope of emulating their lessons in this bioregion once again. With unsentimental reason and respect, might we learn
from first peoples how to share a mutual community of reciprocity between
human and nonhuman life?

Globalism and Its Discontents

All higher species must perceptually distinguish figure from ground and determine wholes from collections of parts. (Humans are perhaps the most
highly skilled animals at pattern recognition, and the life-place concept is a
natural extension of our proclivity to sense patterns—to uncover, in holistic fashion, the necessary "units" of the living environment by which humans and other species are able to survive.) For example, early humans needed
not only to discriminate between similar-looking edible and toxic plant
species but also to assemble the various "parts" of the environment into
constructs that afforded them opportunities to find edible plants in the first
place. This required an ability to associate individual species with combinations of major landforms and other physiographic characteristics.[7]

However, this ability to discriminate has been taken to an extreme in the
last century or so. In the course of evolution, humans have relied on both
"lumping" and "splitting" skills to survive, but dissociation of parts from
the whole, minute examination of certain parts, and the reassembly of parts
via technology without consideration of proper context are today the norm.
Much of supposedly "objective" reality is considered mere social construction. While there is a kernel of truth to the notion that "nature" itself is
just such a social construct, it is possible to take this line of reasoning too
far. Without a tangible, *grounded* (in the literal sense) basis, we lose all connection to nature or bioregion—"constructions" that provide us with our
own, necessary, and proper context. (The recognition of a life-place, or bioregion, then, is perhaps an acceptance of the need for us all to reassemble
the world by integrating the natural dimensions of each of its various regions with a deepening sense that we *inhabit* a specific place.[8]

(Ironically (or perhaps perversely), as scientists continue to "split" the
world of knowledge into ever more narrow specializations, accelerating globalization would have us believe that the world is shrinking and becoming

one homogeneous culture.] Is it? The ubiquity of instantaneous telecommunication, the emergence of English as a world language, the dominance of American pop culture, and the unchecked explosion of capitalism and corporatism might make it seem as if the human proclivity for lumping had at last won out. This interpretation, however, glosses over the deep differences in the nature and culture of humanity. Reassembling a world dissociated by industrial technology and scientific reductionism by means of electronic/capitalistic hegemony strikes many as a cure worse than the disease itself.

▪ In his sequential books *The Network Society* and *The Power of Identity,* sociologist Manuel Castells diagnoses the phenomenon of technologically enabled cultural globalism.[9] (As Castells observes, in an emerging global network society characterized by virtual reality, rapid information, blurred social spaces, dissolution of the idea of time, accumulation of wealth by the few, and social arrhythmia in the familiar cycles of human life, power is being reorganized from the "space of places" to the "space of flows.")[10] But he also notes the emergence of many powerful communal resistance identities, each rallying around a particular value, such as religion, state, region, neighborhood, tribe, family, sexual orientation, or environment. These resistance identities do not fit logically together, nor do they act in consort; in fact, many are totally unrelated to one another or even diametrically opposed. Resistance identities are, however, all communal: they define exclusive communities of resistance to the perception or action of external oppression from the dominant social structure—a process that Castells describes as "the exclusion of the excluders by the excluded."[11] A resistance identity may draw cultural "boundaries" around itself, and within that defined "territory" (whether ideological, geographical, or both) it inverts the guiding premises and expected behaviors presumed by the major social paradigm.

For example, the widespread hegemony of technology presupposes that everyone should acquire computer hardware, software, and requisite skills as soon as these become available. Countering this presumption is a neo-Luddite resistance movement that legitimizes for its participants the act of not buying, not using, or even destroying computers. While the objects of various resistance identities may be different, the processes of carving out ideological territory is similar, whether the resistance identity in question is Islamic fundamentalism, the militia movement, the animal rights movement, the environmental movement, or the feminist movement.

An irony of the current state of civil society emphasized by Castells is that individuals who seek to establish their identity and engage in social action are not likely to do so as members of a "global network society." Rather, they are more likely to participate in various organizations in resistance to it. Notwithstanding the fictitious actors in slick TV ads for dot-coms or the sullen hordes of laptop-clicking, cell phone–calling businessfolk working their way through the airport hubs of the transnational corporate world, few people overtly identify themselves as champions of the "global network society" or wear its emblems. It is as if the network society were a construction built of corporate advertising hype featuring syrupy images of folks chatting happily via Internet and cell phone across continents and cultures. Perhaps the most prevalent feeling about globalism, whether one agrees with it or not, is that it feels external, something that is "being done to us," or at least something that is proceeding without our input or control.

So, as Castells elaborates, it is by means of the resistance identities to network society that people most frequently identify themselves in the arena of social action:

> Thus, social movements emerging from communal resistance to globalization, capitalist restructuring, organizational networking, uncontrolled informationalism, and patriarchalism—that is, for the time being, ecologists, feminists, religious fundamentalists, nationalists, and localists—are the potential subjects of the Information Age.[12]

(I also note, with great interest, the word *localists* in Castells's argument. For the first time in history, a world of subjects (i.e., social actors constructing an identity) is being shaped in part by spatial decentralization while the dominant technical paradigm races toward consumerist homogeneity and corporate economic concentration. If globalism is so widespread and so inevitable, why don't more people overtly embrace it? Society, it seems, has never been in this "place" before.)

Castells also suggests that national governments have become increasingly obsolete as mediators between the global culture-economy and the more localized, specialized communities of resistance; territorial identity and the worldwide resurgence of local and regional movements indeed foreshadow the "reinvention of the city-state as a salient characteristic of the new age of globalism."[13] Unlike past decentralization following the collapse of empires, this form of decentralized social identity is driven by and is in direct opposition to economic centralization. In this strange postmodern condition, the idea of literal and figurative common ground on which a culture can aggregate is the subject of considerable debate. We now enter truly uncharted cultural territory, where a strange admixture of global and local identities pulls us to and fro. As the globe "shrinks" and becomes more "accessible," so, too, does our social resistance increase and our affinity for the local deepen. In both culture and geography, there is something inherent in humanity that does not want us to become one.

Reinventing Common Ground

The list of critics of the globalizing world is long and expanding. Joshua Karliner comments on the coming "corporate planet"; William Greider suggests we will have "one world, ready or not." One particularly astute observer, Canadian John Ralston Saul, describes current postmodern culture as the "unconscious civilization," which has become numbed by marketplace hegemony, is being led blindly by a "manifest destiny" of technology, and is dominated by corporatism. In Saul's conception, corporatism includes not only the more obvious transnational corporations but also the immensely scaled trade organizations, federal bureaucracies, ubiquitous technical networks, labor unions, and national/international environmental movements. Corporatism, according to Saul, is the social phenomenon that has taken away our shared languages and given back to us multiple jargons. It has substituted simplistic ideology for reasoned analysis and has eroded ideas of democracy and true participation and the ideal of a common good. If one were to take stock of the character of corporatism, one would find it to be not "micro-soft" but "macro-hard": ubiquitous, enormous, and capable of deflecting most of the criticism leveled against it. Saul admits that reversing the corporatist erosion of individual, citizen-based democracy may be an impossible goal, but he places faith in the most noble and time-tested of humanist ideals to carry on the struggle for equilibrium: common sense, creativity, ethics, intuition, memory, and reason. If applied separately, these might lead to more severe erosion of democracy. If applied in an equilibrating fashion, however, they are powerful tools against the pressure of corporatist ideologies.[14]

In a world of broad corporatist networks of special interest, Saul reasserts the need for specific communities of *dis*-interest. In Saul's conception, far from being apathetic, a community of dis-interest is a collective manifestation of civic duty practiced in a specific place *without* expectation of personal gain—like serving on a jury. Jurors have no stake in the outcome of their deliberations, but they participate out of a sense of contribution to the local practice of democracy.

A similar observation and subsequent call for reform is made by Daniel Kemmis, who, in his seminal book *Community and the Politics of Place*, notes how people occupying the same geographical region seem trapped by their so-called public posturing to endorse either the myth of rugged individualism or the mire of regulatory bureaucracy in choosing sides during land use conflicts. Meanwhile, the shared values of place and region are ignored. Kemmis advocates a return to republican (small *r*) values. His view is that government should facilitate the *best* of human civic behavior rather than the worst—bureaucratic insularity, confrontational stalemate politics, fear of litigation, or public "hearings" where no one listens.[15]

To read Castells, Saul, and Kemmis is to conclude that the *role of place and region is vital to the politics and culture of a democratic community.* As Kemmis emphasizes, civic participation needs a tangible object—a sort of "table" around which the "*res*, the public thing of the 'republic' . . . could gather us together and yet prevent us from falling over each other."[16] This tangible object is the shared *place* itself, which is to say, the community, the bioregion, the *life-place:*

> That we inhabit a global economy has become commonplace. What
> is not so universally understood is that the organic integration of the
> global economy is drawing into play suborganisms that refuse to be
> ordered by anything other than their internal logic.[17]

As the long-entrenched politics of left versus right, individual freedoms versus heavy-handed government, and "Wise Use" rhetoric versus environmental monkey-wrenching are caught up in the rush of globalization, a political vacuum is created. That vacuum draws into itself the possibility of a new politics focused on region, community, and identity—a place-bounded resistance identity capable of transcending bipolar politics in favor of regenerative civic democracy.

Today, however, a new equilibrium is being reached between communities of *interest*, which tend toward the global, and communities of *place*, which tend to be local. Although the bioregional movement traces its roots back to radical social theory and early left-wing environmentalism, the modern move toward equilibrium is being driven as well by the social experimentation embodied within ecosystem management, place-based civic democracy, ecologically based regional planning, alternative economic theory and practice, and a host of related "relocalization" efforts. This has resulted in something uniquely absent from the typical liberal-conservative spectrum. Grassroots, multistakeholder efforts on behalf of natural regions or watersheds have been labeled "Wise Use"/industry scams by the green left because of their alleged efforts to dupe locals and violate federal land management policies as often as they have been branded government/"enviro" conspiracies by the right wing for their supposed assaults on personal free-

Figure 3.5 After years of legal conflict, the many "stakeholders," or parties of interest, along lower Putah Creek celebrate a signed accord by acknowledging the need for water for humans and water for fish and wildlife. Photograph by Robert Thayer.

doms and individual property rights. The truth, which neither the traditional right nor left wishes to admit, is that broadly enfranchised, local, grassroots efforts to identify with and care for natural regions are so powerful, so ultimately democratic, and so basically popular with the American people that they threaten the huge, entrenched political organizations on both sides.[18]

The Nature of Life-Place Culture

The failure of the traditional government-agency, single-resource approach to meet multiple resource management needs has led to a considerable broadening of the cultural assumptions of the "original" bioregionalists. When coupled with emerging trends in ecosystem management, regional planning, grassroots bioregionalism, alternative economics, and certain strains of social criticism, this multidimensional response suggests a cluster of descriptive and prescriptive principles that could begin to define a life-place culture. As people from more sectors of society and the economy are negatively affected by global trends, a convergence of local interest on the life-place seems inevitable. When valley farmers can no longer find buyers for their crops of apricots or tomatoes—crops that have helped define the region for decades—they may discover new friends, and, perhaps, even new markets, among their nonfarming neighbors. When energy users in California realize they are hamstrung by out-of-state energy suppliers, price manipulators, and regulators, they may turn instead to more local energy solutions. When formerly adversarial groups find themselves, for better or worse, inhabiting the same bioregion, and facing the same limits and potentials, an embryonic life-place culture may arise.

How might a seasoned life-place culture be characterized? First and foremost, it would be a collective human endeavor. In addition, it would be

- framed by the nature of the region (identifying with and growing more attached to place)
- concerned with all life, human and nonhuman
- scaled to territories comprehensible to human perceptions, affections, and activities
- focused upon or catalyzed by tangible objects of shared social and natural value (watersheds, species, habitats, disenfranchised groups)
- based on face-to-face communication in real time and space
- enriched through horizontal networks of civic engagement
- built on mutual trust (neighborliness) in spite of differences of opinion
- grounded in respect for and dependence on local wisdom and knowledge
- balanced between freedom and obligation (negotiating a middle path between annihilation of open country at one extreme and eco-monkey-wrenching at the other)
- supported equally by common sense, creativity, ethics, intuition, memory, and reason
- enfranchising all potential "stakeholders" equally
- equitable and socially just, featuring symmetrical power arrangements
- capable of creating social capital, or building "capacity" for problem solving, among a broad base of citizenry
- innovative in establishing institutional cooperation and horizontal linkages

- reinhabitory, or invested in the future (fostering life as though one's future grandchildren would be living in the same place and doing the same things)
- as supportive of communities of place as it is of communities of interest
- based on quality of life over time, including the means of making a living in place
- regenerative (careful to perpetuate valued social institutions, ecosystems, and physical/natural resources over the long term)
- respectful of natural boundaries and systems that often straddle illogical political demarcations
- evolutionary (capable of being "grown" over time, rather than being forced upon or superimposed over existing political frameworks)
- adaptable to change from without or within

A life-place culture, then, is an alternative mode for contemporary humanity that recognizes the limitations and potentials of the immediate regions in which people live and strives to relocalize the affections and actions of inhabitants in a manner that is socially inclusive, ecologically regenerative, economically sustainable, and spiritually fulfilling. The culture of reinhabitation is life-place culture: the rediscovery of a way to live well, with grace and permanence, in place.

Charmed by a Stone

In April 1991, three friends and I ride bicycles in the sixty-mile Tour of the Lost Valley, our mid-forties age feeling like twenty to us as we climb the narrow, winding tarmac from Williams toward Lodoga, in the westside foothills. It is a cool, sunny day following a rainstorm, and the foothills are as intensely mint-green as could ever be imagined. While resting at the top of the big climb, wolfing down energy bars and chugging polyethylene-bottled water, we are pleasantly buzzed by a golden eagle. To the east, the patchwork valley stretches out to the Sierra foothills, and to the west lies a rolling green carpet of grasses, blue oaks, and wildflowers that could serve well as an official billboard for the "real" California.

By this year and this ride I am thoroughly caught up in a search for knowledge of my home region. I have explored the innermost Coast Range foothills by foot, bicycle, canoe, and automobile. After eighteen years, I feel completely at home amid the agricultural environment of the valley. Gradually I have come to realize that, in contrast to what I believed upon my immediate arrival here, there has been an abundant native population in this place, and *not* all indigenous California people died in the disease epidemics of 1833 and 1834. Perhaps I am typical of many other white Americans: vaguely aware that primal peoples once lived on "my land" but rather ignorant of who they were, exactly where they were, *how* they lived here, and most of all, whether any are *still* here.

On that April day I do not recognize or know the significance of a small object that I pick up from the ground while resting against my bicycle. It is made of hard, black-and-white-flecked stone—something like granite. It appears to be manmade, uniformly round in cross section yet tapered at both ends. I ponder it briefly, thinking it may be a sample intended for testing the strength of rock, or perhaps a balustrade from an ornate stone garden fence. I put the stone in my bike jersey pocket, complete the ride, and, upon arriving back home, stow the object away in a "junk" drawer.

Three years later, while researching the first peoples to live in this region, I see with astonishment in an anthropological text an illustration of the exact object that I found: a four-thousand-year-old "early horizon" steatite charm stone. The function of such stones is still debated, but charm stones were found in native graves dating up until a thousand years ago. The one I found precisely matches the form and material of charm stones found in the earliest horizon of archaeological exploration. It is thought that such charm stones were suspended over spots in the stream to "charm" the fish into being caught. My stone, I suspect, accompanied a load of local gravel brought to buoy up a new asphalt "river." Looking at the stone, I imagine it hanging vertically from a branch and wonder which species of fish it was intended to catch, which hands so carefully hewed it out of a larger piece of stone, what the particular worldview of the individual who made it was, and whether, perhaps, that person wondered, as I do now, who had come before him in that place.

For those of us come only recently to a territory, it is difficult to imagine the hundreds of generations that have passed down intimate knowledge on how to live there: fathers and mothers teaching daughters and sons the best means of surviving and thriving in this place; whole communities of humans and nonhumans so entwined with the land that any slim boundaries between self and other, sky and earth, water and soil, animal and human, must have been inconceivable. How could the land not have been sacred to them? What else could explain the persistence of people in place over such a long time that entirely separate languages evolved within distinct watersheds draining only a few thousand hectares?

The charm stone now sits in a leather pouch upon a small meditation altar in my home office. It symbolizes for me an acknowledgment that we are all "dancing on sacred land." Over the years, I have made it a hobby to piece together every shred of information possible on these indigenous peoples who were here long before me—where they lived, what languages they spoke, what foods they gathered, what fish they caught, what animals they hunted, what gods and spirits they beckoned, what dances they danced— and where they are now. Can we use the echoes of their culture to help us reassemble and reinhabit our fragmented world?

4 Fulfilling

CELEBRATING THE SPIRIT OF PLACE

The solution is simply for us to join the earth community as participating members, to foster the progress and prosperity of the bioregional communities to which we belong.

THOMAS BERRY, 1988

In a simple and straightforward book, *The Dream of Earth,* the solitary American monk and essayist Father Thomas Berry suggests a solution to what he considers the primary challenge of humans: to move beyond anthropocentric toward more biocentric norms of progress. One of the first ethicists to recognize and advocate a bioregional approach, Thomas Berry describes a bioregion as a geographical area of interacting life-forms constituting a "self-propagating, self-nourishing, self-educating, self-governing, self-healing, and self-fulfilling community." According to Berry, "The future of the human lies in acceptance and fulfillment of the human role in all six of these community functions." *Fulfillment,* the sixth of Berry's bioregional characteristics, is the focus of this chapter. A bioregion is self-fulfilling if all of its participants can achieve the highest efflorescence of being, from the flowering of the tiniest plants to the celebration of the greatest ceremonies of human culture.[1]

In what ways might immersion in a life-place help its individual participants achieve this lofty goal? Here I shall suggest another bioregional hypothesis, the Spiritual Hypothesis: *Immersion in bioregional culture and attachment to a naturally defined region offer a deepened sense of personal meaning, belonging, and fulfillment in life.* The bioregional proposition is a *hopeful* and *purposeful* one, allowing environmental views to be joined by traditional wisdom, to evolve into shared visions, and to result in constructive actions on the ground. Bioregional practice is a *deep* proposition, allowing the possibility of lifelong learning in and about one's own place— an inexhaustible locus for a continuing practical, general education. It is a *healing* activity, allowing one to embrace the culture of nature and the nature of culture—to experience membership in a community including plants and animals as well as other humans. It is *place centered* in that it re-

71

verses the contemporary tendency of the dominant culture and economy to become global, consolidated, remote, and alien. And finally, in a world where time seems to accelerate or conceptually disappear, a bioregional or life-place perspective *gives time back to us*, allowing us to see the past, experience the present, and anticipate the future. Attachment to a life-place, then, can serve as a powerful antidote to the often mentioned ills of the contemporary world.)

For me, the process of belonging here, in my own life-place, has been gradual and based on experience. To belong is to attach to the space, embrace the spirit, and find personal meaning within that reciprocal relationship. The stories that follow are the best way I can illuminate these processes.)

Watershed Rituals

One of the most moving moments of my own bioregional participation came during the 1995 Shasta Bioregional Gathering on the Russian River in California. Bob Glotzbach, the conference organizer, asked each of us to bring a container of water from our own watershed at home. En route to the gathering, I stopped by Putah Creek. Mindful that I was to participate in some bioregional ritual of which I had no previous knowledge, I filled the jar with great concentration, aware of precisely where I was in my home watershed. Upon our collective arrival, we gathered in a circle on a flood terrace of Austin Creek, which flows to the Russian River and out to the Pacific Ocean. One by one, we announced ourselves and our watersheds, and poured the water from our containers into a very large collective glass vase, which remained conspicuously on display on a stump in a central place throughout the proceedings. I remember looking intensely at this vase from time to time, marveling at the creativity of the ritual and how so many different watersheds were represented by the vase sitting on the redwood stump. In the closing ceremony, we gathered again, thanked the water for nourishing our lives, spirits, and actions, and poured the collected contents into Austin Creek.[2]

In the absence of overt rituals marking attachment to and care of the land, people at times strive to create them. I am no exception. A colleague, David Robertson, and I have begun to lead tours of the Putah Creek/Cache Creek watershed region for the general public. David has studied the Yamabushi, a Buddhist sect in Japan whose practitioners circumambulate their mountain domain in a clockwise direction. For the Yamabushi, such practices fuse the notion of mandala, a representation of the cosmos, and the place itself. A similar practice is entered into by the Australian aboriginal people, who know and re-create their world by means of "walkabouts," ambulatory pathways that stop at particularly important places. At each point, the world, with all its beings, is "sung" into life and its continued existence guaranteed through ritualized chants and symbolic actions. To abandon such actions would mean the collapse of the world as these aboriginal practitioners know it.

As coconspirators in a not-so-subtle attempt to help our neighbors similarly re-enchant their watershed, David and I have devised a clockwise, ritualized tour of Putah and Cache Creeks. (Since we are realistic Americans, however, ours involves driving as well as walking.) It is important to us to engage the participants in the full dimension of the place: the geography and geology; the pre- and post-European-contact history; the flora, fauna, and ecosystems; and the current economic base and popular culture. We arrange stops at rock formations, native American archaeological sites, diversion dams, pop art sculptures, wineries, small rural towns, irrigation canals, flood control structures, and wildland sites, and we are writing a comprehensive guidebook that continues to evolve as the trips are repeated.

Foremost, we hope to accomplish two things. First, we wish to help participants understand that all aspects of the place are connected and are not just an assortment of independent dimensions, like discrete majors in some university course catalogue. Second, we wish to encourage our touring companions to consider the watersheds in a deep and reverential manner. This is a delicate subject and raises the daunting notion of spirituality, which is the reddest flag one can wave in academe. However, we do these tours beyond academic walls and, anyway, (how could the land beneath us *not* be sacred? We all owe our lives to it in one way or another and had better come to know it.)

The tour starts at an abandoned bridge over the original fork of Putah Creek, deprived of water since the turn of the twentieth century, when farmers diverted the flow into the "South Fork" to take Davisville out of flood danger. Under the bridge where we stand once swam schools of salmon, blackfish, sturgeon. Valley oaks grew in abundance. Patwin people known as the Puta-toi lived here in semisubterranean houses, danced in common dance halls, gathered acorns, and hunted waterfowl and fished in the adjacent seasonal wetlands and river flows, now tamed by dams and levees. We start the tour off by chanting in the Patwin language *Saltu k'ewe Puta-toi* ("spirit home of the Putah people"), a concoction of words I have culled from the few authoritative lexicons of the Patwin language that have been assembled. Then we ask (with appropriate caveats about voluntary participation) people to follow us in a special chant that strings together the native

Figure 4.1 David Robertson explains a Putah-Cache watershed tour chant as novice participants scan their word sheets. Photograph by Robert Thayer.

names of all the former River Patwin, Hill Patwin, Lake Miwok, and Pomo towns in a clockwise course on our tour—a kind of metaphoric tone-poem map that we will soon physically follow:

> Putah-to-li-wai-chem-o-cu-le-yomi-ka-da-yomi-ku-pec-tu-tu-le-yomi-
> al-i-ma-tinbe-kuy-kuy-teb-ti-lo-pa-ko-pe-i-mil-ki-si-moso-chu-rup.

We instruct our participants to sound out single syllables and the occasional disyllabic couplet in the same, monotonic rhythm, one beat between each dash. During the practice run, they mumble and stare. Some feel awkward, but most others gamble and make their voices heard when we do it "for real" the second time. With this rather unusual beginning, we board the bus and proceed with the tour, which takes us to several valley locations: the point of diversion of the creek by Anglo farmers in the late 1800s; groves of valley oak trees; experimental agricultural plots; Main Street in the city of Winters, where an earthquake wrought severe damage in 1892. We course along the Spanish land grant boundaries of "Rancho Río de los Putos," mentioning the ongoing linguistic debate as to the real meaning of the name.

At the Solano Diversion Dam, we discuss water projects in general and the particulars of the legal battle to win more downstream water to keep Putah Creek alive once Solano County diverts it for irrigation and development. Impounded and diverted streams are a given fact of the contemporary California landscape. To underscore the need for us to learn how best to take the water humans need but leave enough for the life downstream as well, we engage in another deliberate ritual. Passing paper cups of water from above the dam in fire-brigade fashion, we walk around the dam, gather at the diversion canal, and pour half of our water into the canal "for people," then walk to the real, undiverted outflow and pour the remainder of our water into the live stream "for the fish" while chanting a portion of the Hanya Shingyo, a Buddhist sutra emphasizing the simultaneity of form and emptiness. By now, participants have accepted the fact that their tour leaders are "unusual," to say the least. They begin to figuratively "go with the flow" even as we literally drive upstream against it.

We stop where Monticello Dam pinches Putah Creek into a reservoir at Devils Gate, a severely stratified and upturned notch in the Blue Ridge, formed by ancient seabeds pushed in front of the overtopping continental plate, like dirt in front of a bulldozer, as the Pacific plate subducted beneath it. We talk of the nature of place making, acknowledging that this is a confluence of water and rock, of physical nature and human structure, of life and death. Behind the dam extends Lake Berryessa, named for the recipient of a now mostly submerged Mexican land grant. The imposing rock strata at either edge of the dam are sedimentary mudstones and siltstones laid down horizontally, one layer at a time, by ancient seas. Their currently upthrusted verticality speaks of the hidden power of the crustal movements beneath.

Berryessa also inundates the former agricultural town of Monticello, and our tour stops at the Bureau of Reclamation headquarters to talk of water impoundments, recreation, vegetation, and wildlife. We chant once more, this time reciting the names of the now-defunct Spanish and Mexican land grants, again in clockwise order along our tour: *"Ran-cho-ri-o-delos-pu-tos-ran-cho-lagu-na-de-santos-ca-lle-can-ya-da-de-capay-ran-cho-ri-o-jesus-ma-ri-a-ran-cho."* David leads us in reciting a simple chant-poem he has written to acknowledge the long-flooded town:

Mon-ti-cel-lo-under-water
Mon-ti-cel-lo-deep-down
Mon-ti-cel-lo-we-remember-you
Mon-ti-cel-lo-don't-forget-us.

By this time, our guests begin to notice the similarities in the peculiar, dissociative rhythm of these chants. Patwin, Miwok, Sino-Japanese, Spanish, and English: they all sound related, and all relate to the place around which we travel. The form-emptiness reference of the Hanya-Shingyo of the last stop seems somehow more meaningful as we gaze at the reservoir's surface and talk of time cycles and passings. Geological formations, native villages, Mexican land grants, Anglo-American towns have all come and gone. We shall pass, too, although no one mentions it. One day either the reservoir will silt up and become a meadow or the dam will fail and the Berry-essa Valley will return, to be inhabited by who-knows-whom. In the swirl of space-time, we are only *here, now*. Both facts are equally important. We depart for the next stop.

Our route takes us past unusual serpentine geology, where mercury, manganese, nickel, chrome, and other elements often toxic to plants form a unique biota adapted to our watershed, including rare Sargent cypress trees. Low-elevation gray foothill pines mark our passage, with cones large and sharp for digging into mineral soil before being opened by fire. We nod to the two sentinel Douglas firs that mark our passage from one plant ecosystem to another. Our tour then takes us to two stops representing extremes in our culture, the first being Registered State Historical Marker #839, "Litto's Hubcap Ranch," where an assortment of 2,500 hubcaps are displayed in the landscape. Litto's forces us to confront where we are—by some standards this chrome collection might represent "nowhere." But such a density of shiny, round road paraphernalia could also be considered a collection of mandalas, reminding us that if we got here by car or bus, we are always connected by the asphalt road to the mainstream of American culture. No sense sitting in a motor vehicle with chrome hubcaps making fun of a hubcap ranch.

The next stop is the sophisticated Guenoc Winery, occupying the former site of a Lake Miwok village, then a Mexican land grant, then an estate purchased by famed nineteenth-century British stage actress and socialite Lillie Langtry, whose portrait graces the labels of the expensive wines shipped from this dry, beautiful watershed to points all over the world. Lillie was, like many modern stars, a talented sophisticate who orbited in the upper echelons of British and American society, subject to both widespread adoration and intense media scrutiny. Arriving in the remote upper Putah Creek watershed, one valley over from Napa, she vowed at this site to make the world's best claret, and the tradition of fine wine took root here.

We tour Middletown, a one-traffic-light community with a world-class pancake cafe and a brand new local microbrewery—Mount St. Helena, named for the mountains seen from the street front that are the source of the water used in the brewing process. We pass next through the ecotone ascending the Putah Creek headwaters into yellow pine country reminiscent of the Sierra. Putah Creek is no longer the familiar, turbid valley stream but now courses clear and cool through white alders, dropping between pools and boulders. At a safe pull-off close to the source, we filter the stream water, then drink a toast to Putah Creek. One person refuses to drink, no matter how thoroughly filtered and apparently cool and clear the water. She cannot believe this is the same stream she has held in such low esteem down below. We chant more in Lake Miwok, and then once in Australo-Aboriginal: *"wal-ya-ji-wanka-run-ya-yir-ni"* ("Land is life"). It sounds strangely like all the other chants.

Over the Putah divide into the sibling Cache Creek Basin, we descend to the outflow of Cache Creek from Clear Lake, formed by volcanic damming and river capture by the downcutting Cache. I bottle some of the Cache head-waters for ceremonial use later. At Anderson Marsh State Historic Park, we share lessons in lakeside ecology, water rights, Pomo origin stories, early Anglo-American history, contemporary planning issues, and avian migration patterns. Downstream along the north fork of Cache Creek, we stop at a small Hill Patwin ruin and discuss the culture that endured for ten thousand years, until the past century, directly beneath our feet. We encourage our participants to look for shards of obsidian formerly imported for the making of arrow and spear points by indigenous residents. One woman finds a large flake. Someone else points out the pile of empty shotgun shells from contemporary target practice discarded nearby, and we ponder the odd juxtaposition of detritus from two very different hunting cultures.)

Downstream still, we visit a tule elk reserve, where state Fish and Game personnel hope to keep alive a threatened species once endemic to our downstream plains but now forced to move uphill, displaced by extensive agriculture in the valley. We talk of pollution—boron and mercury in the Bear Creek tributary—and see a bald eagle fishing that apparently has withstood both so far. We refresh ourselves at the mini-mart adjacent to the mammoth Cache Creek Indian Casino—a Las Vegas–size facility—that has brought needed vitality and unwanted controversy to this nearly defunct Indian rancheria. David dashes into the casino and emerges with twelve dollars in winnings, considering the whole thing a harbinger of future tour success.

Stops we wish to make are omitted as we race the sun past the agricultural center of Woodland to the outflow of Cache Creek at the Settling Basin, an enormous structure designed to intercept sediment and keep it from clogging the even more colossal Yolo Bypass, which must handle Sacramento River overflows in high-flood events. Countless ducks bob in the waters of the bypass. Tundra swans and Canada and snow geese vee overhead as the sun glows pink in the west. We turn and scan the distant western hills from which we have come, pointing out both the Putah and Cache notches in the horizon ridge line. We have orbited two hundred miles around our own region. I break out the captured bottle of Cache Creek headwaters; we make our last educational comments, discuss the trip, then chant in English some lines from the Hanya Shingyo: "Gone, gone, gone beyond, gone beyond beyond," repeating it more softly each time until it dies in the evening sunset. We pour the headwaters offering into the outflow of the Settling Basin and cheer the creek.

After our first tour, word spreads, and more people show up for our next tour a month later. Of course, the watershed tours are merely a start. Awareness must precede attachment, which necessarily precedes constructive action. There remains the hard work to be done: endless community meetings, planning sessions, creek cleanups, fund-raisers, scientific research, and, most important, remaining connected with our neighbors who must make their living in close physical relationship to the land. But mind and place have fused, and Putah-Cache country grows in the conscience of a few more people now. This is an auspicious beginning.

The Putah Creek Cafe

Winters, California, is a pleasant slice of small-town America located at the intersection of the Sacramento Valley floor and the first few rollers of interior Coast Range foothills. This is fruit and nut country: Winters is known for almonds, walnuts, apricots, peaches, plums, nectarines, and some of the best-tasting oranges in the world. Grazing land ties the oak woodland and chaparral of higher elevations to the rich loam soils of the flatland below. An interstate freeway bypass route from Oregon and northern California to the San Francisco Bay Area touches the east side of town, while Putah Creek courses down from the higher Coast Ranges westward to be dammed at Lake Berryessa (actually a reservoir) and siphoned off shortly thereafter to points southward in Solano County. The remaining summer trickle of the creek passes under the old railroad bridge on the south edge of Winters. One block north of the bridge, with the address 1 Main Street, is the Putah Creek Cafe (figure 4.2).

Inviting guests in through a corner entrance fronting diagonally on two streets, the door to the cafe opens directly upon the pastry display cabinet. If serving good pie is a dying art, the cafe is a living gallery of accomplishment. Amid the varieties of muffins and fruit pie (considered by this author paramount in the universe) are vacuum-wrapped char-roast meats prepared on site and multicolored art nouveau Putah Creek Cafe T-shirts featuring a great egret framed by cattails and willow. "Putah Creek—Let It Flow!" bumper stickers from our local volunteer creek advocacy group are

Figure 4.2 The Putah Creek Cafe: an "ordinary" restaurant with extraordinary meaning to those living in the Putah Creek watershed. Photograph by Robert Thayer.

free for the taking on the counter. Public announcements of the "passing" of local citizens are left by the counter for locals to see.

The interior is familiar and homey, with knotty pine paneling, simple colored china decorating a high, surrounding wainscot shelf, exposed brick walls from early-nineteenth-century construction, and the quintessential Naugahyde booths and chromed, swivel counter stools of the American cafe, all spotless. Behind the counter are the crisply functional coffee and espresso machines, and the kitchen is also visible from the restaurant interior: what one sees, one gets. The flowery wallpaper is pleasantly understated; floors are heavy Mexican tile. Streetside are potted succulent plants in earthen pots.

The adjoining dining room uses the exposed brick walls as an art gallery, featuring watercolor paintings by local artists. By the south window is a large, framed color photograph, taken directly outside the cafe from a cherry-picker truck, of just about the entire population of Winters cramming Main Street in June 1992, celebrating the one-hundredth anniversary of the 1892 earthquake. I have seen numerous customers point out themselves, friends, or relatives in the photo, mere specks in a sea of several thousand. On the opposite interior wall is a permanent collection of color photographs of lower Putah Creek taken by Steve Chainey and other members of the Putah Creek Council. These are modest, focal scenes, but they are highly effective in creating a sense of place. This is truly a bioregional restaurant and, in spite of fancier competition elsewhere, certainly an important high point in my culinary landscape.

I have asked the manager, Janet, and my favorite waitress, Shannon, if I might interview them for this book. They have nervously agreed. True, I am a loyal patron who tips well and compliments them on their service to humankind, but I usually show up in smelly bicycle clothing after a dozen miles of hard riding. This time I plan to dispel their unease by arriving showered and clean-shaven. I mull over how to reward them for the interview and reject the notion of flowers in favor of two bottles of local wine from a high-class vineyard much farther up the Putah Creek drainage. I get out my notebook and ask them questions about the significance of their workplace, the Putah Creek Cafe, to the sense of the region.

Janet grew up in the area and once owned her own establishment in nearby Woodland, one major drainage north. She responds to my question about community by emphasizing that the cafe "brings folks into contact who might not normally associate with one another." There are the early-morning farmers who talk about weather; there are horseshoers, salespeople, local businesspeople, professors, bicyclists, Harley riders, tourists, retired folks, college students, and an occasional politician or ex-university administrator. There are the "liberal folks," Janet says. And then there is "everyone else." She has never seen a fight or unpleasantness, and it is common to strike up a conversation with a total stranger. Shannon describes the "counter culture," meaning the solitary, loyal locals who eat individually at the counter, most of whom the servers know on a first-name, conversational basis.

I ask about the name "Putah Creek Cafe" and about the relationship to the creek itself. The owners named it Putah Creek Cafe before either Janet or Shannon arrived seven years ago, they say. Shannon has heard an occasional chuckle about the name from nonlocal tourists. "Putah" sounds like the Spanish word for "prostitute," but local wisdom traces the name to the Patwin word for a native fish once a popular food source for people living along the creek. The creek itself, however, seems to be slowly surfacing in the consciousness of customers. "Up to a few years ago," Janet says, "people didn't even admit we had a creek." Poor diverted and bedraggled Putah won't win any beauty contests, but as the focus on restoring the creek sharpens, business at the cafe increases. Or vice versa. Which is cause and which effect is not clear.

Ultimately, it is the food, ambiance, prices, and service that bring the customers back. Shannon says she is "proud of what she serves to people"—good food at modest prices; Janet says the cafe makes customers "feel like they are coming home." She describes the local origins of some of the food she features—greens, tomatoes, and strawberries farmed nearby, lamb from nearby Dixon, and pie made a few miles south in Suisun. Once, many restaurants were like this; today, however, many have fallen victim to the "progress" of globalization and its fast-food chains. Putah Creek Cafe, on the other hand, has just expanded its dining room. It occurs to me that Putah Creek Cafe has succeeded because it is our bioregion's kitchen—a place for sustaining not only the body but the mind and the soul of the place.

Local *Re*-Creation

In the quiet of a morning in November 1996, just before my birthday, I am paddling Putah Creek where it is all flatwater between old beaver dams. The small furry creatures swimming just a few dozen yards ahead of my canoe do not seem like beaver, though: their motion is far too playful, not like the plodding, methodical purposefulness by which I've learned to recognize beaver at a distance. These small heads appear and disappear, roll, snort, blow bubbles, come toward one another, then part. They are otter, and nothing about their character seems to mean business at all. To watch river otter play while you yourself are at play is a remarkable experience of interspecies kinship unlikely to be forgotten.

Yet unfortunately, contemporary human culture often forgets the importance of play—or at least doesn't give it the credit it deserves. In the 1960s and 1970s, outdoor recreation was an openly admitted planning goal of nearly every governmental jurisdiction, from federal to state, regional, and local. Yet following the passage of California's "tax revolt" Proposition 13 in 1978, public recreation has been on the defensive, and the various governmental agencies have placed nature-based recreation on the back burner or off the stove entirely. In the 1990s, the largest word/concept on the land planning marquees has been *restoration,* and the practices of conservation biology and restoration ecology have emerged to capture the imaginations of managers and the budgets of agencies and philanthropic organizations. For the most part, this was long overdue; in the Sacramento Valley, the "nature" that has been eradicated in the course of humanized occupation simply must be replaced before anyone can be expected to appreciate it. But there is still a strong role for recreation to play in life-place culture, for, like the otter, humans bond with the world in part by making it fun—by challenging and seeking out the "wild" within it and within us. If civilization has rendered the world gray, loud, and predictable, seeking out the land's quiet green-and-blue corners is most certainly a necessary return to our hunter-gatherer origins. My quests into my own life-place have been excursions in search not of food or shelter but of meaning and belonging. For it is when I am paddling a stream, pedaling the backroads, or padding down some trail that I feel most capable of paying attention to the place. The tools I have used in my quest (in addition to my car) are my hiking boots, bicycle, canoe, binoculars, camera, notebook, and the company of friends and family.

Ninety-nine percent of Americans no longer make their living directly from the land. I am one of the majority. Our engagement with the land therefore depends a great deal on how we *play* with it, or within it. Yet the Sacramento Valley, a region long characterized by private land ownership, has relatively few semiwild places for recreation: limited river and stream corridors still intact and accessible to the public; few open foothill trails for people to explore; almost no woodlands or intact grasslands. The nearest legitimate, publicly owned "nature" trail to my house in Davis is forty miles away on Bureau of Land Management land in Cache Creek Canyon.

Most regions of North American have long grappled with the need for accessible nature and open-space opportunities. The Sacramento Valley lags some thirty years behind such notable examples as the Chicago Wilderness, the Boulder County open-space system in Colorado, and the East Bay Regional Park District around San Francisco Bay. Our bioregion will, quite simply, be a very poor place to live if the new population growth expected in the next three decades has no "nearby nature" places to seek experience and contact with the nonhuman dimensions of life.

There is considerable resistance to the prospect of publicly accessible open space among rural and agricultural landowners in the Sacramento Valley. In recent years, ecological restoration specialists have tacitly allied themselves with the agricultural sector in discouraging the consideration of pub-

Figure 4.3 Boaters negotiate the "Mad Mike" rapids on the wilderness run of Cache Creek, closely observed by previously successful paddlers. Photograph by Robert Thayer.

lic access to natural and restored river corridors, wetlands, and grasslands, believing (perhaps justifiably) that such efforts would scare away the landowners from further participation in joint ventures to conserve and restore the valley's natural ecosystems. In some instances, this strategy has succeeded, as in the case of the Middle Mountain Foundation's protection of the Sutter Buttes through a private land trust.

However, I believe an important component is being omitted from this equation: the general public itself. Issues of illegal trespass, for example, might be resolved by the provision of adequate, *legally accessible* open-space resources and sufficient management structures to accept liability and policing tasks. The experience of the Chicago Wilderness, an extensive holding of restored prairies and wetlands adjacent to the Chicago metropolitan area, suggests that well-managed public access actually increases a sense of belonging and care for the region. Open space certainly has economic benefits, too, raising property values and increasing quality of life in the region.

The Sacramento Valley is in for some dramatic population and quality-of-life changes in the future, as the age-old American right to settle anywhere within national borders collides with the rights of landowners to develop their property or to exclude the public from it, or both Hopefully, the region will evolve an ethic that not only acknowledges private property rights and protects the agricultural productivity and heritage of the area but also allows a growing public at least some access to the natural systems endemic to the region. Without enfranchisement of the growing nonagricultural population, there seems little hope of either protecting agriculture or enhancing the region's biodiversity.)

Open Space and Belonging

I would like to suggest a number of axioms relating the experience of nearby nature to the sense of belonging to a bioregion:

- A community's sense of *belonging to a life-place* (i.e., its level of attachment to and concern for the welfare of the natural region) is directly proportional to its ability to access the representative natural character and spaces of that region.

- Illegal trespass and damage to private property are *inversely* related to the opportunity to legally access nearby nature (not *proportionally* related, as some imagine).

- Accessible open space is essential to the willingness of valley residents to accept denser, more compact communities, leading to the preservation of farmland.

- Adequate public access to the "nearby nature" represented by an ecosystem is essential for the public to embrace ecosystem management and restoration.

As a private, local citizen, a planner, and an academic, I've given great thought and considerable action to these issues, and were I not able to deepen my own participation in this life-place through active outdoor recreation, you would not be reading this book. I suspect that I am not alone; most of us need experience with the nature of a place to belong to that place. I've reached a number of interrelated conclusions in my several decades of such experience. First, the opportunity to find local wildness, in spots where one might least expect it, is itself an enlightening experience. Through exploration of those fragments of nature closer to home, less spectacular patches of ground gain a depth of personal meaning beyond that of those far removed. Does it really make sense to drive two hours on a crowded freeway to experience "pristine nature" in the Sierra when one might visit a natural area two miles away with a somewhat less spectacular landscape? Second, the result of the latter exploration is a heightened ability to see deeper and more meaningfully into the nature of home. There may be powerlines in the viewshed and a junked car here and there, but one also learns the intricacies of local ecosystems and may see finer patterns more vividly than one does on more remote excursions. Third, by exploring local natural places, one may weave a tapestry of understanding of the living beings with which we share territory. One result is the evolution of volunteer organizations aimed at protecting that newfound biodiversity.

There is a necessary connection between direct life-place experience and true belonging. It is not a "virtual reality" proposition. If we are not directly tied to the land through our vocation, then we must attach to it by avocation.

(To really *belong* is to *immerse oneself within;* there are no substitutes for "being there.")

Big Head

It is 1996, and I am now deep enough into this region that I begin a search for its quintessential talisman—some physical form I can make that will keep my hands busy and my creativity productive for a time but will endure as an emblem of my belonging to this region. I am searching for a symbol of avowed spiritual bonding, much like a wedding ring, but one that symbolizes dedication to a territory rather than a spouse. Yet our valley is not popularly associated with any particular insignia: no Golden Gate Bridge, Hollywood hill sign, or Half-Dome; no surfboards or sweeping, picturesque vineyard. In the past, there have been scattered attempts to find regional icons here, and candidates for such status have included the usual valley oak tree silhouettes, California poppies, cottonwood leaves, old-fashioned windmills, and water towers. The native Patwin were not a showy people either; they produced few nonutilitarian artifacts and a simple basketry with only a few abstract motifs. Flicker-feather headbands, made and traded by the Patwin, Miwok, and Pomo, might do, but they would not really be mine, and the gathering of feathers in today's environmentally conscious climate is taboo. Instead, I hope to create a symbolic object that ties upstream and downstream together and says something about the past and present of this place.

Sometime around 1,700 years ago, a change occurred in the types of nonutilitarian ornaments that were buried in the graves of prehistoric peoples of middle California. Archaeologists labeled this change the beginning of a "late horizon" period that apparently lasted from about 300 A.D. until about

Figure 4.4 A Patwin "Big Head" dancer prepares to enter the earth-covered ceremonial lodge. Drawing by Robert Thayer, based on Patti Johnson, "The Patwin," in *Handbook of North American Indians*, vol. 8, *California*, ed. Robert Heizer (Washington, D.C.: Smithsonian Institution, 1978).

1500 A.D. One such ornament commonly found was a shortened, banjo-shaped pendant of abalone shell or some similar shell or bone material. Later versions of this ornament were recognized with confidence by archaeologists as "Big Heads"—human figures with a large head and small, stubby arms and legs. The figure is associated with the pivotal central California Kuksu cult and its dance rituals involving large headdresses worn by dancers impersonating powerful spirits (figure 4.4). Dances were performed in semi-subterranean dance lodges located at larger village sites. Big Head figures were unique to central California burial sites and seemed to have a geographical range of their own.

I study the archaeological palette of ornamental objects, including the more ubiquitous oblong charm stones, and read the works of Alfred Krober, Robert Heizer, and Albert Elsasser. Two impressions settle in my mind. First, the Big Head pendants unearthed in the lower Sacramento Valley are unique to the place, and second, the Big Head, or Kuksu, cult later became one of the signifying rituals of the region for several hundred years, spreading out from here to influence a large portion of the West, ultimately in the form of the Ghost Dance of the late 1890s. Virtually all first peoples of the lower Sacramento Valley at the time of contact were identifiable by Kuksu ritual practice. While Big Head figurines are not found beyond the archaeological burial record of the late horizon, they were clearly a link to the dances and impersonation rituals, which continued nearly until modern times and were noted in the recent ethnographic record.[3]

An idea comes to me that I should fashion my own, modern interpretive version of the ancient, "downstream" Big Head burial pendant but make it out of an "upstream" mineral. Serpentine, being soft, blue-green, and workable, is the obvious choice. It underlies the outer edges and very origins of our life-place and defines much of the headwaters ecology of our two local creeks.

My first attempts are miserable failures; I mistakenly pick pieces of a related, look-alike material, talc, which crumbles repeatedly under my tool pressure until my retired-geologist neighbor apprises me of my error. With the selection of a new source of serpentine and a few hours behind a face mask working at my grinder, the pendant emerges, later to become a familiar Western-style bolo tie. Pleased, I make a second version as a gift for Lacey.

But an irony of sorts soon emerges, at first embarrassing, but ultimately altogether appropriate. In the course of my ongoing bioregional education, long after the two pendants are complete, I learn that some serpentine minerals have high concentrations of asbestos and that I have been slaving behind a grinding machine, possibly inhaling life-threatening particles all the while. The weird thought enters my mind: *"News flash! Eccentric professor dies of asbestos-induced lung cancer after making a figurine based on a two-thousand-year-old religious cult!"* I am generally not superstitious, but the thought does enter my mind that I may have no business messing with a couple thousand years of ritual without really knowing what I'm getting into or what may have been the true purpose of the large-headed figures that have inspired my modern craftsmanship.)

Instead, I prefer to bank on my good intentions, not dwell upon my mineralogical ignorance. I prefer to believe that if there are such spirits, they will forgive me for trying to honor this place as they did. I have not stolen their essence, only borrowed it. In the end, this is a simple story of a piece of earth, a place, a precedent, an idea, an action, and an irony, all aimed at acknowledging my evolving attachment to this natural region. Lacey and I designed our own wedding rings; perhaps these pendant creations are how we are to become wedded to this place. From these pieces, I make my peace here.

A Deep Home Place

As any lover knows, affection breeds nicknames. My various personal explorations of this region leave me searching not only for emblems but for the proper appellation to describe our natural home—one that matches the depth of my growing attachment to it. "Putah-Cache country" is okay—certainly easier off the tongue than "the Putah Creek and Cache Creek watershed region," which my colleagues have often shortened to the "P-C watershed." But such terms are simply too clinical and do little to communicate the nature of the place.

Years after beginning my self-directed research into the lands of these creeks, I came across some records of the settlements of the Lake Miwok people, some of whom still inhabit a tiny chunk of their original territory along the Putah Creek drainage between the south end of Clear Lake to the north, what is now Lake Berryessa to the south, the Mayacmas Mountains to the west, and the Blue Ridge to the east. Here, in their ancestral lands, place-names took on dimensions far beyond mere description or labeling. One name jumped off the page into my imagination: *Tuleyome*. This name referred in the Miwok tongue not only to an ancient village located along Copsey Creek, a small tributary of Cache Creek in the Excelsior Valley, but to the contemporary residents, the ancient ancestors, and the entire surrounding territory inhabited by the Lake Miwok people. Literally, *Tuleyome* means "deep-home-place."[4]

(Upon learning of this name, I realized it captured the primary purpose of my quest and the reason for the writing of this book: it was to discover, both specifically and generically, our Deep Home Place, that region where the heart has taken root and "home" territory has sprung forth.) *Tuleyome*, a name marking a place at the head of the watershed (the village lay near the divide of the Putah and Cache Creek drainages), also includes the sound of the word *tule* (an unrelated Spanish noun for "bulrush"), a characteristic plant of the marshes once home to the River Patwin far downstream, where I now live. *Tuleyome* seems to tie upstream to down, just as the Big Head pendant had done through form and material. The pronounced word, "too-lay-yo-me," soon became a self-contained place-poem with a mantra-like mental reverberation. But the plurality of a region demands that names be tried on and tested by many locals over long periods of time. I won't force my candidate name on either residents or readers, but for now I am content—just this once in print, and silently thereafter—to name this corner of the universe Tuleyome: the Deep Home Place.

Some months later, my good friend John and I are making our first descent of the wilderness run of Cache Creek, putting our whitewater canoe in at the Bureau of Land Management trailhead by the North Fork and paddling downstream into the wild heart of our watershed. The immense flows of the previous month's flood have now receded, leaving thousands of fish carcasses stranded at high waterline—washed down from their spawning and rearing beds in Anderson Marsh at the outflow of Clear Lake to die and scatter on the sand, drape over rocks, or catch in low tree branches. The sweet, acrid odor of decaying fish permeates the air as we paddle, and every place the canoe touches shore, we see the fresh tracks of the bears who come to the stream corridor to gorge themselves on time- and sun-seasoned fish carrion. Bald eagles join the feast as well, and they cry in protest when we disturb their meal by passing underneath the cottonwoods and oaks where they perch.

In late afternoon, we camp by a side stream, eating our dinner while gazing across at the immense grassy plain of Wilson Valley, dotted by huge valley oaks. Turkey vultures ride the thermals of evening heat rising from the open grassland, and blooming redbud shrubs splash accents of magenta on the landscape before our eyes. After a time, we walk downstream along the bank, following vague directions given to me by a friend who has worked diligently to have this place federally designated as official wilderness. He has mentioned a Patwin village ruin accessible on the bluffs by the side stream where we have camped. As we ascend the steep bank, I see the faint, shallow depressions in the green grass amid a gallery of fine blue and valley oaks. John and I don't say much, walking slowly around the one large and five smaller shallow floor pits of the former Hill Patwin dwellings. John examines the ground closely for flakes of obsidian. I sit down quietly by the edge of the former dance lodge and begin to play my cedar flute, stopping occasionally to listen to the silence. I imagine the many ceremonies held within the security of this small circular spot to ensure a stable, fecund, and continuing earth. I envision the Big Head dancer entering the dark room through the small backlit door, with his enormous flicker-feather headdress filling the door frame. This place, I learn later, is Kui-kui, or, ethnographically, the "Sweet Place." The archaeological record shows more or less continuous inhabitation for at least five thousand years prior to 1850 or so. But at this moment, in the quietude of the evening, in this special place, I wonder how I might borrow the power necessary to help my own culture restore the world to its proper balance once more.

5 Imagining

CREATING ART OF THE LIFE-PLACE

Facts carry the traveler only so far: at last he must penetrate the land by a different means, for to know a place in any real and lasting way is sooner or later to dream it. That's how we come to belong to it in the deepest sense.

WILLIAM LEAST HEAT-MOON, 1991

Through the car window on the trip south, I gaze at the subdivisions of South Sacramento as they grade into open pasture country punctuated by dairies, each with its characteristic mound of manure. Lacey is driving; we are en route to Stockton. Even though the windows are closed, a faint aroma makes its way into the car interior. It is not really as bad a smell as is commonly reported: I've grown accustomed to it, since my own campus is marked at its west entrance by a conspicuous dairy barn, and its odor is the olfactory mascot of the U.C. Davis Aggies.

Flying through the flat country east of the delta while the sun dips, we arrive in Stockton at dusk, and we walk up the steps of the Haggin Museum, an aging mansionlike structure set off by itself amid a romantic park setting. The entrance lights glow warmly. We are here to view an exhibit mounted by my colleague and friend Heath Schenker—artist, landscape architect, social art historian, and, now, fledgling museum curator. Heath has been pursuing the art of California's interior as a labor of love for some years and, partly motivated by her unflagging sense of social justice, has assembled the painting, photography, early maps, crate labels, and other visual media, past and present, that depict, express, comment upon, or otherwise celebrate the Central Valley. Her exhibit is entitled "Picturing California's Other Landscape." The title is well chosen, for the territory she covers in her exhibit is the oft-overlooked, flat, functional geological bathtub basin that lies between the better-known and more photogenic Sierra and Central Coast Range.[1]

We don't spend nearly sufficient time viewing the works, which are an astonishingly varied collection depicting nearly every conceivable literal or metaphoric point of view on the Central Valley lands, but we are soon ushered into the small lecture room for a panel discussion among three con-

Figure 5.1 Picturing Yolo County (1996). Photograph by Heath and Phoebe Schenker, from Heath Schenker, ed., *Picturing California's Other Landscape: The Great Central Valley* (Berkeley, Calif.: Heyday Books, 1999), 116.

tributing artists, with Heath moderating. First to speak is José Montoya, and to hear his warm, jocular wit and see his vibrant Chicano poster art allows us to look upon a plain place through new eyes. Montoya's Central Valley is a highly peopled one, where individuals, buildings, expressions, even nuances of the brush are charged with political gravity. Montoya laughs a great deal, with the pleasure of an old warrior looking back on his people's battles for the soul of the soil and city.

Paul Buxman comes next. Trained originally as a painter, he returned to take over the family farm, then rediscovered painting, and now both farms and paints. Buxman has sacrificed not a small tributary of his potential cash flow from crops to sit afternoons in his fields painting his impressionistic renditions of ordinary agricultural landscapes: old stacks of grape stakes, irrigation ditches, orchards. His neighbors are accustomed to his request to set up his easel in their fields as well. I am sympathetically moved by one painting in particular, a close-up of stacked irrigation pipe that, through Buxman's eyes, becomes a thing of beauty and transcendence. Buxman is a likable, pink-cheeked, and cheery-souled man, and instant rapport breaks out as he engages in friendly banter with Montoya, whose compatriots Buxman has frequently hired as farm laborers. For a moment, art has reached beyond class boundaries and united these two men from different sides of an economic rift that has split this valley for decades.)

The third artist, Mary Swisher, is soft-spoken, but her photography speaks with a powerful—and also humorous—voice. Hers is a fresh perspective that reveals yet another dimension of place. Of particular note is a shot of a slender girl—her daughter—in a large, numbered football jersey standing in front of an enormous metal ball several times her height, in the foreground of a seemingly endless, unplanted agricultural field. A horse grazes lazily to one side, near the backdrop of a single tree against the horizon, while a scattered collection of worn-out tires appears in the left rear. Girl, field, horse, tree, tires, and ball (it is actually a discarded rocket fuel tank) meet in awkward juxtaposition,(straining to create a place from the vastness of space.) (It is a feeling familiar to those who know the valley and struggle to make it their home. In the omnipresence of the unlimited horizontal, one accepts what simple vertical place markers one can get) Swisher provides the triangulating vision to the social perspective of Montoya and the simple visual pleasures of Buxman's farm home. A complex, yet somehow lovingly and subtly humorous, picture of California's "other landscape" has been framed in the minds and hearts of the audience.

The State of the Art of the Heart of the State

Some places, like some people, hide a depth of character and inner beauty beyond that which immediately meets the eye. Heath Schenker's exhibit and its accompanying book, entitled *Picturing California's Other Landscape: The Great Central Valley*, address this oversight in historic terms, and it is from her own essay anchoring her book that I now paraphrase. From the earliest recorded paintings, maps, photography, and advertising, a nascent valley aesthetic emerged from the brushes of early-nineteenth-century artists, reflecting the Picturesque school inherited from Great Britain by way of the eastern United States. The Picturesque often focused on scenes of nature, giving minor attention to humans and their artifacts, and fed the ideology of Manifest Destiny: transcendent nature captured to legitimize the Anglo-American colonization and harnessed to its utilitarian purposes. For example, in William Hahn's bucolic 1875 painting *Harvest Time*, a wheat-threshing operation emphasizes the background scenery of golden plains and foothills, while children relax in the foreground, watching their dog retrieve a ground squirrel.

In the 1930s, a group of painters calling themselves the California Scene extended the subject matter to include the valley's regional artifacts and occupations. River commerce, farming, and ranching were included within the accepted scope of the works. Gradually, this gave rise to a more critical social realism, aided by a nascent Chicano art movement. Artists like the two brothers Malaquias and José Montoya, native painter Frank La Pena, and a host of others painted a vision of the valley seen through the eyes of the displaced or marginalized: migrant farmworkers and native Californians. The environmental movement of the 1970s launched yet another wave of visual interpretation, with artists commenting on the degree of change wrought upon the land by agribusiness and large-scale irrigation. The valley held an eerie beauty, beneath which was a set of structural social and environmental realities controversial at best, deadly at worst. But, in the same way, the valley revealed a stark utilitarianism, from beneath which a fresh aesthetic could be coaxed to the surface.

The age of photography brought its own interpretations of this unique landscape. Writing of the photographers whose work is featured in Schenker's *Picturing California's Other Landscape*, David Robertson, local photographer, friend, and colleague, lists three major challenges: a ubiquitous, flat horizon line that just "won't go away"; the immensity of the sky, with its cloudless, blue summer blaze, its winter blanket-gray, or its thick and visually impenetrable tule fogs; and the lack of a featured foreground after plowing has removed vegetation and homogenized ground patterns. Of course, photographers have surmounted these challenges in their own way. Another book, *Great Central Valley: California's Heartland*, which features the starkly revealing photographs of Robert Dawson and Stephen Johnson alongside the writing of Gerald Haslam, native son of the Kern and San Joaquin areas, was perhaps the first "coffee table" book to unsentimentally advance the argument that the valley warranted memorable landscape status in its own right, taking its place on travel bookshelves next to the Big Sur, Yosemite, and Golden Gate tourist classics.[2] As the progress of art became more realistic and less formulaic, the quirky realities and utilitarian overtones of the valley became better suited to art's new honesty. We may have only seen the beginning of the evolution of the state of the art in the heart of the state.

An Artistic Hypothesis

In the past decade, Johnson, Haslam, and Dawson's *Great Central Valley*, Schenker's *Picturing California's Other Landscape*, and Stan Yogi's collection of writing and poetry about the valley, *Highway 99*, have circumscribed a new, Spartan valley aesthetic in both picture and word.[3] An Artistic Hypothesis of sorts can be advanced accordingly:(*A distinctly regional art, aesthetics, literature, poetics, and music can evolve from and support bioregional culture.*)

"Bioregion" seems too straight a jacket into which to try to force a relocalized art; art doesn't like constraint. Yet there is something undeniably synergistic in the relationship between a naturally definable place like the Central Valley and the visual and literary meanings springing from it. The risk in producing an art localized to this region lies less in the possibility of trivializing or ignoring the relationship between region and vision than in the likelihood that such a multiple, complex relationship will be oversimplified. Corollary to the Artistic Hypothesis about life-place is the presumption that the complexity of possible interpretations is likely to parallel the intensity of the relationship; the more dearly the place is held in the heart, the more different ways there are to hold it. Folks who have lived in and loved the valley have often kept that affection to themselves. Books like the three named above may allow these emotions to move out of the closet.

The valley is of course a cultural landscape, but beneath that culture lies a strong skeleton of topography. The valley is physiographically a strikingly vivid space, and the aesthetic views of it have been similarly vivid.(When one examines the valley's natural geography and the cultures that have sprung from it, the potential for art to both respond to and shape the spirit of inhabitation becomes apparent.)The books by Johnson, Haslam, and Dawson, Yogi, and Schenker, the photography of David Robertson (of which more below), and the works of many new artists who have emerged to paint, shoot, or otherwise interpret the valley serve as ample evidence that art and life-place are mutually interdependent.(And, when given "permission" by the "outing" of such works, valley residents are freed to experience this place for themselves with their own, new eyes and deepened perceptions.)

For some years after our tenth wedding anniversary, in 1990, Lacey and I sought a celebratory gift to mark our successful passage; we searched for a work of art, yet none appeared on the horizon of our mutual agreement. At a gallery at the long-loved and now defunct Nut Tree, down the interstate in Vacaville, I came across an exhibit of paintings of the delta and valley by William Tuthill.(*Blue Slough*, the only aerial perspective, caught my attention. I later took Lacey to the exhibit, and she responded as I had. We have now gazed upon *Blue Slough* for nearly a decade, always finding within it new, but somehow familiar, emotional territory. It seemed the ideal art to grace the cover of this book.)

In the short span of years since I saw that first Tuthill exhibit, art of the valley has proliferated. What was once a forgotten, blank canvas now seems to have acquired both paint and purpose, and not just on the walls of county fair pavilions, but in tony galleries. I wouldn't call it a movement quite yet, but artists, it seems, have awakened to the subtleties of this region. Perhaps it is merely the challenge of coaxing visual or metaphoric significance from the horizontal, or perhaps it is something more fundamental, like acceptance of where one has located. Keep your eyes peeled—there is certainly more to come.

The Art of Serendipity

Artist or not, if one begins looking deeply, the aesthetic of place often reveals itself simply. On my own watershed explorations, I have captured a number of favorite images. The flooded walnut orchard on Putah Creek Road caught both David Robertson, the seasoned photographer, and me, the novice, by surprise and resulted in my slamming on the car brakes. Yet the aesthetic was so accessible that it begged to be captured on film (figure 5.2).

The photo that I casually refer to as "Cache Creek Weird" (figure 5.3) required more physical effort, though the serendipity was similar. Paddling across the normally high-and-dry Yolo Basin in the first of many wet years, Lacey and I neared the outflow weir downstream from the Cache Creek Settling Basin, and there, thronelike, sat an abandoned couch, flotsam, no doubt, brought down from upstream and positioned by hobos, teens, or other ad hoc interior/exterior designers seeking a high vantage eastward across the Sacramento Valley plain.

Of most power, mystery, and serendipity is the "Glory Hole" (figure 5.4), a surreal, hyperbolic-sectioned overflow drain looming within view of Monticello Dam, which forms Lake Berryessa out of Putah Creek. Designed by civil engineers in the 1950s solely for hydraulic utility (to maintain laminar flow at high output), it has become a de facto exemplar of sited sculpture. It is a focal point of the frequent visitors to Monticello Dam, and when the Glory Hole spills, word gets out and the locals flock to experience the smooth curve of water that drops beyond perception only to emerge downstream, hundreds of feet below, as atomized spray. Competitions could have been held, famed sculptors retained, and no more compelling form could have been found to signify the deepest mysteries of the Putah Creek watershed. Sadly, it has become a mystical symbol etched into local legend. Once, at a joint lecture given by David Robertson and myself, we showed a slide and made metaphoric mention of it as a black hole into which all the mysteries of the watershed, on occasion, seem to disappear. Some months later, a member of that audience, plagued by depression, ended her life by jumping into the Glory Hole, an event interpreted some years later in a beautiful poem by Rachel Dilworth. Places, it seems, are marked and made by their tragedies as well as their triumphs.

THE GLORY HOLE
  Rachel Dilworth

As though from a pitcher to a glass, water slips
over the rim and down the hole in a smooth fall,
caves—almost softly—in. The Glory Hole will never be full.

Go out in a blaze, I guess. God, looks like a thrill.

The floods have browned the liquid in the reservoir
and the influx towards the hole moves thickly, shifted by pulls
so broad and deep they're indistinguishable.

Like she went right down a bathtub drain. Right down.

You can see just inside from the road, can tell
the water wall is thinner than it first seemed,
that speed quickly picks up once clear of the edge.

Bet inside she thought, Shit—forgot rappelling gear.

A sharp reflection off the backside of the dam
plates the rim of the hole with sun, draws an elliptical
outline round the thing, crowns it with the clouds.

At least, on the way down she saw things no one will.

On the other side, the dam is the big screen at a drive-in
projecting static. You can hear the spray crackle
at its base. Everything that side is black and white.

You see that chute there, that's where she came out.

Water vomits from the one unstuffed plug
that relieves the dam, as though from a fire hose,
as though to snuff the drastic canyon.

*Heard she hung there twenty minutes before she did it. Think
maybe she just slipped?*

It doesn't seem there is enough to see.
We want more for the indignity of death,
for having to imagine her body as it shot out
and how cold the fall felt, and for having to palate the joke—
that in her glorious burst skyward as freed water hit water
and splayed up, up, so beautifully up,

she was already dead, dead since the base of the sinkhole
or dead since the cement-walled middle; that inside, water is dark:
that there's just no way to stage it right.[4]

Figure 5.2 Flooded orchard near Putah Creek (1996). Photograph by Robert Thayer.

Figure 5.3 "Cache Creek Weird" (1996). Photograph by Robert Thayer.

Figure 5.4 "The Glory Hole" (1995). Photograph by Jacob Mann; used by permission.

Tule Fog Haiku

As anyone who knows the Sacramento Valley can attest, our perception of place is colored (or, more accurately, *grayed*) by frequent tule fogs in December and January. Extensive ground surfaces, like plowed fields with little insulating plant or tree cover, cool rapidly through long-wave re-radiation during the night, and ground surface temperatures drop below the dew point, creating great masses of fog that lie like cold blankets across the land, sometimes in layers several hundreds of feet thick. Valley residents know that a simple trip upslope in elevation brings relief and warm sunshine, but the oppressive fog works its way into the cracks between one's thoughts, inspiring a multitude of emotional responses. Recently, Gary Snyder, the poet laureate of reinhabitation, casually suggested to our campus bioregional group the idea of an informal fog haiku festival, which we proceeded to institute ad hoc via the e-mail list-serve. The results were astounding. Some of the following examples, when read together, offer an artistic interpretation of place that anyone can appreciate—and any valley dweller can appreciate deeply.[5]

Angry strangers gripe,
What the heck is a tule?
Fog snagged on thousands . . .
              Maria Melendez

Creek Tule fogged-out
In the gray breath of winter
Red Tail shriek piercing
              Dan Leroy

What little cat feet?
Carl Sandburg never saw this
Lioness linger.
              Linda Book

Fog: Valley's *koan*
Practice form in emptiness
Clear the mind, not sky
              Rob Thayer

tree after tree row
fades back into tule drape
closeness shows distance
              Laurie Glover

Morning: gray damp air,
dry grass; noon: sun, shorts, shirtsleeves;
Winter or summer?
              Amy Boyer

The Lure of the Local: From Lippard to Robertson

I am incapable of speaking with great authority on the subject of art, so I turn to the authority of Lucy Lippard, prolific author and keen observer of public art. In her important book *Lure of the Local,* Lippard suggests some ways to capture the imagination of a life-place in a local art that "merge[s] with and/or illuminate[s] a place." In Lippard's words, such an art would be

- SPECIFIC enough to engage people on the level of their own lived experiences, to say something about place as it is or was or could be

- COLLABORATIVE at least to the extent of seeking information, advice, and feedback from the community in which the work will be placed

- GENEROUS and OPEN-ENDED enough to be accessible to a wide variety of people from different classes and cultures, and to different interpretations and tastes

- APPEALING enough either visually or emotionally to catch the eye and be memorable

- SIMPLE and FAMILIAR enough, at least on the surface, not to confuse or repel potential viewer-participants

- LAYERED, COMPLEX, and FAMILIAR enough to hold people's attention once they've been attracted, to make them wonder, and to offer ever deeper experiences and references to those who hang in

- · EVOCATIVE enough to make people recall related moments, places, and emotions in their own lives

- · PROVOCATIVE and CRITICAL enough to make people think about issues beyond the scope of the work, to call into question superficial assumptions about the place, its history, and its use[6]

By way of concrete example, let me use this framework as a way to look at the photography (figures 5.5a–b) of David Robertson, whose works capture a unique character of the valley.

David's medium of choice is the large-format Polaroid camera, and I frequently see him pass by my house in his aging pickup, his signature white plastic chair and assorted found-object props conspicuously scattered about the bed of his truck, en route to some exotic corner of the Putah or Cache Creek watersheds. His method of engaging the place is deliberately open-ended: if he is shooting collaborative photography, his subjects (more like co-artists) figure spontaneously and heavily in the final artistic outcome. (Once the specific site is found, the search for meaning commences, and "the silver-sided Muse" is evoked from the ambience and invited into the camera.) Robertson doesn't "take" photographs; he coaxes them into deliberate being, posing himself (always) with props and people in wild collages that mix humor, serendipity, nature, culture, and irony. In addition, there is (always) some deliberate environmental manipulation of the Polaroid film: he might dip half-developed film in seawater, rub it in dirt, or expose it to sun or rain.

One never knows—especially not Robertson himself—what to expect from these photographic dances with place. (Viewers must work to make their sense of *his* sense of things.) Yet when all is completed, and Robertson's photography is hung, circulated, or published, Lucy Lippard's framework is silently revealed. Often collaborative, always appealing, and generous and open-ended to the max, it is just specific enough, just "simple" and "familiar" enough, to hook us before demanding that we work hard to decipher its (or create our own) layers of significance. As for the evocative, provocative, and critical dimensions, Robertson's work precisely fits these criteria. (His photography hovers on the edge of rationality, but all who participate in his experiments or seriously view his work are somehow changed in their relation to the region. He is not an easy study; it takes work to understand what he is all about, but then that is also true of most places. Robertson

Figures 5.5a–b "True Communionism" (top) and untitled photograph by David Robertson; used by permission.

demands that we expend the same kind of energy in engaging his photography that he would want us to expend in finding out just where we are.)

Artists in Bioregional Residence

One of Robertson's many contributions to raising the artistic awareness of the local life-place is his Artists in Bioregional Residence (AiBR) program. Now in its fifth year, AiBR was born of a desire to have the watersheds of Putah and Cache Creeks interpreted through the eyes, ears, and hands of local artists. Applications are taken from painters, printmakers, poets, photographers, storytellers, fiction writers, musicians, weavers, and sculptors who, in exchange for a very modest honorarium and brief residency, would create art that in some manner responded to or commented on the watershed region. It has been, by all accounts, a resounding success. One of the more memorable contributions is by Stuart Allen, artist and photographer, who worked with light to outline the shores of Lake Berryessa and illuminate, both figuratively and literally, the threatened blue oaks characteristic of our foothills. And one writer of fiction and nonfiction, Amy Boyer, stayed on with the program, serving as our Web site coordinator while continuing her place-based creative writing. She now teaches a successful extension course called "Write Here" in the community.

Using written and graphic material from the AiBR recipients and from the larger faculty-student group, as well as his own photography, David has edited and published ten small, superbly reproduced folios entitled *Putah-Cache* (1 through 10), which are distributed through our local bioregional word-of-mouth networks and are available by order from our Web site. *Putah-Cache* folios treat the reader to a taste of the highest-quality art and writing to emerge from the life-place, and they whet the appetite for more knowledge and engagement.

Landscape Architecture: The Ultimate Bioregional Art

My profession, landscape architecture, which sprang from a general yearning to bridge nature and culture, was brought into the public consciousness and named by Frederick Law Olmsted nearly a century and a half ago. First popularly manifested in the creation of New York's Central Park in 1858, landscape architecture soon become known as the discipline that provided intentional territory for human use and enjoyment of the outdoors. While "landscape gardening" curricula emerged in the late nineteenth century at

Figure 5.6 West Davis Ponds. Landscape architecture by Deering Design; environmental consulting by Jones and Stokes; photograph by Robert Thayer.

a number of land grant colleges, the first program in landscape architecture was offered at Harvard in 1900. Landscape architecture spawned the profession of city and regional planning several decades later. From the outset, landscape architects have sought to discover the *genius loci*, to make *place* out of raw space.)

As a source of inspiration for landscape architects, the Sacramento Valley is rich with natural potential. Once a land of vast permanent marshes, seasonal wetlands, riparian forests, and native bunchgrass uplands, the valley has strained under the weight of paving and the pull of the plow to the point where the "soul" of the place has nearly dropped out of sight. Recent landscape architectural efforts have placed this regional nature back at center stage. A notable example is the West Davis Ponds (figure 5.6), a mere hundred yards from where I sit typing these words. With the help of local landscape architect Paul Deering and restoration ecologist Steve Chainey, city of Davis personnel and Audubon Society chapter members collaborated in reconfiguring a weed-filled, trapezoidal storm drainage detention basin into a complex, dynamic, and visually appealing waterfowl habitat. Permanent ponds surround nesting islands in the dry season, while winter storm drainage fills an irregular frame of seasonal ponds. In spring, wading birds such as avocets and stilts appear, and many of the once seasonal Canada geese have settled here permanently. (Perhaps the most striking acceptance, however, is by the people of the community, who cherish this new bit of constructed nature, honoring it with frequent walks and careful surveys through binoculars. The original suburban houses that first turned their backs on this once-ugly engineering necessity are now joined by upscale mansions poised strategically for views of the nesting islands and tule marshes. Property values—as well as bioregional awareness—have gone up.) *Nɜꞓɔhgī Ldꞓ Ɛɜ/led*

Imagining

(To live in a place, well, most certainly, requires an imagination. Without imagination, humanity mires in mediocrity and stagnation; to imagine, to create, is to survive and thrive.)

Yet imagination often gets short shrift. (True creativity has an otherworldliness to it. We are often suspicious of truly creative people because they often push the boundaries of our socially constructed realities farther than is comfortable for us to tolerate.) For the most part, however, the artwork that springs from imagination is not a navigation system but merely a hand-drawn map of alternative routes, not a windshield but a side window, or perhaps even a rearview mirror. (The possible futures glimpsed by art are like views through a kaleidoscope. But walking through life looking through a kaleidoscope is certainly preferable to walking blindfolded.)

Life-place—the notion that humans might learn to live more permanently and responsibly within territory constrained by the nature of place—is certainly an act involving both individual and collective imagination. (Imagination precedes most of the accomplishments of history and culture.) Consider some of the other major accomplishments of a creative human society: freedom, social justice, democracy. Each of these notions began as an imagined alternative to a less positive reality before it took root in collective consciousness. For the most part, we can only guess at the role of the artist in these most significant of human achievements. In the birth of each of these concepts, the picturing of an alternative reality, aided by art and imagination, must have moved from the singular to the collective mind. Art, I would argue, is likewise essential to life-place.

One of my favorite books is a specifically reinhabitory or bioregional novel, perhaps the first of its kind, set in the watershed one ridge over from Putah Creek. In *Always Coming Home,* Ursula Le Guin creates an "archaeology of the future," writing of a hypothetical people named the Kesh who reinhabit the valley of the River Na (geographically similar to the Napa

River of today). The Kesh "lived in the future" in five "houses" or clans; each was marked by an element (obsidian, blue clay, serpentine) and a cardinal direction (north, south, up, down), and the membership of each included certain animals (domestic, wild, flying), plants (wild, cultivated), festivals or dances, and artistic or craft endeavors (wine making, glassblowing, tanning, weaving, irrigating, bookmaking, smithing).[7]

Le Guin, the daughter of anthropologist A. L. Kroeber and author Theodora Kroeber, also created for her fictitious Kesh people a literature, poetry, folklore, artistic iconography, and intricate place geography. (The original hardback edition even came with a tape of completely original Kesh music.) Strangely, the Kesh people occasionally uncover remnants of a former technological civilization (presumably ours) that has long since perished, and all the information ever recorded in human history is in a remote mountain computer "data center" from which the Kesh people have intentionally distanced themselves. The information is available anytime but is seldom used by the Kesh, who prefer to live closer to the land, to their houses, craft occupations, artistic traditions, dances, and embodied wisdom.

Le Guin's novel is a rich tapestry of culture that the author has invented to give us a glimpse of a possible reinhabitory state of being with respect to the earth. In my frequent trips over to the Napa watershed for work or pleasure, I can never look at the landscape without my perception being colored by the Kesh. Le Guin has, for me at least, animated the place and permanently influenced the way I construct my idea of the region.

Several years after I had read *Always Coming Home*, Le Guin spoke on campus, and I was delighted to discover from her talk, which centered on the book, that she was cautiously optimistic about the possibility of "reinhabitation." A great portion of her own soul, she said, had been captured in *Always Coming Home*. Her book has in turn become somewhat of a literary landmark among those of us toying with the bioregional notion, as if some of that soul has passed from her to us and from us to our students and friends.

Like a growing cadre of similar literary "ecocritics," David Robertson maintains that a good portion of today's fiction, nonfiction, and poetry is inspired by the ecology of region, especially that which explores the resonance of people and place. Perhaps this gravitation toward life-place themes is in part a reaction to the many alienating and displacing forces at work in the global arena, and in part a celebration of the local and familiar. Whatever its impetus, regional art is flourishing today.

One notable such effort in my own backyard is the Program in Nature and Culture in the U.C. Davis English Department, where participants study the relationship between literature and the ecology of the wild. And in the watersheds of Putah Creek and Cache Creek, cross-disciplinary research, education, and outreach have brought about a productive synergy, with literary and artistic interpretations of these local watersheds now paralleling scientific, ecological, and political data-gathering efforts. A celebration of "Putah Creek Week" in Davis in 1995 featured an exhibit of artworks inspired by the creek. Paintings and photography sold briskly at the opening reception.

As individuals and groups form stronger bonds of identity with natural regions, the value of localized arts, literature, and music rises concurrently. In Le Guin's novel, the "Initiation Song from the Finders Lodge" is sung by Kesh elders to the young initiates who have chosen to be the explorers and emissaries to the "outside world." Yet in the final lines they are admonished to remain spiritually centered in place:

> May your soul be at home where there are no houses.
> Walk carefully, well loved one,
> walk mindfully, well loved one,
> walk fearlessly, well loved one.
> Return to us, return to us,
> be always coming home.[8]

6 Trading

EXCHANGING NATURAL VALUES

A bioregional economy would seek first to maintain rather than use up the natural world, to adapt to the environment rather than exploit it or manipulate it, and to conserve not only the resources but also the relationships and systems of the natural world.

KIRKPATRICK SALE, 1985

Rice Bowl: Economic Realities in the Sacramento Valley

It is September, and great plumes of smoke rise from the rice fields of the Butte Sinks, forming mushroom heads as the ascending columns are pushed laterally and broadened by the upper wind currents. In the shadow of Sutter Buttes, my assistant Jake Mann and I are taking photographs of the home bioregion. We have followed one of the smoke columns to its source: the burning stubble of a recently harvested paddy, or "check," as the growers refer to it. In this instance, the farmer is riding his small ATV, wielding his backfire torch, properly overseeing the controlled burn according to both state law and common practice. As Jake and I shoot 35-millimeter shots of the activity, the farmer approaches us. He is smiling, and he greets us politely, but we immediately sense an understandable discomfort in his tone of voice. Quite soon, his pressing question emerges: "Are you reporters?" "No—we're college instructors!" is our honest reply; we are preparing to take university students on a comprehensive field trip focusing on the nature and culture of the Sacramento Valley bioregion. We assure him that we are only after real-world knowledge for our students, and we explain our philosophy that learning should be local and not contained by walls. Upon hearing this, he opens up a little, and the exchange begins.

The Sacramento Valley is a "rice bowl," growing short-grained rice and some wild rice on poorly drained ancient flood basin soils, producing higher yields of grain per acre than any other rice-growing region in the world. Many of the growers belong to cooperatives or sell directly to subsidiaries of multinational corporations. To prevent rice blast, a fungus disease that attacks new rice plants, the stubble is routinely burned after fields have dried out following harvest (figure 6.1). After decades of this practice aroused

Figure 6.1 Rice stubble being burned from a field in the Sacramento Valley. Photographer unknown; from the archives of the College of Agricultural and Environmental Sciences, University of California, Davis.

both consternation and controversially documented respiratory complica-
tions among the region's expanding nonfarming public, laws were passed
declaring a five-year grace period, now expired, after which farmers had to
find alternative means of disposing of rice straw, and specifying a maximum
percentage of acres a rice grower might burn each season. The first five-year
period was later extended when the growers found few cost-effective re-
placements for rice stubble burning.

I mention to the farmer that I eat local rice, enjoy it, and have some sym-
pathy for his situation, inquiring as to the relative costs of various practices
of controlling the fungus. He replies that he pays twenty-five dollars per
acre for air quality permits to burn his rice, and that using the roll-and-
flood method (inundating the field and pressing the rice stubble into the
mud to speed natural decomposition) would cost him twenty dollars per
acre for the water and fifteen dollars per acre for the roller, or thirty-five
dollars per acre.

As Jake and I drive away, I wonder how the price of twenty-five dollars
per acre for burning permits was calculated and why the government
doesn't set the fee high enough to encourage rolling and flooding, which
would eliminate the air-quality impacts of rice growing. Or perhaps the state
government should augment the fees rice growers pay, chipping in the additional ten bucks per acre out of the general fund to protect the state's residents from the detrimental atmospheric and health effects of rice burning
and to "pay" rice farmers for a needed public value. Like so many related
issues in North America's farming heartlands, this issue raises a number of
thorny questions: How can rice farmers be expected to pay extra to remove
rice straw when they are hamstrung by the fluctuating global market for
rice? How might local consumers of rice, some of whom, like me, are concerned equally with the livelihood of the region and its environmental quality, contribute to a solution? Should the expense of nonburning control
methods be passed to consumers of rice (thereby jeopardizing the competitive position of valley rice growers in global markets), or should it be borne
by all regional residents who want clean air to breathe? Is it reasonable to
expect rice growers to take the extra costs of nonburning controls out of
their own pockets? Since rice is often grown with irrigation water priced
under its actual market value, what is the real cost of producing rice in this
region? How might the recognized benefits of rice fields as migratory waterfowl forage be quantified and figured into the equation? Most of us local folks eat rice, I'm sure. Is there a "bioregional" solution to this problem
of rice burning?

Such are the dilemmas a life-place faces when confronting the collision of the globalizing economy and the need for local inhabitants to participate in assuring the environmental quality and sustainability of the regions they inhabit. In the whole of the Sacramento Valley bioregion, from Mount Shasta to the Sacramento–San Joaquin Delta, the top twenty agricultural crops, roughly in order of cash value, are rice, tomatoes, almonds, grapes, milk, cattle and calves, walnuts, hay, nursery products, peaches, prunes, seed crops, corn, pears, wheat, safflower, beans, honey, turkeys, and melons. Eighty-three percent of the almond crop and 60 percent of the prune crop are exported to foreign markets, as well as 15 to 25 percent of the rice, tomatoes, walnuts, and grapes.[1] With such a complex harvest, the bioregion produces considerably more food than could possibly be consumed locally; most agricultural production goes to processing and distribution markets serving California beyond the valley and the rest of the United States. In short, we are a food-producing and -exporting region, operating under the classic economic principle of comparative advantage. We are a breadbasket to the continent and, increasingly, the world.

Natural versus Unnatural Economies

The economic component of the bioregional hypothesis represents the practical nexus of the entire question of "natural" relocalization. A life-place perspective implies that a bioregion should be able to provide for its human residents over the long term without degrading the ecological stability, collective community, or natural resources of the region. However, without hard-nosed thinking about making a living sustainably from a finite natural region in an increasingly global economy, life-place theory is mere wishful thinking. The problem is twofold. The first difficult task is to reconsider economics from the standpoint of the environment per se; the second equally difficult task is to assess how an "environmental" economics might apply to a specific local region like ours, which has evolved within the confines of traditional economic theory in response to continental and global markets. In rethinking our economy "bioregionally," the gravest mistake is to discount valley residents' century-and-a-half-long experience in drawing a living from these rich soils. Instead, the economic challenge of this life-place might be best framed as an investigation into scale, context, and perpetuity: How might we farm better, and more *permanently*?

Herman Daly is the acknowledged dean of environmental or ecological economics. He points out that while *microeconomics*—with its emphasis on prices and cost-benefit analysis—takes *scale* into account and is conceived of as part of a large whole, *macroeconomics,* the study of broad economic issues such as income, labor, capital, and GNP, is assumed to be an isolated system, not part of anything larger. Herein, says Daly, lies the fallacy of macroeconomics:

> The macroeconomy is an open subsystem of the ecosystem, and is totally dependent upon it, both as a source for inputs of low-entropy matter/energy and as a sink for outputs of high-entropy matter/energy. *The physical exchanges crossing the boundary between the total eco-logical system and the economic subsystem constitute the subject matter of environmental macroeconomics.* (Italics in original)[2]

The problem clearly emerges in a simple diagram (figure 6.2a): as the macroeconomy (represented by the square) "grows," it becomes larger with respect to the finite capacity of the larger ecosystem (represented by the enveloping circle). Hence, the constraints on the economy change, and we move from an era in which manmade capital was the limiting factor to one in which "natural" capital is the limiting factor. Ecosystem functions for noneconomic activity are thereby reduced as the economy grows.[3]

Daly's elegant theory can be understood when one imagines a pair of simple "before-and-after" views of the Sacramento Valley bioregion. Prior to intense population by Euro-Americans, land use in the Sacramento Valley was dominated by grasslands, permanent marsh and seasonal wetlands, riparian forests, and unconstrained rivers and streams. Subsequent agricultural development has transformed most of the valley land into agricultural land and has expropriated most of the water for agriculture, leaving the ecosystem functions significantly debilitated. Yet existing macroeconomic models have no means of accounting for the near-total loss of marshes, grasslands, valley oak woodlands, free-flowing rivers, natural floodplains, aquifer recharge areas, vast flocks of migratory waterfowl, and immense schools of migrating salmon. Agriculture, now the valley's dominant land use, ebbs and flows in consort with global commodities markets, which take no account of ecological conditions in the Sacramento Valley.

Even with the significant theoretical contributions of Herman Daly and others, surprisingly little information exists to tie the relatively new environmental economics to local or regional issues. Environmental economics has so far concentrated on global-scale concerns such as air pollution credits, energy development, carbon taxes, food surpluses, and international trade. Daly's circle diagram representing the large ecosystem remains just that: a generalized biosphere ecology, undifferentiated by region. To a certain extent, the conspicuous absence of a sustainable *regional* economic theory or practice can be explained by the fact that the economic structure of

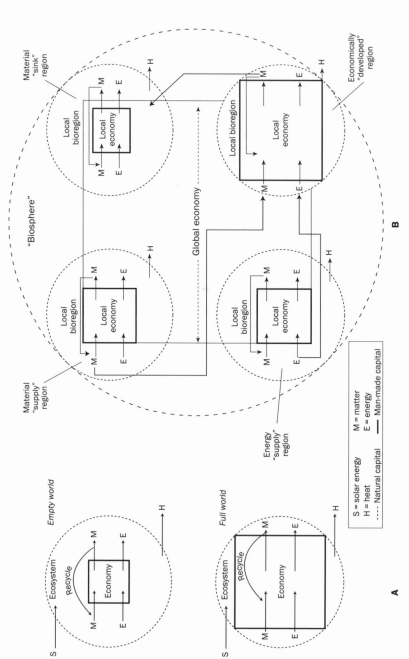

Figures 6.2a–b Ecosystem/economic subsystem diagrams. *A, left:* Daly's diagram of the economy is an open subsystem of the enveloping ecosystem; as the economy grows, with respect to the ecosystem, natural capital, rather than human-made capital, becomes the limiting factor. *B:* A bioregional version of Daly's concept. The "global" economy actually consists of a network of interconnected regional economies. Local ecosystems are subject to regional inequities of the "global" economy; some bioregions are degraded to support the supply or waste needs of remote, developed regions. Figure A from *Beyond Growth*, by Herman E. Daly, copyright © 1996 by Herman E. Daly, reprinted by permission of Beacon Press, Boston; *B* based on original by Robert Thayer.

the world is globalizing. New, liberal trade agreements, growing transnational corporations, and rapidly expanding telecommunications all presume a future "unified" global economy. In this paradigm, each region's economy is reduced to providing goods and services for world markets under terms dictated by the global economy and at great peril to regional carrying capacity and self-sufficiency. Within this framework, "national economies" play an ever-receding role.

What is needed is a new theory that embeds the macroeconomy within the "larger ecosystem" (i.e., Daly's biosphere) and accounts for economic effects on local natural subregions. The larger ecosystem is essentially an interconnected, hierarchical set of smaller natural ecoregions, each of which possesses a particular ecological structure and function (figure 6.2b). The increasingly globalized macroeconomy, then, is actually embedded within many smaller bioregions, the sum of which compose the biosphere. Matter and energy flow from the natural capital of each of these natural regions into the macroeconomy, and the macroeconomy delivers products, waste matter, and waste heat back to the biosphere via its specific bioregions. A simple example from the Sacramento Valley serves to illustrate. From the soil and water of the valley, rice is grown, delivered into the global rice commodity market, and consumed by valley residents, other Americans, and Asians. As a result, less water is available for waterfowl and fish, air is polluted with particulate carbon from rice field burning, and money flows into the coffers of global corporations, local growers, middlemen, shippers, and farm laborers, with some of the immediate economic benefits "trickling down" through valley towns and communities. Although the natural capital—free-flowing water; clean air; intact marsh, riparian, and upland ecosystems—has been exchanged for currency by means of rice, no feedback to the price system takes this loss of natural capital into account, and production is instead limited only by labor costs, world commodity prices, chemical inputs, and water availability.

This phenomenon has two ramifications. On the one hand, consumers of California rice in, say, Taiwan, do not pay higher prices as Sacramento Valley bioregional ecosystems are damaged because there is as yet no mechanism to reflect the loss of our natural capital. Further, Taiwanese consumers of Sacramento Valley rice will never see or personally experience the loss of natural capital in our bioregion because they live quite literally on the other side of the world; they cannot be expected to adjust their rice-eating behaviors to save our ecosystems because it is simply not on their cognitive horizon: out of sight, out of mind. So the degradation caused by our local rice economy is separated, economically, ecologically, geographically, and perceptually, from the point of consumption. This near-total lack of economic feedback is antithetical to the way ecosystems actually function.

The above example is, of course, an oversimplification. But it does not take an advanced degree to live in the Sacramento Valley and understand that something is critically wrong with the way global economics fails to account for local environmental impacts. Let us again examine rice farming to illustrate the limitations of the classical economic approach. In addition to providing one of the world's essential staple crops, what other local services might rice farmers be equipped to provide the nonfarming public? The answers: habitat for waterfowl, aquifer recharge, flood control, soil conservation, air quality, salmonid stream flows, wildlife observation, hunting areas, natural beauty, and outdoor recreation. Yet are they paid for any of these potential services? Hardly. We (the nonfarming, largely urban/ suburban public) expect the rice farmer to provide all of these secondary services out of pocket as part of the costs of doing business. Even the current label *grower* denies the more holistic purpose carried by the term *farmer*. Growers only grow, while farmers, in the classical, true agri*culture* sense of the term, might again provide an entire suite of related stewardship benefits if we could find the mechanism to pay them to do it.

Yet even as economic theory struggles to incorporate environmental externalities, much can be observed about how local communities and businesses respond to, and in some fashion compensate for, emerging globalization. According to the popular and ever-optimistic futurist John Naisbitt, "The world's trends point overwhelmingly toward *political* independence and self-rule on the one hand, and the formation of *economic* alliances on the other," a phenomenon he describes as the "global paradox."[4] Characteristics of this paradox, which rests on the notion that the "bonding commonality of human beings is our distinctiveness," include a larger world economy, but with smaller, stronger, more efficient parts. In a new twist on Rene Dubos's slogan, Naisbitt suggests that the world must now "think locally and act globally."[5] It is perhaps through this new distinctive "tribalism," as Naisbitt calls it, or "resistance identity," as Castells might characterize it, that a means for feeding back economic information into the health of local bioregions will be found.[6]

Jane Jacobs and Regional Economics

In her seminal work *Cities and the Wealth of Nations,* Jane Jacobs presents four key concepts of direct or indirect implication to the economics of bioregions: *import replacement, city regions, improvisation,* and *faulty currency.* Together, these form the most sophisticated argument for a possible bioregional economics to date.[7]

IMPORT REPLACEMENT

To be self-sufficient and vital, cities and their surrounding regions must replace imports with their own raw materials, goods, services, and expertise. Most cities, Jacobs contends, are not vitally import-replacing. Overdependence on export to other markets and regions or on administrative, tourist, or cultural services without provision that a significant proportion of goods and services be consumed within the city itself makes for an inefficient (and incomplete) local economy. By replacing imports, cities and the surrounding regions they influence can (1) enlarge markets for local and nearby rural goods, (2) increase the numbers and kinds of local jobs, (3) increase transplants of city work into the local region, (4) create new uses for the technology of rural production, and (5) grow city capital.

CITY REGIONS

Jacobs debunks the idea of "national" or "global" economies, saying that they are tenuous artifacts beyond the scale of human needs. Instead, Jacobs posits the city regional economy as the true, classical means of providing necessities for people. Cities and regions that become mere "supply regions" for the global market and do not replace significant imports doom themselves to economic stagnation and dependency on this artificial national/global economy or, worse, on subsidies and bailouts. However, when a city with its immediate geographic surroundings provides a full component of essential raw materials, services, and goods for local/regional consumption, it naturally becomes a city region: a complex, import-replacing economy with a high degree of self-sufficiency.

IMPROVISATION

What allows cities to become import-replacing city regions, according to Jacobs, is *improvisation.* Citing the example of Taiwan, Jacobs paraphrases the Taiwanese's own question: "If our cheap labor can be put to work by foreigners, why can't we put it to work for ourselves?"[8] By investing local capital locally and by exercising a high degree of creativity in the provision of local goods and services, the island of Taiwan has emerged as an economic powerhouse and, due to the island's small scale, its own city region. This is not to suggest that Taiwan is a stellar example of a healthy island bioregion; it is not. Taiwan has largely ignored pollution control and environmental health measures, and it is now struggling to catch up to the rest of the developed world. However, Taiwan's economy is healthy, strong, diverse, and *complete* in the sense of being an import-replacing city region; as of 2001, Taiwan remained surprisingly resilient to the economic downturn that has plagued other Asian nations. The strength of the Taiwanese economy should enable it to easily pay for the environmental cleanup it so desperately needs, and investments in that sector will undoubtedly reap large long-term economic payoffs.

FAULTY CURRENCY

Jacobs clearly criticizes national (and, by extension, international) currencies: "National or imperial currencies give faulty and destructive feedback to city economies and . . . this in turn leads to profound structural economic flaws, some of which cannot be overcome no matter how hard we try."[9] A national currency can convey information only about international trade conditions and the major exports to and imports from other countries, not about the differing conditions of local regions within the nation. To Jacobs, it is like one brain stem for many pairs of lungs, each pair of which may be "respirating" at a different economic rate. This situation often causes a weaker or less-developed region to be unable to pay the high prices for goods and services from the dominant regions without losing its own economic improvisational ability and becoming a supply region to the stronger areas of the nation. In short, national currencies enable nations to model the world, with areas of economic decline coexisting alongside thriving dominant regions.

Jacobs, writing over a decade prior to the North American Free Trade Agreement (NAFTA), the General Agreement on Tariffs and Trade (GATT), and the current World Trade Organization (WTO), states that when cities and their surrounding regions begin to lose important export work to foreign imports, they have no defense and no means of self-correction. Not only are global trade agreements and international currencies destructive, according to Jacobs, but something that functions like regional tariffs and export subsidies is necessary to protect city regions and to foster the improvisation needed to replace imports and derive local economic solutions. If the city region is the genuine unit of economic activity, it should have the automatic equivalent of tariff and export subsidies as well as of currencies, allowing it to remain as self-sufficient as possible. From there, it is not too far a stretch to suggest that the city region and the "bioregion" might evolve to describe the same territory as more and more economic activity would begin to be based upon quality of life and other measures of environmental quality, such as clean water, clean air, and renewable energy.

Had Jacobs written her book more recently, she would have no doubt concurred with Paul Hawken, who, in *The Ecology of Commerce,* writes that global or hemispheric trade agreements like GATT (which led to the WTO) and NAFTA "are little more than thinly veiled blueprints for the expansion of trade by multinational corporations. They have little to do with small business, community concerns, or cultural diversity, and only in passing will they consider the environment."[10] In short, WTO and NAFTA are antithetical to the bioregional perspective, placing the carrying capacity of bioregions at risk and encouraging the generation of a global mosaic of huge, centralized supply regions (e.g., Canada provides the lumber and hydropower, California and the U.S. Midwest grow the food, Mexico provides the cheap labor, Japan manages all the multinational manufacturing webs, and so forth). It takes little imagination to envision the ecological destruction and resource depletion implicit in such a reality because the true costs and environmental and social impacts of such monolithic service to global markets are most often exported to third-world countries or impoverished regions within developed countries.[11]

The thermodynamic inefficiencies of the global free-trade paradigm have been ignored by the international corporations as they have built complex manufacturing webs wherein assembly plants are constructed near the cheapest labor supplies, mines are located in the most regulation-free countries, and a powerful international lobby suppresses the price of fossil fuels so that imports and exports across the oceans to tie this trade together remain unrealistically cost-efficient. Much of the supposedly free international trade is between divisions of the same multinational corporation in different countries, which send partially assembled components or partly processed raw materials to subsidiary divisions in other nations without paying tariffs, thereby covering up the natural, physical inefficiencies of shipping or air freight and the differences in labor rates, prices of necessities, and costs of living between the exporting and importing nations.

In the end, the free-trade, global, corporatist paradigm often destroys local communities and formerly self-sufficient economies, mines what would otherwise be renewable resources, reduces environmental protections to the lowest common denominator, cheapens the value of work, wastes billions of BTUs in needlessly shipping goods and materials (which might have been locally provided) across vast oceans and continents, and exports the environmental and social impacts of its economic activity beyond the perception of its primary consumers. Global corporatism is antithetical to sustainable development and highly destructive to the carrying capacities of local, natural regions. Furthermore, it actively discourages alternatives to itself. Thus, in the face of such an apparently unstoppable juggernaut, a bioregional economic perspective is often ridiculed as wishful thinking, yet it need not be.

Exchanging Natural Values: A Bioregional Economy?

What, then, might be a relocalized economics supportive and respectful of the limits and potentials of a life-place? Perhaps the best way to consider this life-place potential is to turn to a basic notion of primitive economies: that of *trading natural values*. When first peoples generated surpluses of a sustainably harvested resource, they traded these natural values to others. In my region, flicker feathers and dried salmon were traded upstream; obsidian came down in return. Among Hill and River Patwin peoples, low population densities made it likely that none of these commodities would be overharvested. No fossil fuel was involved in moving these physical substances back and forth, and while the existence of a shell bead "currency" has been suggested, the proportions of things traded to things obtained locally was probably small when considered in economic terms. In any event, the enveloping ecosystem containing the "natural capital" was still large in relation to the manmade capital of the first people's subsistence-and-surplus-exchange economy.

A simple principle behind life-place economics—the bioregional economic paradigm—is as follows: *Use local resources and materials locally; then trade only surpluses.* This flies directly in the face of the modern economic law of comparative advantage—the global economic paradigm—which suggests that regions capable of exploiting a particular commodity should do so monolithically, with all other material wealth being obtained by receipts from the sale of that "global" commodity.

One of the least acknowledged benefits of local consumption of local materials is the spatial and cognitive feedback it gives both producers and consumers. This is true for locally grown produce and other physical necessities, such as energy, water, building materials, and aggregate for construction. For example, the citizens of Yolo County, in the Cache Creek watershed, were presented some years ago with alternative ballot measures: one that would have banned gravel mining along lower Cache Creek altogether and one that relegated gravel mining to off-channel sites, directing ten cents per ton of aggregate extracted from the corridor toward restoring the creek. Since Yolo County's population growth averages about 3 percent per year (typical of the lower Sacramento Valley region), the citizens approved the second option, which ensured that gravel needed for local growth came from local sources. This protected a vital perceptual feedback loop: local growth could be measured and monitored against local impacts, and local revenues could be redirected toward restoring the creek corridor itself. The entire process could be envisioned by local residents in a perceptual feedback system: the faster the growth, the more gravel needed, the higher awareness for restoration. While aggregate is basically a nonrenewable resource, it is far better and more economical in the broadest sense to control the process locally than to fuel new urban growth based on aggregate mining from some remote location.

Yet to presume some magic, idealized transformation to a bioregional economics when the entire world seems to be headed in the opposite direction would be naive. Local regions must *consciously* take steps to sustain and fairly exchange the natural values embodied in their own regions through deliberate, locally controlled policies. One "natural" value easily overlooked is the potential to improve, protect, and capitalize on local environmental quality. Economist Thomas Power argues that managing regions for environmental stewardship is wise, necessary, and, ultimately, cost-effective. It is not just an excuse to develop a tourism industry, which can be a double-edged sword; "the primary economic contribution of protected landscapes and communities is attracting not tourists but rather permanent residents and businesses, which stimulate and support diverse economic activity."[12] Power's conclusion reinforces the previously mentioned arguments of Jane Jacobs and Daniel Kemmis: a city region develops best when it preserves and enhances the abilities of local citizens to respond to economic opportunities, replaces imports to the greatest extent possible, adjusts its extractive industrial base to one that can be sustained over the long term without despoliation, and seeks the highest quality for its natural resources, ecosystems, and quality-of-life amenities.

Characteristics of a Life-Place Economy

Weaving together these various strands of theory, we can devise a framework for a true life-place economy. Ideally, it would involve the following characteristics:

- loyalty and commitment to the local place, a sense of pride in residency, and a high degree of participation by citizens in local affairs of all types

- a desire to preserve natural assets, cultural integrity, and lifeways of the region in perpetuity

- a high degree of self-sufficiency in the production of essential food, water, energy, goods, and services

- a willingness on the part of local consumers to support local businesses for the necessities of life, with an understanding that "price" does not always equal "cost"

- a creative, entrepreneurial society capable of innovating to respond to changing economic forces and making use of local resources, goods, and services in unique ways beneficial to the life-place

- a healthy skepticism toward large-scale tourism that might harm local culture, economic self-sufficiency, or ecological integrity

- a healthy skepticism toward externally owned businesses and industries wholly "imported" from outside the region

- a formalized means of rewarding local production, consumption, and reuse of resources, goods, and services through incentives, local taxes, local currencies, cooperatives, farmers' markets, and community-supported agriculture

- an understanding that the consumption within a region must be matched by a willingness to accept responsibility for the environmental and social impacts of that consumption

- a means of nurturing the flexibility, adaptability, and overall educational level of regional residents in a manner that encourages them to stay and commit to a productive life in place

- a sense of civic responsibility, citizenship, and pride in the public good beyond sheer commercialism, corporatism, and privatism

The irony of the above framework is that it is quite "conservative," but in a new meaning of the word, one providing an alternative, third position with respect to both global corporatism and "wishful-thinking" environmentalism. Ultimately, the business of the land pays for preserving the land; the economy, then, extends the efficiencies and limits of the ecosystem in a process of exchanging natural values. In this model, natural values are the ultimate currency standard.

Scale and Boundaries

To maintain any hope of a more bioregional economy is to presume that the bioregion's geography might eventually be better respected in people's economic activities. The key here is *scale*. Regional economies in the industrial era have been structured largely by political boundaries, transportation corridors, market distribution networks, immense power and water delivery systems, and numerous fragmented governmental jurisdictions—geographic determinants more likely to violate than to reflect bioregional carrying capacities.

At some point, the sheer displacement of resource and economic activity *sources* from *end uses* becomes so large in scale that natural regions become compromised. Intense arguments over the appropriate scale of energy and water developments and the distances that both these resources should be allowed to travel before being used have marked politics in California and the Pacific Northwest for decades. The Pacific Northwest has begun to seriously contemplate whether it can have both extensive hydroelectric power *and* sustainable salmon fishing components in the economy. An *either-or* choice between the two seems to dominate policy decisions. Prior to California's 2001 energy woes, a significant political movement evolved for the removal of several hydroelectric dams in the Columbia River Basin to bring back spawning and rearing habitat for salmon. For the Pacific Northwest, the tradeoff between salmon runs and hydroelectric power represents a crucial balancing act between two clashing economic forces of the bioregion and marks an acknowledgment that carrying-capacity limits may have already been reached, if not exceeded.

Normally, the Pacific Northwest exports hydroelectric power, providing about 9 percent of California's electricity. Yet when California energy use began to exceed its supplies and the 2001 drought reduced Northwest hydroelectric capacity to just above 50 percent of normal, the issue grew more complex. Should the Northwest export what little excess hydropower it could muster to California at high premiums? Should it build new dams in anticipation of more years of drought? Or should it remove some dams in a biological gamble to restore its salmonid fisheries, a keystone of its economic and cultural identity? One wonders how the people of the Pacific Northwest will resolve this dilemma; both abundant hydropower and immense salmon runs characterized the region for decades. With the costs of hydroelectric power surging, and the loss of an adequate surplus to sell to California, the "costs" of losing the salmon habitat and fishery by continuation of the extensive hydropower dams now seem necessary to bear. But are they?

Have the costs of decimated salmon runs been adequately internalized in the costs of generating hydroelectric power? One might conclude that a national/international currency does not adequately reflect the relationships between regional resources and economic activity in the Pacific Northwest.

To paraphrase and extend the conclusions of Mark Reisner in his books *Cadillac Desert* and *Overtapped Oasis*, both water and power flow toward money.[13] Two maps that reveal this condition well are of water impoundment and transport networks and the sources of natural gas production for central California (see figure 6.3 and, later in this chapter, figure 6.5). Both maps show immense dislocations between *sources* and locations of *end-use consumption*. Long-distance transport of energy and water across vast territory hinders regional self-reliance and keeps consumers from perceiving the relationship between benefits and true costs of consumption. Large resource scales lull consumers into dangerous dependencies and exaggerated expectations, as the recent energy crisis in California has illustrated.

A bioregional economy implies a stronger *convergence* between the boundaries of natural ecosystems and the boundaries of local economic activity: a better set of checks and balances between the limits and potentials of a region to provide resources, energy, water, food, goods, and necessary services for itself and the propensity of the local economy to export singular resources, commodities, and services into the globalizing economy. The importance of scale cannot be overemphasized. Clearly, the California "economy" (if such a state economy can be said to exist) has been based on unrealistically low and artificially supported costs for generation and transmission of both power and water. Recent energy shortfalls in California have wildly accelerated the cost of importing vast quantities of energy from out of state. Likewise, much of California's agriculture is supported by federal subsidies for water and power, thereby drawing on general fund contributions by other states and regions. (Since I am in a college of agriculture, my salary as a University of California professor is tied to this agroeconomic activity and is supported by such subsidies.) In the case of California, federally subsidized prices for water and the once unrealistically low cost of electrical power have resulted in a population in southern California vastly in excess of any natural carrying capacity and a northern California threatened with becoming yet another ecologically degraded "supply" region.

Similar examples can be made of other geographical scale domains: northern hemisphere cities suck the resources of southern countries, exporting their environmental-impact "footprints" across continents and oceans. The global paradigm assumes that the world will adjust to the exploitation of

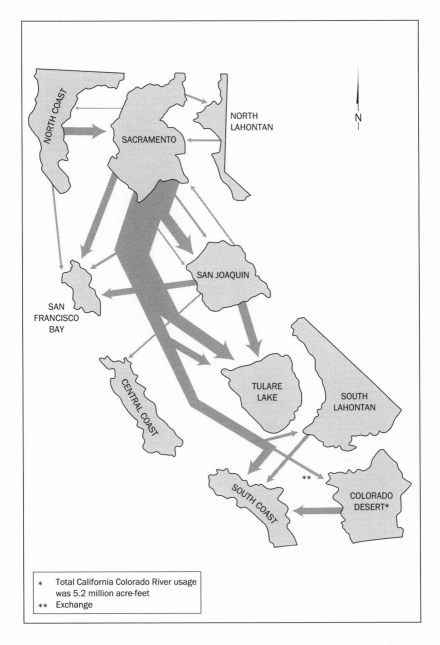

Figure 6.3 State water transfers in California (at 1990 level of development; in thousands of acre-feet per year). The Sacramento Valley region is a major exporter of water to the rest of the state. From California Resources Agency, *California Water Plan Update* (Sacramento, Calif.: Department of Water Resources, October 1994).

certain regions as resource supply regions and the designation of others as sinks for energy, water, manufactured goods, wastes, political influence, or economic power. The result of this thinking is unfortunate; there is nothing inherent to the current globalist paradigm that might respect the limits of a particular bioregion's carrying capacity to contribute resources to the global economy. When one local supply of a resource or commodity burns out, the global economy merely looks elsewhere for a replacement supply, ignoring the resource depletion or community costs and accounting only for the costs of extraction. In other words, the global paradigm has yet to determine a means of accounting for natural or human capital, rather than financial capital. Yesterday's defunct copper mine in Montana becomes tomorrow's burgeoning copper mine carved out of the Amazon rainforest. Just as Montana failed to prevent despoliation of its mined landscapes, so too will the Amazon be unable to prevent similar despoliation without substantial activism and involvement by local dwellers.

Economic bioregionalization requires (1) a means of internalizing the very high real costs of long-distance transport for providing necessary physical resources and goods and (2) a severance tax on resource extraction and unsustainable harvesting rates of renewable resources. Free trade, however, is antithetical to both of these necessities. Not only is free trade a flawed political idea and a disaster in terms of entropy and ecology, it is also a highly dangerous cognitive disconnect. Removing the responsibility of living within ecological carrying capacities from a society's immediate, perceivable region disrupts the perceptual feedback that tells us how we are doing on the face of the earth away from our area of immediate concern. This cognitive separation is directly parallel to Jane Jacobs's criticism of national and international currencies, which also provide faulty feedback. A cruel simplification of this fact is that such long-distance, fossil-fuel-driven, subsidized, and hence artificially low-priced trade has allowed the world's population to grow far in excess of the planet's carrying capacity. In short, fossil-fueled trade deludes the world into thinking it has become more efficient when, instead, it has become more entropic. A finer-grained mosaic of demand, supply, consumption, and recycling—a provision of necessities derived from and attuned to the nature of local regions—is the best hope the world has for sustaining regional populations at steady-state levels without depleting renewable resources, disrupting environmental service functions, or wrecking ecosystems.

Yet all is not lost. If we consider the essentials that any economy must provide—food, energy, water, material goods, services—we find a surprisingly healthy groundswell movement toward economic relocalization. For a variety of reasons, people are now challenging the implicit assumptions embodied in global business as usual. Let us now look at some of these alternatives.

Foodsheds: Relocalizing Agriculture

Agriculture is the very foundation of any economy; the procurement of food resources has been the dominant work of humans since humanity evolved. Yet the modern food economy is global in scope, subject to the vagaries of international speculative markets, addicted to nonrenewable hydrocarbon energy supplies, highly mechanized, and increasingly separated in distance and perception from the lives, concerns, and control of consumers. Furthermore, the contemporary production of food is an entropic nightmare: a ten-calorie equivalent investment of fossil fuel is needed for mechanized plowing, seeding, harvesting, fertilizing, processing, and shipping to produce a single useful calorie of food value in many staple crops. Furthermore, adding the costs of shipping food commodities increases the investment in caloric energy expended versus caloric energy used by the food consumer. We are, as many observers have commented, essentially "eating oil." Herman Daly points out that "more than half of all international trade involves the simultaneous import and export of essentially the same goods. . . . Americans import Danish sugar cookies, and Danes import American sugar cookies. Exchanging recipes would surely be more efficient."[14] Agriculture as it is now globally configured is therefore most certainly unsustainable. The agricultural output of many countries is far less than they consume. By measurement in calories, Japan is only 37 percent self-sufficient in food production; the remainder of the caloric input of the Japanese diet is imported, paid for by receipts from Japan's strong export market.[15]

In a work entitled "How Great Cities Are Fed," W. P. Hedden coined the term *foodshed* to suggest the spatial dimensions of how food is produced, distributed, and finally consumed by the metropolitan public. Arthur Getz, referring to the foodshed as "the area that is defined by the structure of [food] supply," describes how our modern food production and distribution systems have effectively eliminated the concept of seasonal foods and severed the tie between agricultural producers and food consumers, to the detriment of communities and the environment. John Hendrickson suggests that the foodshed is a useful heuristic device for consideration of alternative, sustainable food systems. He advocates increasing research on foodsheds from the standpoint of bioregional resources, limits and potentials, cropping systems and farming practices, urban farming and gardening, nutrition, energy, recycling, regional economics and communities, education, and ethics.[16]

In the past several years, a regional and community-based food system movement has slowly been gaining momentum. Wisconsin's Center for Integrated Agricultural Systems publishes a newsletter, *The Wisconsin Foodshed*, that highlights regional food news "from field to table." Joan Gussow and Jennifer Wilkins of Ithaca, New York, have done original work on seasonal and local diets. Among other things, they have created a popular poster that interprets the basic food pyramid of the Food and Drug Administration specifically for the northeastern region of the United States, offering tips on which plants to grow, when to plant and harvest, and how to combine, cook, and "season" (literally and figuratively) regionally compatible foods. Gail Feenstra, a nutritionist with the California Sustainable Agriculture Research and Education Program, manages research, education, and outreach in community food security, community-supported agriculture, direct marketing, regional food guides, and foodsheds.[17]

In my home town of Davis, a popular farmers' market offers a wide variety of organic and locally grown foods and has been a pillar of the local (and *re*localizing) community for several decades. As a simple teaching exercise, I frequently ask students to consider their personal foodsheds, challenging them to map the geography of their own food consumption. Under my supervision, my former student Eric Roberson drew a foodshed map of the Davis Farmers' Market (serving as the basis for figure 6.4) and found that the foodshed was only about 250 miles wide. In contrast, the typical food items in a supermarket travel an average of about 1,300 miles from source to dinner table, defining a geography roughly ten times as wide and one hundred times as extensive in area. With more local, intimate foodsheds, consumers can become more involved in decisions about how their food is grown, how their local ecosystems can be protected, and how the entire food delivery system can be made more regenerative or sustainable.

One aspect of a relocalized food system is the emergence of community-supported agricultural enterprises, or CSAs. For several years prior to our now weekly ritual visits to the local farmers' market, our family "subscribed" to an organic farm forty miles away, paying a quarterly fee in advance to receive a weekly box of fresh, seasonal vegetables delivered to a small distribution point at a neighbor's house. The number of CSAs, especially near large cities and suburbs, is growing as people realize the value of knowing who produces their food, how it is grown and harvested, what inputs are used, how the farm laborers are treated, what the farm looks like,

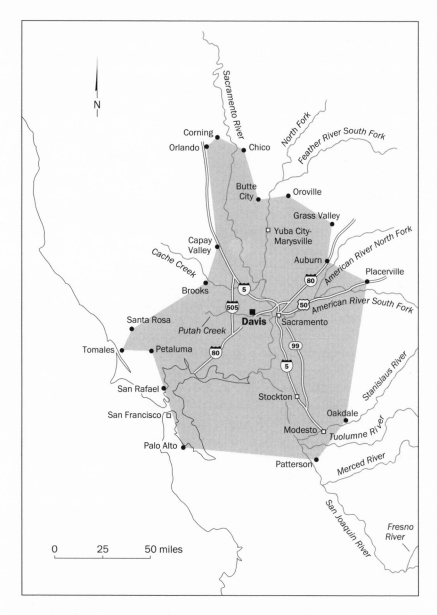

Figure 6.4 The "foodshed" of the Davis Farmers' Market. Map based on original by Robert Thayer and Eric Roberson.

and how it feels to participate in food production. Community-supported agricultural enterprises, like farmers' markets, facilitate a direct line of feedback between producer and consumer while minimizing the entropy inherent in conventional agriculture and food distribution.

Two recent trends point to an acceleration in the relocalization of agriculture. First, as of this writing, widespread consumer concern over the prospect of eating transgenic foods has caused European boycotts against certain imported American agricultural products. The enormous snack manufacturer Frito-Lay asked its suppliers not to sell it corn that had been genetically engineered. Second, there are now over thirty certified farmers' markets in the Sacramento Valley bioregion alone; this is a trend that appears to be nationwide as well. These indicators point toward more local concern for the sources and methods of food production and more direct feedback between producers and consumers of food.

Community Utility Districts: Relocalizing Energy

America's electrical utility system has been characterized by both small public utilities and large, publicly regulated, investor-owned power monopolies such as Pacific Gas and Electric Company, Consolidated Edison, and Southern California Edison. These utilities produce and distribute electrical power through a vast, continentally interconnected system of transmission lines referred to commonly as "the grid," ranging from enormous 530 kV trunk lines to various substations and step-down transformers to single-user power lines to homes and businesses. In spite of the ubiquity of overhead wires, utility poles, and transmission line towers, most citizens "tune them out" of their perception. Few people really comprehend the mysterious geography of energy, not knowing where or how "their" power is generated, what mix of fuel types provides their electricity, or what the environmental consequences of their own energy consumption might be. While nearly everyone has a detailed mental map of local highways and roads, few readers of this book are likely to ever have seen an actual map of their region that showed power plants, electrical substations, and transmission lines. The recent chaos in California electrical energy delivery caused by deregulation has further blurred any semblance of geographical relationship between "sources" of power and the locations of end uses; deregulation has erased what slight understanding the public may have had regarding the geographic logic of electrical power delivery.

With minor exceptions (most notably SMUD, the Sacramento Municipal Utility District), the Pacific Gas and Electric Company, a stockholder-owned private utility, controls most power generation and distribution in California's Great Central Valley, which includes the Sacramento and San Joaquin bioregions. As I type these words, more than half of the electricity powering my computer is from coal or natural-gas-fired fossil fuel plants like the two-thousand-megawatt PG&E plant in Pittsburg, California, about fifty miles away. About 20 percent comes from hydroelectric plants such as those on the Feather River and other eastern tributaries of the Sacramento. A small percentage (5 percent) is generated by the Geysers geothermal plants in the upper Putah Creek watershed, 1 percent from wind power plants at Altamont Pass and the Montezuma Hills, and a tiny amount from generators powered by methane recaptured from the Yolo County Landfill, only five miles away. Nine percent of my electrical power is imported from the northwestern hydro regions of Oregon and Washington. Of the "fuel mix" producing electricity to type these words, *only about 10 percent is renewable and relatively benign to environmental quality.*[18]

The electrical power delivery system is notoriously inefficient: only about one-third of input power reaches its delivery points to provide necessary heat and light. Nearly two-thirds is lost in transmission-line reductions, conversion inefficiencies, and waste heat. The high voltages needed for long-distance delivery of electrical power are especially susceptible to transmission-line losses.[19] To make our local matters worse, in 2001 California experienced an unprecedented energy crisis. Yet it was not a crisis in a physical or technological sense—other regions of the United States continued with adequate power supplies, reasonable prices, and uninterrupted electrical service, while California endured rolling blackouts both winter and summer, exorbitant and highly inflated prices for natural gas, and overall political and economic chaos in its electricity delivery system.

In 2001, California electrical rates rose to 50 to 100 percent higher than the national average. In spite of the emergence of renewable energy-generating technologies in the 1970s, many of the larger California utilities invested heavily in nuclear generation, leaving them with considerable debt on power plants that were eventually no longer cost-effective to run. During the utility deregulation that swept the country in the late 1990s, California, the first state to institute rate restructuring, managed to pass a thinly disguised bailout of the major utilities' bad investments (euphemistically, "stranded costs") in nuclear power by convincing voters they were actually getting a 10 percent rate reduction when, in essence, they were buying bonds to pay off bad debts for nuclear plants such as PG&E's Diablo Canyon. Instead of holding private stockholders responsible for the bad investments, the entire ratepaying public was saddled with retiring the utilities' debt. Also, under a poorly studied and hurriedly passed legislative mandate, private California utilities divested themselves of local power plants while investing heavily in out-of-state power production capacity, thereby abandoning some of the responsibility they had previously borne toward their regional constituents. Instead, PG&E's parent corporation became yet another global energy provider, with a substantially weakened spatial allegiance to California. As of this writing, the "local," in-state subsidiary utility of PG&E has declared bankruptcy, and its sister utility, Southern California Edison, teeters on the brink, propped up only by nervous politicians of both parties, from the governor on down. Interestingly, the latest California energy crisis is a totally bipartisan debacle. Although both Republicans and Democrats try to pin the blame on each other, nearly all state politicians have accepted campaign donations from the utilities, including the successive Republican and Democratic governors, as well as state legislators of both parties who hurriedly passed the misguided deregulation legislation in the first place.

According to consumer advocate Ralph Nader, deregulation has the potential to create unregulated energy monopolies. Utilities that were formerly restricted to one region (PG&E, for example) form unregulated "sister companies" that then buy energy assets in other regions—an unplanned phenomenon similar to the merger mania occurring after long-distance telephone service deregulation and the breakup of AT&T. The recent collapse of energy giant Enron is a case study in the problems of deregulated energy. Furthermore, the "green power" marketers who emerged in the immediate wake of deregulation purportedly sold consumers "renewable energy" at a premium. Critical analysis has now exposed most green energy marketeering as a sham. The so-called "renewable" energy sources (1) are already fully developed for captive ratepayers and are now being resold (thereby shifting the burden of additional generation back to conventional, polluting fossil fuel plants), (2) include power produced from very large environmentally destructive hydroelectricity projects, or (3) are merely vague promises to develop renewable energy sources sometime in the future. Very few of the many green energy schemes would actually lower energy rates for residential consumers or would increase the percentage of renewable electrical capacity by replacing nonrenewable capacity. There is also no regional tracking or certification system that might allow verification of green marketers' claims to a more benign fuel mix for generation of electricity. Finally, of the few actual providers of genuinely renewable power, several are owed money by now-bankrupt utilities like PG&E and have ceased providing power to the grid.[20]

In summary, electrical energy deregulation in California, as elsewhere, is now moving into uncharted waters. No one is sure that the outcome will provide the degree of competition, local control, or renewable and environmentally friendly energy once touted by the politicians. Deregulation of energy opens the distinct possibility of a backslide toward large unregulated monopolies marketing least-cost power production via large coal and fossil fuel plants that have been exempted from the constraints of the federal Clean Air Act. We are moving from an era of publicly regulated, regional electrical monopolies (such as the "old" PG&E) to an era dominated by a handful of unregulated continental energy conglomerates that act as a price cartel with poor or nonexistent ties to the many actual regions they supply; Enron was the salient example. In short, energy production is becoming a global phenomenon controlled by a few huge corporations and is less and less a regional delivery system controlled by local consumers.

A simple arithmetical analysis of California electrical energy reveals some startling facts. Seventy-five percent of the electrical power is generated in-state, while 14 percent is imported from the Southwest and 11 percent from the Northwest. However, of the 75 percent, a majority is generated using natural gas supplies originating from outside California. Only 16 percent of the natural gas consumed by residents, businesses, or power plants in California is actually from California gas wells (figure 6.5). A summary of the fuel sources for California electrical power is offered in table 6.1.

So, while California is a global economic powerhouse with the world's sixth-largest economy, it, like Japan, seems to be far from self-sufficient in energy and must rely on external sources for nearly half of its fuel supplies, whether hydro, coal, gas, or nuclear. California "pays" for these energy imports by widely exporting agricultural commodities, high-technology products, services, and popular culture. Yet California has immense untapped resources of sunlight, wind, and biomass, and the Sacramento Valley bioregion itself contains most of California's primary natural gas deposits. The current California energy reality is the antithesis of the principles espoused by Jane Jacobs in her analysis of vibrant city regions. In addition, the environmental impact, or "ecological footprint" (see next chapter), of California extends far beyond its boundaries. While all the world's regions import certain commodities and export others, it is the *scale* of importing and exporting compared to the potentials and limitations of natural regions that is the principal subject of this chapter. In terms of electrical power, Cali-

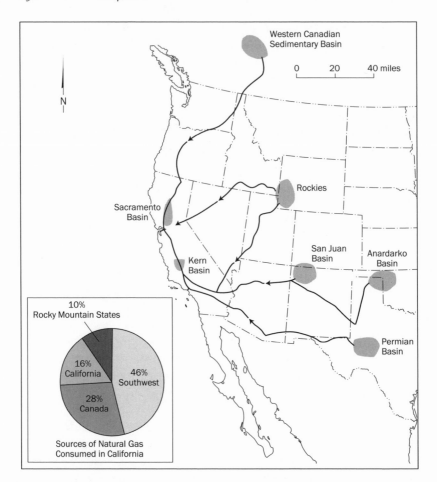

Figure 6.5 California produces only 16 percent of the natural gas it uses to provide for its electrical needs. Most of that comes from wells in the Sacramento Valley bioregion. Based on map by California Energy Commission, "California Energy Facts," www.energy.ca.gov/html/calif_energy_facts.html, retrieved January 2000.

fornia misses a substantial opportunity for both regional efficiency and more self-sufficiency.

Fortunately, the chaos of deregulation has created the potential for establishment of small utility districts that may aggregate the buying of power by informed consumers, set rate structures to facilitate local energy goals, develop new, renewable sources, and provide power to known, regionally defined constituencies. The need to move from nonrenewable, environmentally consumptive energy sources to renewable, environmentally be-

TABLE 6.1   Fuel Sources for California's Electrical Power

Fuel	In-State Production	Out-of-State Production	Total
Coal	7.2%	12.6%	19.8%
Hydro	11.3	8.8	20.1
Natural gas	4.4	3.5[a]	31.0
	(with California gas)		
	23.1[b]	(23.1)	
	(non-California gas)		
Nuclear	16.2[c]	(16.2)	16.2
Renewables	12.2	—	12.2
Other	0.6	—	0.6
TOTAL	52%	48%	100%

SOURCE: California Energy Commission Net System Power Data, 1999.

[a] Electricity "shipped" into the state using natural gas from elsewhere (e.g., the Southwest).

[b] Domestic production assuming out-of-state fuel. In other words, I consider electricity generated by gas-fired plants within California, using gas from out of state, to be "out-of-state" power.

[c] Geographical source of nuclear fuel not known, but could be out of state.

nign energy technologies is now widely accepted. The public prefers solar and wind for generating electricity and believes the government is spending too little on renewables research and too much in support of the fossil fuel and nuclear industries. Deregulation allows the potential relocalization of energy through community control of fuel policy, generation, pricing, distribution, and maintenance.

A look at the energy resources in the Sacramento Valley reveals that we have above-average annual direct sunlight, ample biomass resources from agricultural by-products, natural gas reserves along the spine of the valley, geothermal and wind resources along the western-edge coastal mountains, and hydroelectric power along the eastern border with the Sierra. The most efficient use of energy is "source-to-end-use matching," where the energy used to perform a particular task is directly suitable to the task and is located nearby. In several dairies of the adjacent Sonoma region, for example, methane generators from captured cow manure power the dairy and farm equipment, with virtually no distant power transmission required—a virtually sustainable energy relationship. Locally controlled utilities are more apt to facilitate source-to-end-use matching of energy, with the result that greater efficiencies in production versus use can be achieved.

Just such a local utility is being proposed in Davis, a community already world renowned for its solar energy utilization and the first city in the nation to have instituted an energy conservation building ordinance. The Coalition for Local Power is currently moving to establish a Davis Municipal Utility District (DMUD), whose overall goal would be to gradually reduce dependence upon fossil fuel until the community is powered solely by sun and wind. DMUD is but one of many local utility districts being proposed in the aftermath of energy deregulation. However, it is not the only harbinger of a more relocalized, renewable energy future for the Sacramento Valley bioregion. Existing renewable energy plants in the bioregion already provide over 250 megawatts of generating capacity and include small hydropower plants, biomass plants that burn forest or agricultural waste, landfill gas-burning generators, and photovoltaic arrays that produce electricity directly from sunlight. The region's considerable incident solar radiation and its vast agricultural by-products offer ample renewable energy by which to fuel a local, "bio-regenerative" electricity supply.

What, then, might be the characteristics of a truly relocalized, "bioregional" energy system?

LOCAL/COMMUNITY CONTROL

· Aggregated purchasing by local community or communities within a bioregion

· Local boards of directors capable of translating the community's or region's wishes for reliable, affordable, renewable, and clean energy into specific action

· Local ownership, not ownership by larger conglomerate corporations or out-of-region investors

LOCAL, RENEWABLE FUELS

· Use of local, renewable energy resources, not remote sources via power line transmission

· Investment of receipts from use and sale of nonrenewable energy into renewable development gradually, until renewable capacity eclipses nonrenewable sources and renders them unnecessary

· Direct visual, spatial, economic, and land/resource planning feedback among producers, distributors, and consumers of energy so that customers know where their energy comes from

NEW CAPACITY

(NOT ALREADY DEVELOPED AND PAID FOR BY EXISTING GRID)

· Development of new, alternative renewables, not merely purchase of power from those already developed

· True premiums charged to ratepayers that pay either for *new,* not previously contracted supplies, increases in energy efficiency, or rate subsidies to low-income residents and small, locally owned businesses

END-USE MATCHING

· Matching of energy source with energy use. *Examples:* rice biomass generates power to operate rice mills and dryers, dairy wastes produce methane, sawmills are run on wood-chip-generated power

· Grid-connected photovoltaic systems that allow south wall and roof surfaces of buildings to generate power nearly equivalent to electricity consumption within the buildings themselves

PRICING, EFFICIENCY, AND RATES

· Rates set by the community/region on the basis of its own goals, not just short-term economics

· Community/region's subsidizing of investments in new renewable capacity and conservation

In the inevitable transition from nonrenewable to renewable energy supplies, bioregions are the obvious venue in which to consider economies of scale and local control over energy resources. Bioregional energy systems would be large enough to provide a resilient mix of fuel types and distributed power plants but small enough to give residents and local officials a sense of feedback and substantial control over their own energy destiny and over the environmental impacts of their own energy demand. In short, bioregions like our Sacramento Valley are ideally scaled to create energy from the "interest" on natural and human capital, rather than consuming resources and destroying ecosystem functions in remote bioregions elsewhere on the planet to provide "our" power. The emergence of a demand for "green energy" marks the desire on the part of consumers to have an influence in how their energy is generated; a local community-based, bioregionally scaled utility is the obvious way to ensure that such demand results in a more regenerative system of electrical power.

Rice Straw: Relocalizing Materials

In the Sacramento Valley bioregion, agriculture is the dominant industry. One of the main crops is rice, the cultivation of which is controversial not only because it requires so much irrigation (in the semiarid regional context of California) but also because the most cost-effective way of disposing of the after-harvest rice stubble is by burning it, which pollutes the air and affects the respiratory health of regional residents. A shallow look at our rice industry by an uninformed outsider might therefore lead to the conclusion that we really have no business growing rice in this region. Upon deeper examination, however, one might begin to recognize the great role rice fields have begun to play in serving as wetland forage for migratory waterfowl when the fields are allowed to accumulate winter stormwater. Even deeper examination would reveal that rice stubble is a useful resource just waiting for the right set of economic incentives, price signals, and creative marketing to take its place in an exemplary cycle of industrial ecology and bioregional resource sustainability.

In the past ten years, rice farmers have come under increasing public and governmental pressure to find ways to reuse rice stubble instead of allowing it to go up in smoke. At least six different uses are being tested or developed for the straw by-products of rice: fiberboard, construction-ready straw bales, quality paper, erosion control blankets, animal feed, and chemical specialty products.[21]

FIBERBOARD

Rice straw contains a high degree of silica, which makes it difficult to decompose in the field. The silica content and relative durability of the straw also make it potentially useful as a low-cost, versatile, lightweight building product with excellent dimensional stability, moisture- and fire-resistant capacity, machinability, paintability, and strength. Experiments with rice-straw fiberboard reveal potential widespread application in the furniture and building industry for use in flooring, cabinetry, door faces and cores, moldings, sound walls, office partitions, and insulating panels. Rice-straw fiberboard, unlike some current wood-based products that it might replace, has no out-gassing of formaldehyde and offers 15 percent savings in weight. At least two companies are now building plants to produce rice-straw fiberboard in the heart of the rice-growing region, Colusa County, in the Sacramento Valley bioregion. Soon we may be able to eat rice while sitting on flooring made partly of rice, eating on tables built partly from rice as well.

STRAW-BALE CONSTRUCTION

A building technique so simple and straightforward as to intimidate those accustomed to more complicated methods is alive and well in the form of whole rice-straw-bale construction. In this proven, inexpensive process, full-dimension rice-straw bales are placed on poured foundations, stacked like large bricks, reinforced with rebar, covered with wire mesh and stucco, and painted, resulting in a curtain wall of enduring beauty, simplicity, and thermal efficiency. The celebrated architectural buildings of the Real Goods Center in Ukiah, California, designed by architect Sym Van der Ryn, elegantly demonstrate this technique at a fraction of the cost (both in dollars and BTUs) of other construction techniques. In the past several years, county planning offices in the Sacramento Valley have allowed straw-bale construction into their suite of permitted building types, and straw-bale houses have been built in most of the counties in the bioregion.

PAPER

Recently a process has been developed by a former forest paper products researcher to make high-quality writing paper out of rice straw.[22] The procedure, when compared to the detrimental processes of timber-derived paper, is extremely environmentally benign, producing both paper and a secondary by-product from the straw that can be returned to the rice fields as a fertilizer. Initial tests of the prototype product have been successful enough that Bank of America, the Gap, Esprit, and Patagonia have all agreed to use the product when it can be delivered competitively in bulk, and several newspaper chains and environmental organizations have enthusiastically endorsed the process. The developer envisions a chain of small-scale rice-paper mills located up and down the Sacramento River Valley to reduce the transport distances for the rice straw, allow dispersal of the by-product to nearby rice fields, and provide local employment. With its reputation as a populous government center and paper-pushing bureaucracy, the city of Sacramento and the state government itself would presumably be major consumers of rice-straw paper.

EROSION CONTROL FABRIC

In tests conducted in Brawley, California, rice-straw erosion control fabric blankets performed very well in simulated rainstorms on 40 percent slopes, besting wheat-straw blankets by a considerable margin. Rice-straw erosion fabrics are now being tested in other states as well, most importantly in

Texas's Department of Transportation, whose testing facility results are respected by other state departments of transportation. With erosion control measures on the upswing, the potential market for rice-straw fabrics could potentially expand at a rapid rate.

ANIMAL FEED

The high silica content of rice straw makes it a less directly palatable feedstock than other alternatives, but tests by the U.S. Department of Agriculture forage laboratory show that a 20 percent mixture of treated and acid-stabilized rice straw is readily consumed by dairy cows. The prototype fermentation treatment process for the rice straw results in higher carbohydrate conversion by livestock than that of alfalfa hay, a ubiquitous western feed crop. Experiments on various processes to convert rice straw to animal feed show considerable promise, and the propinquity of rice fields to significant livestock populations would guarantee very short distances from rice field to processing plant to livestock "consumers."

CHEMICAL SPECIALTY PRODUCTS

Perhaps the most interesting reuse of rice straw on the horizon is the "biorefinery concept" being advanced by the Arkenol Company. Although proprietary, the process, called *concentrated acid hydrolysis*, involves the conversion of rice straw and similar rough organic feedstocks into sugars via acid hydrolysis, with gypsum and lignin as additional by-products. A fermentation process then transforms the mixed sugars into a number of additionally useful products, such as ethanol for transportation fuel or fuel additive. The process requires only moderate thermal energy, since it would operate by burning lignin, one of its own by-products. It would produce no waste stream other than useful products (ethanol, industrial carbon dioxide, lignin, gypsum, and yeast), making it environmentally benign and relatively easy to site with respect to other land uses. Water would be entirely recycled throughout the industrial process.

It remains to be seen whether these or other evolving rice-straw utilization techniques will capture markets of sufficient size to make an impact on the rice-straw disposal challenge in the Sacramento Valley bioregion. As of this writing, AB 1686, authored by valley Assemblywoman Helen Thomson (D-Davis), has passed the Assembly and is headed for the state Senate. The bill would create market incentives to speed the development of above-mentioned and other rice-straw by-products. The benefits of these rice-straw reuse industries would be many. Less diesel fuel would be consumed in shipping Northwest-timber-produced paper into the region. A resource that might otherwise go up in smoke could be recycled at a profit, providing local jobs and returning nutrients to the rice fields. The improvisation implicit in the process would create local expertise in our own bioregion that could spin off to other agricultural industries. A wide range of bioregional residents—rice farmers, environmentalists, stockmen, paper-consuming governments and corporations, local building industries, asthma sufferers, the regional air quality control board, the birds and microorganisms dependent upon rice growing, and, no doubt, the politicians—would all benefit from a successful rice-straw reuse program. In essence, the rice-straw challenge for the Sacramento Valley is typical of the kind of bioregional industrial ecology that must emerge worldwide if we are to build a more sustainable material culture. The best scale in which to resolve these material issues, however, is one life-place at a time.

"Buy Your Region": Relocalizing Consumer Purchases

In the current rush toward e-commerce, it would be easy to assume that all future consumer purchasing will be done at home with the click of a mouse. This assumption, however, presumes that people actually *wish* to denature their own shopping experiences and to take the fun out of that age-old pleasure: *buying things,* whether they are necessities or luxuries. It's my contention that consumers are neither stupid nor callous and that recent trends toward "big-box" retailing and "e-buying" have reached or will soon reach their natural, human limits. There is simply too much fun to be had, and too much local benefit to be shared, by keeping the act of consumption within the community of consumers themselves.

Allow me to tell a story of deliberate purchase directly influenced by my regional allegiances. It reveals that although our tastes and desires may be based on values formed in part by global influences, with our own purchases we either reinforce or drain vitality from our home regions.

While on a trip to Volcanoes National Park on the Big Island of Hawaii, I had an opportunity to browse the art gallery in the park museum. There, on display for sale, was a collection of exceptional Hawaiian-made artifacts, including a stunningly beautiful, handmade Koa-wood rocking chair. At the instant of "test-sitting," I felt as though the craftsman had somehow re-

motely x-rayed my body and tailor-made the chair to fit me; it was so comfortable I could barely stand to extract myself from it. The price tag was exorbitant, but I hung around the gallery long after my family's patience had
worn thin, silently trying to rationalize why I should buy the chair. My
obvious enthusiasm was not lost on the friendly saleswoman, who made a
point of noting how inexpensive (compared to the price) it would be to ship
the chair back with me to the mainland. This, of course, was against my
principles.

At home, I found myself longing for the Hawaiian chair, wishing somehow I had swallowed my environmental ethics and maxed out the old credit
card to buy it. Eventually it occurred to me that I could find a local equivalent. After convincing myself that twenty-some years of diligent university teaching and late-forties athletic delusional soreness entitled me
to a quality rocking chair in which to grow old(er), I began the local hunt
in earnest. My search ended up taking me to an internationally known
woodworker named Robert Erickson, himself a bioregionalist of sorts re-
siding in the nearby San Juan Ridge community, also home to poet and
bioregionalist Gary Snyder. One day Bob called me to say he had located
some really wonderful black walnut "roadkill" from the expansion of Route
113, merely five miles from my house. After negotiating the price with
me, Bob took measurements for both my wife, Lacey, and myself, aver-
aged them a bit, and in three months, produced a chair of greater quality
and beauty than my original Hawaiian affair. I paid plenty for my new chair,
but it will last several human lifetimes, and it is simply one of the most
satisfying purchases I have ever made. It has already given our family
countless hours of satisfaction, all with local talent, local materials, and no
wasted energy.

By the manner in which we execute our consuming activities, we can either add to or subtract from the import-replacing capacities of our local regions. Buying is like voting with money—axiom: *"Buy your region."* Put
your money where your heart is—hopefully, that is somewhere near home.
That is where your dollars can have a local multiplier effect, where your
purchase can help employ local people, and where you help ensure the diversity, flexibility, and durability of trading in local, "natural" values.

Of course, paying a "local surcharge" is something of a luxury. Moreover, most material "necessities" of contemporary life, such as cars, refrig-
erators, TVs, and computers, are no longer manufactured in our backyards.
Yet surprising trends in local buying can be seen if we only look close enough.
Main Street is back; thrift shops are thriving; community gardens abound;
crafts have resurfaced; local vendors line the summer streets of low-income

ethnic neighborhoods; and microbreweries threaten the big-five global beers. The Internet, for all its touted economic impact, still only accounts for less than 1 percent of American consumer spending.[23] The rest must, literally, "take place" somewhere. In the final analysis, buying locally is just more fun!

Ithaca Hours: Relocalizing Money

From time to time, small North American cities improvise processes that increase local ecological integrity and reduce dependence on out-of-region imports. In the 1970s, Davis, California, pioneered building solar utilization and energy conservation ordinances and extensive bicycle paths, reducing the city's energy dependence. In the 1980s, Arcata, California, showcased the regenerative treatment of wastewater to the benefit of many species in its now famous Arcata Marsh, in the process avoiding a costly mechanical/chemical treatment plant. In 1991, Ithaca, New York, instituted an alternative local currency, the Ithaca "Hour" (figure 6.6), that embodies many of the economic lessons implicit in Jane Jacobs's work.

Asked why he created an alternative local currency called "Hours," Paul Glover stated:

> Here in Ithaca we've begun to gain control of the social and environmental effects of commerce by issuing over $51,000 of our own local paper money since 1991. We printed our own money because we watched federal dollars come to town, shake a few hands, then leave to buy rain forest lumber and fight wars. Ithaca's HOURS, by contrast, stay in our region to help us hire each other. While dollars make us increasingly dependent on multinational corporations and bankers, HOURS reinforce community trading and expand commerce that is more accountable to our concerns for ecology and justice.[24]

Hour notes themselves come in one-eighth Hour, one-half Hour, one-Hour, and two-Hour denominations, all printed in colorful inks on local cattail paper. They include slogans such as "In Ithaca We Trust" and feature various pictures, including one subtitled "Ithaca's Children." Each one-Hour note buys ten American dollars' worth of labor for such services as carpentry, plumbing, nursing, car repair, firewood cutting, and farmwork on local organic farms. Hour notes have begun to be accepted by local restaurants, theaters, bookstores, markets, and even some professionals. Participants receive two Hours upon listing their services in a network directory and may receive an additional two Hours every eight months for their continuing participation. Often Ithaca's locally owned stores pay their employees partly

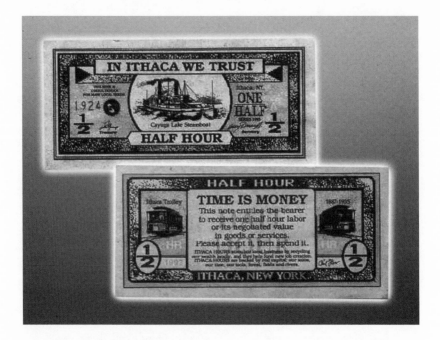

Figure 6.6 A "Half Hour" note—Ithaca, New York's local currency. Photograph courtesy of Paul Glover, Ithaca Hours.

in Hours, which allows them to slowly increase their dependence upon (and investment in) the local currency. Loans are made to local individuals and businesses in Hours without interest, fostering greater self-reliance and expanded ecological outreach. Says Glover: "Hours are real money, backed by real people, real time, real skills and tools. Dollars are funny money, backed no longer by gold or silver but by $4.8 trillion of national debt."[25]

Ithaca Hours has received nonprofit corporate status and is now managed by an elected board of directors. More than eight thousand notes of various denominations have been issued, and over 850 individuals and businesses (nearly 400 of them retail) participate, including credit unions, hospitals, and other mainstream businesses.

With a strong cooperatives movement, a vital farmers' market, community-supported agriculture, and a progressive population, my hometown of Davis, California, in the heart of the Putah Creek–Cache Creek watershed area of the Sacramento Valley bioregion, is ripe for the introduction of a local currency. What would we name such a currency? "Putah-Cash," of course!

Natural Values Emerging

I love the journey from my home near Sacramento and the southern end of the bioregion up Interstate 5 to the region's apex at Mount Shasta. I have developed a deep affection for this working landscape through which I frequently travel. My political background and views (and indeed many of the ideas promoted in this book) might be anathema to some of my agricultural neighbors to my immediate north. Yet there is an immediacy and vitality to our collective landscape, and I value the contributions that all people in this region are making to life in this place. Jane Jacobs herself would appreciate this city region stretching from Sacramento and the delta to Redding and Mount Shasta. The potential for the Sacramento Valley to nurture a more bioregional economy is high, and countless individuals are now contributing their efforts toward making the region work for all of us. We have a plethora of natural assets: an identifiable land territory framed by mountains; beneficial soil, water resources, and climate; a potentially rich biodiversity that could easily be coaxed back to its former glory; a diverse population with considerable innovative spirit; a tradition of hard work and making a living from the land; and a number of quality institutions of higher education. As globalization continues its momentous evolution, our own bioregion may find ways to increase our collective local identity, security, and perpetuity. Perhaps the first and most essential step in securing a more bioregional economy is just to realize that we all live here together in this place. The place depends on us, and vice versa.

7 Planning

DESIGNING A LIFE-PLACE

Bioregional planning is a way of understanding the complexities
of ecosystems as they relate to regional culture.

CLAIR REINIGER, 1997

The truth about life-place (or bioregional) planning reads like a koan, or
Zen riddle: *There is no such thing as "bioregional planning," yet it is happening all the time in every bioregion.* To the Zen monk, koans were a source
of considerable frustration but ultimate enlightenment. Such is the case with
life-place planning. There are, as yet, no professional schools of "bioregional
planning." There is no professional society and no coherent body of theory,
few books in print mention the subject, only scattered examples of such planning might be construed as success stories, and few professionals or academics are willing to suggest that life-place planning might be a feasible or
fruitful endeavor.

On the other hand, countless volunteer coalitions and broad partnerships
of private landowners, government officials, environmentalists, and industry groups now earnestly apply themselves to natural areas and ecological
attributes that cut across or ignore political boundaries. These organizations
often make broad connections between cultural and natural "resources," propose substantive management regimes, and envision comprehensive landscape or infrastructural changes: attributes typical of any "planning" process.
If, indeed, there is nothing as yet called "life-place planning," certainly numerous groups are applying considerable planning effort to various dimensions of the life-place. It is safe to say that, given the momentum of
these practical actions on behalf of natural regions, a convergence of theory
and technique will follow shortly. With this chapter, I hope to speed this inevitable process along.

In April 1999, a diverse group of people has assembled in a ninth-floor meeting room of the Federal Office Building in Sacramento, home to the Western Regional Office of the U.S. Army Corps of Engineers. Long decried as

the governmental agency primarily responsible for converting America's natural waterways and wetlands into a straitjacketed system of reservoirs, canals, and levees, the Corps in recent years has sought a new, more environmentally centered existence as the protector of wetlands and the restorer of some of the "nature" it eliminated in the name of flood control. Those attending this particular meeting are converging around the idea, born of one of the Corps's more visionary employees, of connecting newly restored wildlife areas and wetlands by nonmotorized trails. The ad hoc Ecosystem Restoration Trails group owes its euphemistic name to fear that local landowners are not quite ready for *recreational* trails or, in fact, even the concept of public access. The simple proposition being considered is that the growing populations of Sacramento, Davis, Woodland, and West Sacramento might benefit from access to the natural habitats and wildlife reserves now being reestablished in the local region at the Yolo Basin Wetlands, Stone Lakes Reserve, and the proposed North Delta Wildlife Refuge. Talk and ideas center on connecting these nature reserves with bicycle and hiking trails along the Corps's flood levees and perhaps extending a trail eastward to the Sierra Nevada and westward to the coast and Bay Area Ridge Trail.

At today's meeting are landowners, bicycle-club commuters, planners, state and federal agency people, academics, open-space managers, and local government officials. A presentation by an acquisitions specialist at the East Bay Regional Park District offers the participants a state-of-the-art glimpse of the district's highly successful open-space network. We adjourn, agreeing to meet again armed with additional information brought back to the table by each volunteer participant.

At the next meeting, a month later, several landowners from the Clarksburg area show up. Two of them, fourth- and fifth-generation California farmers, express considerable disapproval of the idea of public access across their land. They fear conflict between crop spraying and public attitudes, potential liability over accidents, and added encumbrances by government on their freedom to farm as they please. It is an archetypal response often heard in rural environments across the continent, but one with considerable weight to it. The small and decreasing farming minority and the vast, expanding nonfarming majority have been drifting apart for decades. But at this meeting, the conversation continues, for the most part cordially. Discussion soon identifies the major hurdles to our regional project as gaining private landowner confidence; allaying fears of liability and loss of "private property rights"; pinpointing responsibility for management and maintenance; creating jurisdictional responsibility for policing and emergency patrol; and, of course, paying for initial improvements and long-term maintenance. A brainstorming workshop with forgiving ground rules enables everyone to lay his or her cards on the table, some mutual understanding and considerable ice-breaking occur, with hand-shakes at the end, and the date for the next monthly meeting is recorded in the participants' calendars.

The Ecosystem Restoration Trails effort is one of dozens of recent initiatives that have emerged from the many corners of the Sacramento Valley bioregion in the past decade. Some groups arise out of contention, others out of opportunity; most spring from the grassroots populace, although a few—like the Ecosystem Restoration Trails effort—start with the agencies. Some efforts persevere and succeed; many others fail and disappear. But the small group of people meeting on the topic of connecting restored natural ecosystems with public trails in the Sacramento area is in many ways a re-action to a vacuum in regional planning, a resurgence in community identity with the natural attributes of the bioregion, and a nascent efflorescence of what might be called *life-place planning.*

Limitations of Conventional Planning

Planning is a short word with an enormous definition. To discuss the presumption of life-place planning adequately, it is necessary to draw some conclusions about its antecedents, most specifically, "urban" planning, "regional" planning, "ecological" planning, and "infrastructural" planning. What I call bioregional or life-place planning is a converging collection of activities that cuts across all of these more traditional planning domains yet owes its existence in great part to the limitations of these conventional planning approaches. Life-place planning essentially addresses a growing demand for comprehensive, ecosystemic social and physical planning, a sort of planning made nearly impossible by the absence or impotence of existing city and regional plans, the top-down "expert" approach to ecological planning, the narrow scope of single-resource agencies, and the myopic pragmatism of engineers.

URBAN PLANNING

Traditional urban planning often tends to be exclusive and to *compartmentalize* physical and mental realities from the top down (exclusionary land use zoning; separate treatment of "engineering," "social," and "civic art" functions; domination by developer/political alliances). In a ground-breaking book entitled *The Life Region,* Swedish editor Per Råberg sums up the limitations of the currently operative pragmatic approach to planning: "Planning for human needs is regarded as one, single sector—the socio-cultural—along with other planning sectors, e.g., the production sector, the communication sector, the technology and political sectors. The planner of our times profiles himself as a neutral social engineer. His task, as he sees it, is to solve technical problems of distribution within the material structure in accordance with the demands of various clients."[1]

And these "clients," according to Råberg, are increasingly fragmented and abstract:

> One important aspect of physical planning during this century is, in actual fact, the shift of the powers of decision to higher and more abstract levels of organization. . . . The currently most powerful interest wins, whatever the long term interests of the community. The pragmatic planning machine of our time has provided us with a gigantic infrastructure, but a community . . . with no heart and no working brain. . . . The planners' division of society into a number of spheres of interest, with the citizen's interest representing only one segment of the whole, frustrates our innermost wish to actively take part in and to survey that space in society that we consider our own.[2]

Råberg's book is but one of many discussing the inadequacies of planning as we now know it. Yet most city planners and local government officials probably would claim that the planning work they do *is* both communitarian and natural. And they are correct, but only in a limited sense. City, county, and regional planners are frequently hindered by the enframing legal structures within which they operate. In California, regional planning is legally toothless and financially bankrupt. Local county and city governments in California have been hamstrung by 1978's Proposition 13, a taxpayer revolt that strictly curtailed the ability of counties and cities to raise tax revenues for local improvements such as parks and open space. Little legislative framework exists to direct development toward or away from particular subregions except by nonbinding agreements between cities and counties operating through memoranda of understanding. The typical councils of governments, or COGs, voluntary nonbinding associations without police power or fiscal resources, are held together by little more than a handshake. Consequently, the default position is often competition among neighboring local governments for scarce resources such as water or employment-producing business. Regional planning, if we are to call it that, is often reduced to a process of rearguard reactions in response to market-driven and development pressure channeled through local political lobbying. It is a process

highly exasperating to a majority of residents, who believe themselves powerless to stop what feels like a steamroller of development turned loose on
their own backyard.

A case in my own community, Davis, serves as an illustration of the feeble nature of so-called regional planning. During the early 1990s, a particularly powerful and wealthy developer proposed to develop many hundreds
of acres of land abutting the northeast edge of Davis, outside of what was
then the city's general plan boundaries. After initially being rebuffed by
the city planning staff and council members, the developer took his proposal to the Yolo County government. Being hard-pressed for an operating
budget, due in part to the recent incorporation of West Sacramento and its
subsequent removal from the county tax base, the county seemed eager to
approve the development, since it would bring considerable revenue into
county government coffers. Because of the favorable response from a county
government in need of revenue sources, the developer went back to the city
of Davis and basically said: If you won't expand the general plan boundaries so I can build my development within the city of Davis, I'll get approval from the county and build it anyway. So the Davis City Council caved
in, approved the development, and signed an agreement sharing the tax revenue between the city and the county, increasing the size of the city by 20
percent, or about ten thousand people, with the stroke of a pen.

As a rather liberal, environmentally oriented university town, Davis
might be expected to actively oppose growth, but the quality of life in the
town is still a powerful engine for local population expansion. Many other
counties and cities in California find themselves in the same position with
respect to their inability to resist growth pressure. Some communities embrace development, growing up to 12 percent in population per year—a rate
no region could possibly sustain for long. Developers say they are merely
responding to demand and exercising their constitutional rights. In one sense,
that is true. However, when the ability of a region's citizens to respond to
growth pressure is squashed by backdoor deals among their elected city
councils, county supervisors, and powerful developers, it is likely that the
resource limits and carrying capacities of a life-place will be ignored altogether and quickly exceeded. *Growth management* is now the euphemistic
term that has replaced the former label *growth control* in the planning lexicon of California.

Yet there is hope, for a genuine tilt toward positive change in the typical
template of development is now discernible. The term *Smart Growth*,
coined by the U.S. Environmental Protection Agency and endorsed by the
Congress for the New Urbanism (an avant-garde, voluntary association of

like-minded planning professionals), refers to a compact, pedestrian-friendly neighborhood design approach and now occupies center stage after a procession of earlier terms: *solar design, appropriate technology, sustainability,* and the like. The rudiments of an alternative means of designing sustainable communities have begun to be established. For the most part, however, this amalgamated movement toward more sustainable community design, having emerged from a rather professionally driven, nationally ubiquitous, and top-down movement, has only recently discovered the idea of "the region," and not necessarily from a grassroots point of view.[3]

REGIONAL PLANNING

In the realm of regional planning, too, significant disconnects exist between the geographies of multiple jurisdictions and the limits and potentials of natural regions. Some planners believe that a bioregional approach is a waste of time since natural regions do not coincide with regions defined by political, economic, or technical means. But the trend toward bioregional planning reflects, among other things, an increasing amount of public attention and concern focused on qualities not adequately contained within such manmade boundaries: air, water, energy, food, biodiversity, transportation, and recreation. As these issues join others addressed by planning, it is inevitable that a more bioregion-wide spatial framework will necessarily emerge.

One of the practical ways to rectify the obvious limitations of existing county and city boundaries and overlapping districts is to aggregate counties roughly according to bioregional similarity. For example, the "Sacramento Valley bioregion" might encompass Shasta, Tehama, Glenn, Butte, Colusa, Sutter, Yuba, Yolo, and Sacramento Counties, which are tied together by mutual concerns over water, agricultural land, and containment of development and by a shared air basin, topography, soil, climate, and seasonal flooding regime. As these shared bioregional dimensions move to the forefront of environmental and political issues, a sense of the Sacramento Valley life-place emerges. For example, the state bond that created Cal-Fed, the federal-state mega-agency mandated to solve water quality issues in the Sacramento–San Joaquin Delta, has had the effect of consolidating Sacramento Valley concerns over the fate of water supplies, water quality, rivers, streams, and impoundments. Cal-Fed is, in reality, driven by southern California interests, which have realized that solving the state's complex northern water quality issues in the environmentally sensitive river delta area is the only hope for procuring reliable supplies of that water for southern agriculture and urban uses. This situation makes for strange bedfellows, for both conservative Colusa County rice farmers and urban environmentalists are suspicious of Cal-Fed's motives, fearing that the construction of a "peripheral canal" around the delta will divert even more northern water out of the bioregion for points south.

Some scholars boldly suggest that political boundaries should be changed to better correspond to such natural divisions among regions. Planner Timothy Duane, for instance, has advocated reconfiguring counties in the Sierra Nevada bioregion to more closely correspond to physical watersheds.[4] What is more apt to occur is the gradual establishment of cooperative bioregional partnerships, operating across political boundaries and focusing on issues bridging social and environmental concerns—which means most issues these days. In time, depending on the relative success of such cross-jurisdiction planning efforts, they may become the norm rather than the exception. Only then are changes from political to bioregional boundaries likely to be considered seriously.

At present, the real costs of protecting networks, corridors, and reserves of land needed for conservation of biodiversity are only beginning to be realized by participating localities and jurisdictions, and means that now exist for equitably distributing the costs of this protection are inadequate. For example, a recent proposal for a relatively modest habitat conservation plan for Yolo County, featuring common mitigation banking for several endangered or threatened species and holistic management of reserves for their recovery, was attacked (for entirely different reasons) by both the Farm Bureau and certain academic ecologists. The scientists saw the proposal as not offering enough in terms of restoring species to health; the Farm Bureau saw it as involving too much "government" meddling and loss of property rights for farmers.

On a larger scale, in the Sacramento Valley bioregion, a tremendous public demand for nature-based recreation and for environmental lands of high amenity value is building as the predominantly agricultural region experiences a tremendous surge in population growth. Yet the Sacramento Valley bioregion is mostly in private ownership. Who will pay for the lands that an increasingly urban population now desires for preservation, conservation, recreation, and scenic value? The historic expectation that such lands will be somehow be provided by "government" without new taxes is but a nostalgic pipe dream. New economic realities demand some form of payment from the beneficiaries (suburban/new urban/exurban residents) to the providers (rural landowners). Without this, Sacramento Valley can look forward to increasing tension, a growing backlog of recreation demand, public misuse of enveloping private property, and perpetual ill will between urban and rural populations.

RESOURCE PLANNING

County planning, never having had much power in California, today has become even less viable after considerable loss of state and federal revenues and increasing numbers of issues that cross county boundaries (such as the Clean Air Act, the Clean Water Act, the Endangered Species Act, and the Central Valley Project Improvement Act). Counties are now required to satisfy many state legislative requirements without adequate state-supported funding and without any means of raising needed funds themselves. Never in this century in California, ironically, has so much wealth been accumulated in private hands and so little been made available for public planning and environmental management at the regional level. Adjusted per capita investment in planning and environmental protection is at an all-time low.

Ad hoc, bioregional approaches have appeared in part due to the failure of single-resource-based governmental agencies to solve comprehensive environmental problems. Traditionally, wildlife, soil, air, water, energy, transit, and parks agencies all engage in planning efforts under separate legislative mandates in isolation from one another. This has merely perpetuated some environmental problems and created others. Occasionally, however, government tries to correct this problem. In 1991, several state and federal agencies with responsibility for managing California's complex natural resources signed a memorandum of understanding (MOU) that produced a policy statement entitled *California's Coordinated Regional Strategy to Conserve Biological Diversity*. The MOU's most significant provisions called for California's natural resources to be managed by coordinated resource management plans (nicknamed "CRiMPS"), which empowered public agencies and private groups to "coordinate resource management and environmental protection activities, emphasizing regional solutions to regional issues and needs."[5] It further stipulated that goals and strategies be defined at the level of a bioregion and that institutions and their policies adapt to reflect a bioregional approach to the protection of natural diversity. The MOU then proposed dividing the state into ten bioregions whose boundaries were refined as the local planning began. The MOU also called for three levels of planning and administration: a statewide executive council, ten individual bioregional councils, and locally organized landscape or watershed associations. In legitimizing a "bottom-up" approach wherein the local watershed and land-

Figure 7.1 Newsletter masthead of the California Biodiversity Council. The California Resources Agency's *Memorandum of Understanding: California's Coordinated Regional Strategy to Conserve Biological Diversity* (Sacramento: California Resources Agency, 1991) created the Biodiversity Council and the first official recognition of the existence of bioregions by California government. Courtesy of the California Biodiversity Council.

scape associations played a key role, the signatories (of which there are now more than thirty) envisioned a role for the agencies of providing politically neutral technical assistance and coordinating the flow of information.[6]

Unfortunately, part of this new vision backfired: the proposed middle-tier bioregional councils never got off (or "on") the ground, being perceived by locals as too much top-down government meddling. While the statewide Biodiversity Council has continued to function, it has done so by leaving the local, grassroots organizations alone, in overreaction to the initial negative public response to the middle-tier councils. The resulting top-down approach basically failed due to lack of support at the grassroots level, yet the bottom-most rung, the local watershed/bioregional groups, have thrived. Experience now makes it clear that operative bioregions will be largely defined (and, perhaps, planned) by the scope of concerns of individual ad hoc groups. Top-down political edicts (like Cal-Fed) or "expert science" designations of bioregions are less likely to result in tangible progress. The participating public has begun to identify with its local natural ecosystems and resources and has discovered its own political power; excluding it from the planning process will occur only at great cost to existing political capital.

As a result of all this, bioregional boundaries are apt to remain fuzzy, flexible, and opportunistic and to vary according to certain vagaries of culture, even if based on scientifically determined watersheds, species distributions, or topographies. The regional representatives of single-resource agencies (e.g., Fish and Game, Forestry, Water Resources) participating in local, grassroots life-place initiatives often experienced a greater sense of purpose in the local, holistic efforts, and greater allegiance to them, than they did in their own resource agencies, a fact that jarred the top-down administrative status quo of their home agencies.

Up until the late 1990s in California, it was assumed that less government was better government and that an expanding economy coupled with low taxes would allow the "marketplace" to resolve the sticky issues of ecosystem management, regional planning, and urban growth. However, private enterprise has shown itself to be incapable of doing the job, and taxpayers seem unwilling to foot the bill either (fewer than one-third of the parks and recreation bond measures proposed in California between 1987 and 1993 passed). Advocates of reduced government assume either that no investments in planning, management, or infrastructure are needed or that they will be covered by the private sector. Advocates of a strong governmental role accuse big business and callous taxpayers of ignoring their social and environmental responsibilities. In this political climate, voluntary, participatory (and often severely underfunded) bioregional advocacy groups have formed to do the necessary planning and management work ignored by big business, government, and recalcitrant taxpayers.

INFRASTRUCTURAL PLANNING

The planning of infrastructure (e.g., water supply, sewerage, electrical power, transportation) is dominated by engineers and features an engineering mentality that considers one dominant, exclusive planning goal at a time. Even the production and distribution of food has taken on a mechanized, industrialized character that has trivialized concerns over food security, employment, energy and water conservation, and the health of both workers and environment. Furthermore, conventional infrastructural planning presumes an indefinite supply of fossil fuels. The structure of the landscape we now inhabit reflects the predominant philosophical viewpoint of

Figure 7.2 The State Water Project's Harvey O. Banks Pumping Station, near the Sacramento–San Joaquin Delta, is an example of large-scale, one-dimensional infrastructural planning. While its foremost purpose is delivery of irrigation water southward, it also contributes to altered channel flow directions, increased salinity, and loss of anadromous fish populations in the delta, as well as considerable energy consumption. Photograph by Robert Thayer.

the twentieth century: the dissociation of the world into its various mechanistic components (irrigation canals, powerlines, and freeways, to name three examples) and the optimization of each of these components in isolation from the others. This is directly counter to the organization of natural ecosystems, wherein multiple functions are the norm.

Bioregional planning anticipates a different, interdependent, complex relationship among and between all attributes and elements of the landscape. When the reliance on renewable resources begins in earnest (as it must), the source, transport, consumption, and recycling of material goods, water, and energy will shrink in scale. This thermodynamic reality is unavoidable and provides a most incontrovertible and instrumental argument for the efficacy of the life-place concept. When we no longer are able to afford to move materials and resources great distances at unrealistically cheap fuel costs, a very close examination of the regenerative limits and potentials of each bioregion will become imperative. The bioregion then will be even less portrayable as an idealized, utopian concept and more defensible as a pragmatic and necessary spatial delineation.

Origins of Life-Place Planning Theory

That a bioregion might become the locus of planning for community, ecology, and sustainability is a relatively new idea. Yet the notion of natural regionalism has been considered by planners and theorists for nearly a century. The theory reaches back to Lewis Mumford and Patrick Geddes. Writing as a self-educated urbanist and social critic from the 1920s through the late 1960s, Mumford promoted a concept of regionalism that balanced the conditions of the natural world with the needs of the human culture inhabiting it. His ideas rested on a highly optimistic critique of the technological culture of industrialism, and he suggested that a science-based "neotechnics" could lead to the emergence of planned cities and new social institutions grounded in ecological regionalism. Mumford drew heavily upon the work of Scottish botanist and geographer Patrick Geddes. Geddes, who had been searching for a way to consider human communities as an extension of the natural world, in turn had absorbed the "sociography" ideas of French sociologist Frederic Le Play and the garden city concepts of Britain's Ebenezer Howard. Geddes's sociographic perspective gave Mumford the foundations of "a humanistic science of society that could be useful in the creation of communities grounded in a sense of place."[7]

One of Mumford's seminal contributions was the founding of the influential Regional Planning Association of America (RPAA). With the cooperation of Mumford and his colleague, forester and planner Benton MacKaye, RPAA articulated numerous proposals that anticipated the soundest of today's regional thinking: the reconsideration of cities in relation to regions; the establishment of carrying capacities allowing both exploitation of regional economic assets and protection of long-term ecological conditions; the development of new civic institutions aimed at conjoining urban and regional values; the connection of open spaces and natural assets in linked systems; and the guidance of regional growth by means of sustainable spatial patterns. These remain the cornerstones of regional theory to this day.

Although he failed to predict the devastating outcome of industrial technology on cities and regions, and although American political culture in general forced him to alter his thinking late in his career, Mumford never lost his faith in the potentials of ecological regionalism, community, and the redefinition of economy and technology along ecological lines. Mumford would no doubt have felt a strong kinship with the bioregional movement of today. As if anticipating this movement before his death, Mumford wrote in the preface to Ian McHarg's epochal book *Design with Nature:*

Here are the foundations for a civilization that will replace the polluted, bulldozed, machine-dominated, de-humanized, explosion-threatened world that is even now disintegrating and disappearing before our eyes. In presenting us with a vision of organic exuberance and human delight, McHarg revives the hope for a better world.[8]

Outspoken landscape architect Ian McHarg, who died in 2001, was not the originator of all the methods he popularized, but the effect of *Design with Nature* and his more recent books on the professions involved in ecological planning was incalculable. Because of the animated poignancy and sheer power of McHarg's oral and written delivery and the persuasive effectiveness of his multilayered, colored-map approach (see figures 7.3a–c), he was to have a lasting and permanent effect on the field of ecological and regional planning. Inspired by his example, countless individuals (including myself) followed McHarg into the profession of landscape architecture and found his theory and methods in regional ecological suitability to be a rallying point for future work. Many of McHarg's followers—Frederick Steiner, Pliny Fisk III, and the late John Tillman Lyle, to name but a few— have made direct contributions to the legitimacy of ecological planning and, indirectly, to the validity of the notion of life-place planning.[9]

McHarg's sophisticated graphic methods, his incorporation of data from scientific disciplines such as geology and hydrology, and his grasp of complex ecological issues elevated the assessment of regional patterns to new heights. More than anything else, McHarg popularized the very notion that *the ecology of a region or extensive landscape could be analyzed, synthesized, and graphically presented.* After McHarg, regions *had* recognizable ecological dimensions, potentials, and limitations. The current, rapidly expanding field of computer-based geographic information systems (GIS) merely reflects and electronically amplifies the approach to regional landscape analysis popularized by McHarg.

Laboring as a nationally less recognized but regionally heroic contemporary of McHarg has been landscape architect Phil Lewis. For over forty years, Lewis has examined the regional landscapes of Wisconsin and the northern Midwest, proposing, refining, practicing, and popularizing a less structured, more spatially intuitive "regional design process," as he calls it. Lewis is generally credited with articulating the concept of environmental corridors (figures 7.4a–b), wherein the mapping of multiple environmental and cultural values illuminates belts of regional landscape worthy of preservation. Lewis is as comfortable mapping economic data and cultural icons as he is illustrating landforms and soil types. Through his Wisconsin-based

Environmental Awareness Center, he has educated countless thousands of residents on the environmental possibilities of the region. Not the least of his "student body" is the state legislature, which structured a Wisconsin Outdoor Recreation Plan following Lewis's detailed inventory. Lewis, with his clear, sustainable vision and goals for the Great Lakes bioregion, is an exemplary life-place planner.[10]

There are numerous other landscape architects and regional planners whose systematic work indirectly reinforces the central notions of bioregionalism, including Carl Steinitz of Harvard and Frederick Steiner of Arizona State University. Jack Dangermond, also a student of McHarg and one of the acknowledged progenitors of GIS, has never lost his determined environmental orientation. His system for computer-based spatial analysis of the ecological dimensions of regions, if sometimes beyond the reach of typical budgets, is considered an ultimately desirable goal for nearly every volunteer regional or watershed association in existence.

Interestingly, in many instances of applied grassroots bioregional action, the process of mapping regional ecological dimensions has served as a neutral activity around which opposing factions could rally and "break the ice," leading to more substantive compromise. In the Trinity National Forest, unemployed forest industry workers are being trained in GIS techniques, while fishermen, ranchers, loggers, farmers, and environmentalists are joining in a mapping process to save the spring-run Chinook salmon on various tributaries of the Sacramento River. In some ways, the map itself serves as a unifying bioregional symbol: to map one's bioregion is to proclaim both the existence and importance of it and the meaningful role of the individual and group within it. Bioregionalist planner and theorist Doug Aberley has dedicated several books to this process and has produced an eye-opening video on bioregional mapping entitled *Maps with Teeth*. His invaluable contribution is his articulation of the role bioregional mapping plays in the empowerment of indigenous and local populations to take charge of their own destinies. Around the world, indigenous cultures are learning to use sophisticated maps as cultural tools by which to resist global industrial intrusions on ancestral aboriginal lands.[11]

From the ecological regionalist proposals of Mumford and the ideas and methodology of more recent landscape planners and environmental designers comes a substantial body of theory and practice truly fundamental to the bioregional notion. The ability to identify and map a region's ecological character and impact in detailed and integrative fashion should not be considered merely pragmatic; such an ability represents a direct contribution

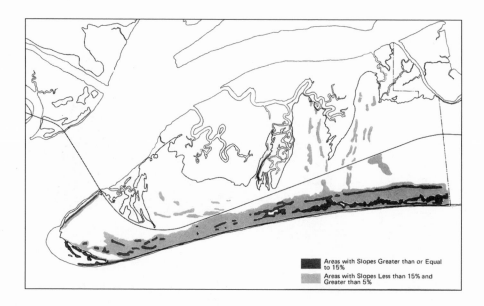

Areas with Slopes Greater than or Equal to 15%

Areas with Slopes Less than 15% and Greater than 5%

Figures 7.3a–c Ian McHarg's popularization of the overlay planning method established the basis for rational and scientifically defensible landscape planning. Inventory data such as slope *(A, above)* and tidal inundation *(B, opposite, top)* are assigned values for development and conservation and combined with other data to produce land use suitability maps *(C)*. After McHarg, it was generally accepted that the ecology of large territories of land could be mapped and represented in both quality and quantity. © The Architectural Archives of the University of Pennsylvania.

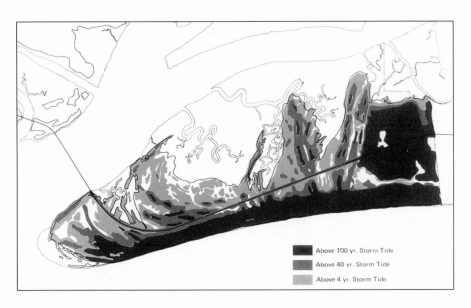

Above 100 yr. Storm Tide

Above 40 yr. Storm Tide

Above 4 yr. Storm Tide

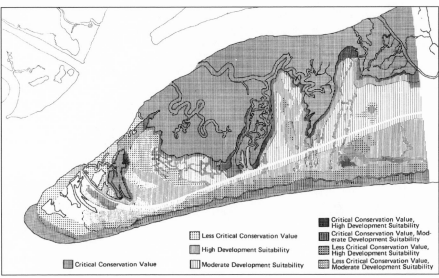

Less Critical Conservation Value

High Development Suitability

Critical Conservation Value

Moderate Development Suitability

Critical Conservation Value, High Development Suitability

Critical Conservation Value, Moderate Development Suitability

Less Critical Conservation Value, High Development Suitability

Less Critical Conservation Value, Moderate Development Suitability

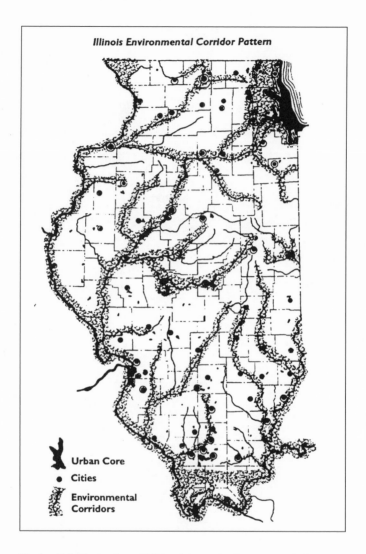

Figures 7.4a–b *A, above:* Phil Lewis's study of the state of Illinois clearly represents the pattern of corridors that emerges when major environmental resources are simultaneously mapped. *B, opposite:* Another study by Lewis identifies a "constellation" of urban development and transportation corridors surrounding the relatively undisturbed natural values of the "Driftless Area," a unique bioregion in the northern Midwest untouched by the glaciation that influenced much of the surrounding landscape. From *Tomorrow by Design,* by Philip M. Lewis, Jr., figures 5.16 and 7.3; copyright © 1996 Philip M. Lewis Jr. This material is used by permission of John Wiley & Sons, Inc.

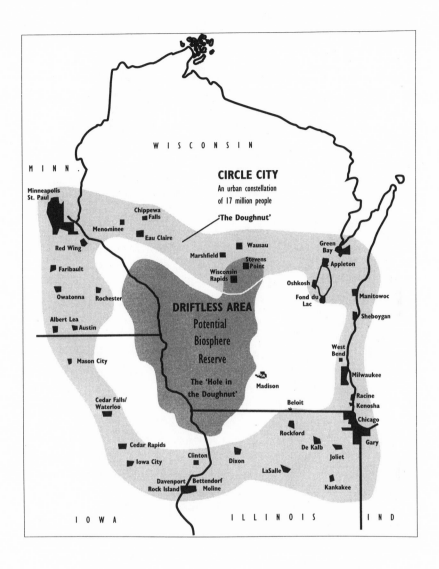

WISCONSIN

MINN.

CIRCLE CITY

An urban constellation
of 17 million people

'The Doughnut'

Minneapolis
St. Paul

Chippewa
Falls

Menominee

Eau Claire

Red Wing

Faribault

Marshfield

Wausau

Stevens
Point

Wisconsin
Rapids

Green
Bay

Appleton

Oshkosh

Owatonna

Rochester

DRIFTLESS AREA
Potential
Biosphere
Reserve

The 'Hole in
the Doughnut'

Fond du
Lac

Manitowoc

Sheboygan

Albert Lea

Austin

Mason City

West
Bend

Milwaukee

Madison

Racine

Cedar Falls/
Waterloo

Beloit

Kenosha

Chicago

Rockford

Gary

Cedar Rapids

De Kalb

Iowa City

Clinton

Dixon

Joliet

LaSalle

Davenport
Rock Island

Bettendorf
Moline

Kankakee

IOWA

ILLINOIS

IND.

to a comprehensive theory and philosophy of life-place as well. The future of our life-places will hinge upon the skillful use and bottom-up applications of ecological planning, mapping, analysis, and synthesis. The physical planning professions have played and will continue to play a major enabling role in the further evolution of the bioregional movement.

An Operative Life-Place Planning Hypothesis

We now come to that activity by which the entire notion of a life-place will most certainly and ultimately be judged: actual planning of the land. In the hierarchical framework I have been describing throughout this book, the bioregional approach transcends wishful thinking in the proposition of life-place planning and takes on serious practical dimensions. If the practical, professional activities associated with regional planning, design, and land management act in service to a vision of the life-place, the result may be a mosaic of uniquely bioregional patterns. These life-place land patterns will vary from region to region, depending on distinct ecological features and unique cultural factors such as land ownership; rural, suburban, or urban context; and the nature of the human communities occupying the places in question. The major distinction that such a life-place planning approach makes relative to typical planning is that the patterns will be driven from the bottom up by a grassroots vision supported by increasing numbers of ordinary citizens, rather than foisted on the land top down by the usual alliance of developers and beholden local politicians. In far too many regions today, this latter method is still the de facto planning reality. But in an increasing number of communities, civic visions of future land patterns that more holistically embrace bioregional values are spreading, driven by nonprofit groups, public-private partnerships, and citizens who are just plain fed up with developer-driven planning.

The practical bioregional hypothesis, then, is simply that for every bioregion there is a unique *method* or set of *practices* of planning, design, and management of the land and that this approach will result in a bioregionally unique set of *landscape patterns*. In the age of fossil-fuel-driven, centralized, industrial economies, the techniques, practices, and patterns of the land became regionally indistinct, and much of the wisdom implicit in local practices has been lost. Today, a time marked by computer telecommunication and the continued fire-sale use of fossil fuels, it remains to be seen whether local wisdom and practice will be permanently resurrected or lost in the ether of the global network. In many ways, as I have said, the bioregional movement is a conscious reaction to the numerous problems and shortcomings of the current technological era.

Owing to the bare-bones budgetary status of most bioregional efforts, many land planning, design, and management professionals must choose whether they wish to work on responsible projects for less money or irresponsible projects for more money. This particular manifestation of cognitive dissonance—between doing right by the life-place and performing the wishes of corporatist clients—is apt to cause a reinvention of the nature of planning work in the bioregion. Often, because there will be lean years, professionals likely will need to resort to dual forms of practice: doing the "real" work for little pay while staying alive with profit-making or tax-revenue-generating developments.

What is likely to persist, and to drive the practical reality toward a life-place of permanence, is the overall vision itself. In recent years I have marveled at the ability of civic groups to converge on sets of well-defined land planning patterns for particular bioregions: denser infill development for areas prone to sprawl onto valuable farmland or critical open space; alternative flood management patterns that return ecological functions to formerly straitjacketed and impounded rivers and streams; networks of connected habitat that provide migratory corridors, recreational trails, and visual amenities; alternative forms of transit that place more emphasis on light-rail, bus, bike, and pedestrian modes; and community support for local agriculture and environmentalist/agriculturalist coalitions to support continued local farming and open space. In many cases, the public converges on these patterns far sooner than it is able to find procedural mechanisms to counteract the development-driven status quo. Whatever the practical realities, it is becoming increasingly clear that a more regionally inspired process—the norm prior to our modern infatuation with centralized, consumptive, techno-economic paradigms—is what we must return to if we are to have a sustained world to (re)inhabit in the future.

Life-Place Planning Emerges

Life-place planning suggests the melding of ecosystem management, regenerative resource use and conservation, regional planning, regenerative systems, and sustainable community design into one multiscalar activity in which each ecological activity or dimension is seen and practiced in relationship to every other. Life-place planning implies that a bioregion is more than just a venue for biodiversity and ecosystem management; more than a collection of "sustainable communities"; more than the proper regional scale for energy, water, or transportation planning; and more than a self-similar cultural region. It is all of these combined, and far more.

Implicit within the possibility of whole-life-place planning is the gradual broadening of the ideas of "the environment" and "ecological planning" into domains formerly considered separately as cultural, social, or political. As environmental issues rise to the surface of public concern, former lines between "human" and "natural" are erased. The disproportionate number of toxic waste sites existing near low-income neighborhoods, for example, has spawned the notion of environmental justice and has illustrated the futility implicit in any separation between environmental and social planning. In essence, the concerns of social planning have expanded outward to encompass "the environment," while ecosystem management and ecological planning have grown to incorporate issues of social capital, capacity building, and human embeddedness in nature. This blurring of former boundaries between culture and nature requires fresh ways to conceptualize land and regional landscapes.

Essentially, life-place planning is an extension and a merging of several formerly independent countercultural thrusts. In the 1970s era of physical or landscape planning, three major and relatively distinct alternative movements each fought a separate, uphill battle against corporate norms of planning and design: ecological planners and rational/scientific overlay mappers; solar design/"appropriate technology" advocates; and a "community design" movement centered in urban core areas that openly advocated urban public space as a means to social justice. Today, remarkable synthesis is in process as advocates for water conservation, renewable energy, landscape restoration, "green" architecture, alternative transit, urban open space, equitable housing, environmental justice, regional planning, and ecosystem management have come to realize their interconnections are more important than their distinctions.

Patterns and Signatures

Physical land planners and designers naturally want planning discussions to reach all the way to the ground—to the actual patterns and forms of human interventions in the landscape. Where does the idea of life-place planning actually touch down? Gradually, a body of theory and practice has begun to coalesce around the notion of bioregional *patterns*.

In 1977, architect Christopher Alexander and his colleagues published an important book entitled *A Pattern Language*. In Alexander's words, a pattern "describes a problem which occurs over and over again in our environment, and then describes the core of the solution to that problem, in such a way that one may use the solution a million times over, without ever doing it the same way twice."[12] Alexander's method is elegant, instructive and useful, for it presumes that the seeds of the solution to a problem (i.e., the "pattern"—see figure 7.5) can be found in the nature of the problem itself and that most environmental planning and design problems lead to generalizable patterns of solutions that can be tailored to particular circumstances.

A Pattern Language, however, is not without its limitations. It describes supposedly universal social principles; Alexander and his colleagues presume that their set of patterns apply to all places, cultures, or regions. Furthermore, their methodology says little about the biological framework in which the patterns (largely human based) are embedded. Finally, there is a sense of top-down origination or authorship of these patterns. Yet in spite of its limitations, the book has become an admittedly useful design and planning "bible."

Landscape architect and educator Joan Woodward, using the specific regional example of the front-range Rocky Mountains in Colorado, extends the concept of patterns by describing four major regional influences that leave their "signature" on the landscape: geomorphic, climatic, biotic, and cultural. The last, cultural, she divides into *protection* needs, *production* needs, and the need for *meaning* among human residents of a region. A life-place planning approach seeks to fuse these such that in providing for production needs, life-places are protected, and the fusion of production *with* protection in the context of land, climate, biota, and culture provides a foundation for a deepening sense of bioregional meaning. Woodward's simple, general framework, exemplified in her book for a specific region, allows a multitude of interpretations and patterns, each of which might guide concrete decisions about the land's surface. Her approach elegantly applies pattern theory to the nature of the region in question (figure 7.6).[13]

Much of bioregional or life-place planning involves the gradual acknowledgment by local communities that *limitations* exist. Acceptance of the need for resources to be kept at regenerative levels is perhaps the foundational pattern of bioregional planning. In my past and current work, I have emphasized a process whereby attributes of a bioregion are identified, mapped, and analyzed, then intermeshed with more generalized goals for sustainable or "regenerative" living systems and combined with locally ad-

TOWNS

Therefore:

Wherever possible, work toward the evolution of independent regions in the world; each with a population between 2 and 10 million; each with its own natural and geographic boundaries; each with its own economy; each one autonomous and self-governing; each with a seat in a world government, without the intervening power of larger states or countries.

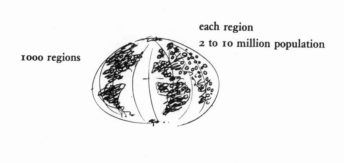

1000 regions

each region
2 to 10 million population

❖ ❖ ❖

Within each region encourage the population to distribute itself as widely as possible across the region—THE DISTRIBUTION OF TOWNS (2). . . .

Figure 7.5 Pattern No. 1, of 253, from *A Pattern Language,* by Christopher Alexander et al., copyright © 1977 by Christopher Alexander, used by permission of Oxford University Press, Inc. This classic text added the notion of generalizable patterns to the lexicon of planning and design and, when blended with McHarg's equally classic work, leads to the concept of regionally distinct patterns (see figure 7.6) and the substance of chapter 8 in this book.

vanced solutions. The result is a series of land patterns that might be called "bioregenerative" in that they represent the best long-term fit of human intervention with geomorphic, climatic, biotic, and cultural influences.

With some tweaking of baseline assumptions, the pattern approach can easily be modified to yield a bioregenerative pattern language, wherein a particular life-place uniquely informs the solutions to its own specific problems.

Figure 7.6 Landscape architect Joan H. Woodward, in *Waterstained Landscapes,* examines the role of water in forming regionally distinct landscape patterns in the Front Range foothills and plains east of Colorado's Rocky Mountains. Each bioregion has its own formative landscape patterns that offer both limits and potentials for compatible development and conservation. From Joan Woodward, *Waterstained Landscapes: Seeing and Shaping Regionally Distinctive Places,* 111. © The Johns Hopkins University Press. Reprinted with permission of The Johns Hopkins University Press.

As will be seen in chapter 8, in the Sacramento Valley bioregion, unique geomorphic, climatic, biotic, and cultural conditions allow generalized, patterned solutions to the problems of agriculture, biodiversity, community design, and human infrastructure. Most of these patterns, moreover, are not new: many are the result of grassroots advocacy and partnerships coupled with stewardship practices that either have slowly evolved or have been relearned from past experience in time and place.

As numerous planners acknowledge, land patterns emerge when the manifestations of a cultural, organic *physiology* interact with the structure of an ecological *physiography*. In simpler terms, humans make characteristic, generalizable marks on the land in the course of providing for their continued existence. Not all of these "signatures," as Woodward calls them, can be sustained indefinitely; indeed, one might argue that *most* of our *current* human patterns *cannot* be sustained much longer. Yet the notion of a generalizable signature or pattern evolving from a land practice or intervention can be modified by the emerging notions of regenerative or "sustainable" design, and its origins can be attributed not to some all-knowing higher authority but to collective local wisdom. In our Sacramento Valley bioregion, most regenerative land patterns can be traced to certain individuals or small groups who have discovered or rediscovered concepts that solve multiple problems. Some examples include irrigation tailwater ponds, multipurpose constructed wetlands, infill urban development, building forms that naturally temper the extreme heat of our summers, deliberate landscape habitat corridors, direction of floodwaters onto rice fields for waterfowl enhancement, photovoltaic electrical production from buildings and parking structures, and levee setbacks for more natural flood control. Most successful applications of these patterns are "labors of love," articulated and disseminated out of a sense of civic duty and affection for place.

In the lower Sacramento Valley, one man, John Anderson of the Yolo County Resource Conservation District, has worked tirelessly to convince his fellow farmers of the advantages of restoring slough and canal corridors, establishing hedgerows to harbor beneficial insects, and building tailwater ponds to protect water quality and conserve soil erosion. For this effort, he is paid mostly in the "psychological currency" of knowing that he has done the best he can for the local life-place and seeing others accept and adopt the wisdom of the conservation practices he advocates. Anderson is not really the creator of these bioregenerative patterns but merely their regional interpreter, defender, spokesperson, and proponent. This model of advocacy for responsible land patterns and practices has recurred time and time again in countless other locations.

When linked together in the landscape, bioregenerative patterns naturally form a "language." One fundamental property of such a pattern language is that it is an interconnected network of relationships, not a linear list of ingredients. Also, while regenerative patterns emerging from different bioregions may have strong similarities, each ends up uniquely adapted to a particular life-place, just as language dialects take on fine-grained regional differences. Patterns of land intervention are applied differently at different scales and in different situations. Different policies and procedures for implementation are likely to evolve under each unique circumstance, even in different sections of the same general life-place. Ultimately, a bioregenerative pattern language is a manifestation of a smaller-scaled, finer-grained, more participatory, democratic approach to land planning and management. Just like words, patterns evolve meaning and are modified by associated use in a place over time.

Examples of Bioregenerative Planning

Nowhere is the fusion of local wisdom, regenerative or "sustainable" principles, and bioregional constraints more evident than in a stellar example of "parallel" grassroots planning entitled *Blueprint for a Sustainable Bay Area*. Produced by a nonprofit corporation, Urban Ecology, Inc. (centered in Oakland, California), the *Blueprint* document moves from the scale of the home to that of the neighborhood, the urban center, and ultimately the bioregion, concluding with specific recommendations for action by individuals, neighborhood groups, planners, educators, developers, businesspeople, institutions, and governments. Supported heavily by foundation grants, generated by a broad coalition of individuals and groups, contributed to voluntarily by numerous experts, and widely disseminated in the Bay Area, *Blueprint* demonstrates precisely the kind of grassroots vision for a life-place that results in tangible land patterns and practical guidelines for a more permanent, sustainable way of living in place.[14]

The *Blueprint* document also acknowledges, however, that currently all is not well in the Bay Area bioregion. Such is also the case in most other bioregions, including the Sacramento Valley. Most existing land and development patterns—fossil-energy-intensive agriculture, low-density suburban sprawl, vast expanses of heavily irrigated turfgrass in a semiarid region, endless development of housing on prime agricultural land—are not regenerative and will be decidedly unsustainable over the long term. It is important to note that the patterns that are least sustainable are also the least regionally unique. Low-density, single detached tract homes tens of miles from city centers can be seen in nearly every region of the continent, along with big-box commercial developments amid great treeless expanses of asphalt parking lots and six-lane freeways with inadequate or no sidewalks. When land development patterns *do* respond to the nature and culture of the region, the result is a more sustainable, unique environment in which the regional flora, fauna, climate, culture, and regional energy, water, and resource realities are more visibly expressed. In some ways, the life-place planning process calls for the generation of a new "vernacular," or a reinterpretation of the expression of local nature and culture in the built environments of a particular region. There is no earthly reason why houses, parks, building materials, or climate-response strategies in Seattle should replicate those in Phoenix or Miami, or vice versa.

Bioregenerative planning evolves from the bottom up from groups of individuals who meet to resolve sticky problems, identify with specific resource conservation issues, protect certain natural or human communities, or seek a deeper moral basis for life itself. It embodies a return to participatory democracy and face-to-face communication requiring time and patience. *Blueprint for a Sustainable Bay Area* offers alternatives to the "official" politically driven planning process and is seeing increased exposure in the places of local government where it is most needed. We are likely to see an increase in the number of similar, unofficial civic planning organizations that see their role as that of "parallel" visionary planning to counterbalance the incremental and unsustainable "business-as-usual" planning and development demonstrated by most city governments. While efforts such as *Blueprint* do not provide professional planners with a road to riches, they can provide considerably more in the way of moral and ethical job satisfaction for their participants.

A Hierarchy of Patterns

The bioregenerative patterns that result from life-place planning tend toward sets of nested hierarchies that respond similarly to different scales within the same region. For example, the ways in which stormwater sheds from built structures, urban development, farmland, and wildlands is a thematic, related concern ranging from the scale of the smallest individual roof drain to that of the largest river floodplain. In many western bioregions, techniques for handling stormwater in a regenerative, sustainable fashion are "fractal," or self-similar, across all scales: allow as much water into the soil *after* development as the soil absorbed in its predevelopment condition; allow the natural groundwater regime, rather than hard pipes and valves, to meter the flows and to provide the necessary ecological functions accompanying natural and constructed waterways. In this example, some of the most advisable patterns for residential-scale drainage are smaller versions of the best techniques for managing floods on large river systems: allow room for the stream to spread out and periodically flood adjacent land.

Similar hierarchies can be articulated for other landscape dimensions, such as food growing, pedestrian and regenerative transit systems, energy production, water harvesting, and biodiversity lands and corridors. Each must be examined in terms of the scale of human intervention on the land and the distances and times required for resources to regenerate. In addition to a hierarchical, fractal format, most regenerative patterns are also *multidimensional* in that they serve more than one purpose—like the natural ecosystems they emulate. For example, the natural drainage patterns described previously not only mitigate flooding but recharge aquifers, provide needed habitat, increase the aesthetic potential of the landscape, and provide open space for recreation and human contact with nature.

New Zealand: Government-Sanctioned Bioregional Planning

Although most successful bioregional planning and management efforts grow from the bottom up, there are occasional instances of effective governmental policies that incorporate both bioregional frameworks and sustainable planning goals. New Zealand is such a case. Tracing its deliberations back to the 1984 World Conservation Strategy (International Union for Conservation of Nature and Natural Resources) and taking its impetus from the 1992 United Nations Conference on Environment and Development (the "Earth Summit"), New Zealand realigned its public policy and reorganized the administrative structure of its environmental agencies, passing two significant acts, the Local Government Reform Act (LGRA) and the Resource Management Act (RMA). The LGRA created a two-tiered local-government framework that gave the responsibility for large-scale and strategic planning issues to the regions, allowing social and economic issues such as urban expansion and transportation planning to be resolved alongside and at the same scale as environmental resource issues. Most significant, the regional councils established by LGRA were based almost entirely on hydrological basins. The RMA, which focused New Zealand's sustainable management strategy, actually wrote into law a set of performance-based regulations for sustaining the country's health, safety, natural and physical resources, and the carrying capacity of air, water, soil, and ecosystems and for avoiding, remedying, or mitigating the adverse effects of human activities.[15]

Attributes of Life-Place Planning

How, then, might a bioregional approach to planning, designing, and managing land differ from other familiar civic, regional, or ecological planning processes? First, life-place planning is highly *regional*. No two approaches are ever identical, nor should they be; instead, they respond to the unique nature and culture of particular life-places. There are apt to be as many different approaches to life-place planning as there are life-places. Second, life-place planning acknowledges that the top-down, "expert" approaches characteristic of more traditionally segmented regional planning are inadequate to resolve complex social, environmental, and management issues. It also realizes that planning done in a vacuum or with inadequate or feeble public input does little to perpetuate the culture but instead destroys it. Real solutions must grow from collaboration, building of social capital, involvement of broad foundations of stakeholders, and the slow but necessary processes of civic engagement. Third, bioregional planning requires the reestablishment of a sense of both *time* and *place*—two notions under severe attack by the momentum of globalism and electronic communication. Life-place planning seeks to restore the necessary concept of time: time for people to weigh and consider alternatives; time for renewable resources to regenerate; time for people to establish mutual communications and build trust; time for learning how the land responds to change, both intentional and unintentional. Since the pace of global corporatism is rapid, this may often translate into the need to initially say "no" to proposed changes. Fourth, life-place planning emphasizes *qualitative* decisions rather than quantitative ones.

It is always dangerous to presume that life-place planning is capable of codification; it is not. However, the cluster of practices that converge on a model of life-place planning may share certain attributes. These life-place processes may

- fit the characteristics, limits, and potentials of the region
- reflect the ecological structure and function of the region
- emphasize local resources and energy sources

· reflect the "deep wisdom" of how best to live in a place over the long term

· mix traditional wisdom with new ecological knowledge

· emerge from a collaborative process of grassroots support by many individuals and groups

· often be carried forward by a single individual as a "labor of love"

· embody the collective affections of various different groups for the place under consideration

· acknowledge and respond to the need for local communities to make a living from the immediate life-place

· foster the community economy and emphasize regional economic self-reliance

· gradually build a wider and more inclusive civic constituency

· ultimately attract the approval and support of local politicians

Not all life-place planning efforts include all of these attributes. However, the trends in such processes are toward increased respect for the limits and potentials of the region; reduction in the scale of physical intervention; a finer-grained, more regional self-sufficiency; ever-broadening grassroots constituency and public support; more incorporation of local wisdom from long-term residents and those intending to stay; intersection of sustainability goals and regionally distinct characteristics; and adaptation to different scales and different situations with similar, but not necessarily identical, outcomes or results. It is, of course, simply too early in the evolution of life-place planning to see many tangible results from successful applications. It is likely, however, that as life-place planning processes achieve increasing success, they will result in landscapes where the patterns of human intervention are adjusted to reveal a more regionally unique sense of place and aesthetic meaning.

Tools for Life-Place Planning

As it matures and evolves, life-place planning will become a highly complex endeavor requiring broadly educated participants with a wide variety of skills, experience, and knowledge of the local region. While the same (or greater) need will exist for scientific and technical specialists in life-placing planning that exists in conventional single-issue, top-down planning, bioregional planning will require the greatest levels of social facilitation, leadership, and group communication skills, since its success hinges on broadening social participation and building community "capacity." Although scientific expertise will always play an important role, with the typical need for specialists in soils, geology, hydrology, ecology, transportation, agriculture, forestry, range management, and so forth, scientific conclusions and positions will be more subject to scrutiny, open to question, and apt to be negotiated as part of the deliberations, rather than objectified as incontrovertible truths.

Mapping will play a key part in life-place planning, not only because bioregional scope must be established collectively for any action but also because certain forms of information elicited from stakeholders can best be recorded on maps and may strongly influence the spatial outcome of the planning effort. One technique is to seek and record all mappable information or "geographic wisdom" from those most familiar with specific places in the bioregion. In this fashion, maps become social research and action tools whose value is at least as great as that of the single-resource data layers (e.g., soils, hydrology, vegetation, slope) typical of top-down ecological planning. Although computer-based GIS (graphic information systems) is helpful, experience has shown that its complexities sometimes overwhelm or bury the important bioregional issues beneath a preoccupation with data validity, operating jargon, and system glitches. When trained personnel put this powerful but complex tool to work, however, the results can be significant. Already GIS has proven itself to be highly effective in regional decision making for conservation and biodiversity, and it no doubt will extend its success to other dimensions of regenerative planning.

Monitoring of ecosystem conditions is another important bioregional planning tool. Since agencies usually have inadequate funds for monitoring conditions on a bioregion-wide scale, that task often befalls volunteer citizens. Each year philanthropic organizations award numerous grants that include training components for citizen monitoring of water quality and quantity, wildlife and fish populations, recreational or transit use, climate conditions, and the like. Problems of methodology and data reliability no doubt will occur in these citizen monitoring projects, but merely spreading the responsibility for data gathering across a broad constituency deepens the public engagement with the region and commitment to the planning process.

Texas architect and planner Pliny Fisk III is well known for his bioregional approach to architectural and building systems, materials, and methods. One of the techniques he uses is *indexing:* focusing on a physical parameter such as water, energy, or food, for example, an analyst can determine how much is *produced* within a given region versus how much is *consumed*. The resulting ratios can be used to gauge relative self-sufficiency versus dependency on external supplies. Periodic measurement of these benchmarks allows relative progress toward or away from desired, sustainable conditions to be determined. For example, Sustainable Seattle, a nonprofit group, has established forty benchmarks that it measures each year. The state of Oregon has institutionalized the benchmark process, enacting into law some 259 different measures of current and desired status, which it uses in the budget allocation process.[16]

A more complex yet increasingly popular tool is "ecological footprinting" (figure 7.7), a heuristic device attributed to Canadian planners William Rees and Mathis Wackernagel that calculates the land-equivalent areas needed for sustainable production of life needs, such as water, energy, food, or wood. Their process has demonstrated, for example, that under present conditions many cities in developed countries such as Canada and the United States require an area on the order of fifteen to twenty-five times the size of their own immediate regions to sustainably provide for their basic physical resource needs. Pliny Fisk III also created a footprinting exercise entitled "The Eco-Balance Game," which can be modified to simulate relative sustainability of site developments of any size, from a few acres to an entire region. As life-place planning evolves, it is likely that the variety of simulations used to assess relative goal achievement will increase. Not all of these will be esoteric "expert" models decipherable only by a computer-literate priesthood. Indeed, the most effective will be those that reveal directly to bioregional residents the progress needed or gained toward sustainable conditions.[17]

In the case of life-place planning, there is no boundary between planning, education, and participation: all are subsumed into a general, reinhabitory culture. Bioregional education, in fact, is likely to be a many-sided dialogue, with local residents teaching experts as well as vice versa, and the whole gamut of stakeholders exchanging views on many interrelated issues. Skilled facilitators will know when and how to bring all participants up to speed before expecting results from group problem-solving processes. (In a world made frantic by the speed of electronic communication, there is still no substitute for the *time* taken by a community to learn about itself in relation to its physical, ecological, and cultural needs.)

Another significant function of bioregion-wide planning is to facilitate communication among nongovernmental groups with similar, compatible, or adjacent areas of concern. Often, groups find they have enough in common

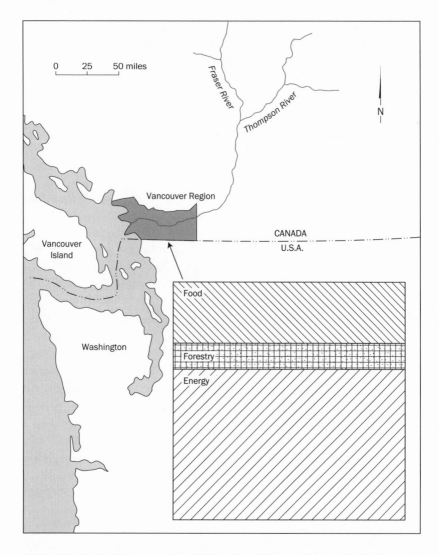

Figure 7.7 Mathis Wackernagel and William Rees have established the highly useful concept of "ecological footprints," in which the physical needs of a person, group, or city can be described in terms of land area equivalents to sustainably produce necessities such as water, food, energy, and building materials. Here, the ecological footprint for Vancouver, B.C., Canada, is shown to be approximately fifteen times the size of the region surrounding the city. Based on original in Mathis Wackernagel and William Rees, *Our Ecological Footprint: Reducing Human Impact on the Earth* (Philadelphia: New Society, 1996), figure 3.5.

to collaborate on grants, watershed coordination, education, or policy formation. While there are limitations to the geographic scale on which such collaborations can reasonably occur, the benefits often include better recognition by funding agencies and increased attention (and, hopefully, subsequent action) from local, regional, state, and federal political bodies.

The life-place planning process can also include region-wide economic assistance. In the north coastal region of California, where dairy farms make up a significant percentage of open space threatened by development, environmental groups have participated in marketing and have advocated price supports for milk. During periods of downturn in salmon fishing and temporary closure of the commercial salmon fishery along the Oregon coast, various groups participated in widespread marketing of the region's tourist potential to offset the economic decline from reduced fishing. Several regions have also launched organic food marketing endeavors. Partnerships between environmental groups and economic development groups have immense potential as more regions realize the synergistic relationship among environmental quality, amenity-based tourism, and economic prosperity.

Due to recent government underfunding for regional planning and environmental protection, funds for public-private partnerships on behalf of natural regions increasingly have come from large philanthropic organizations such as the Packard Foundation, the Nature Conservancy, and the Trust for Public Land. Grant writing, therefore, has become an indispensable tool for bioregional planning organizations. It remains to be seen whether the high level of such funding for collaborative grassroots projects is sufficient or likely to remain so in the future. Critics on both sides say that more of the costs should be borne by government and/or business. For now, though, life-place planning involves assembling budgets dependent on multiple grants, matching funds, in-kind services, and volunteer labor. At the very least, this develops "social capital," even if financial capital is thin.

Well-known land-saving techniques such as conservation easements, transfers of development rights, pooling agreements to trade government lands with private owners, habitat mitigation banking, and community land trusts all serve indispensable roles in the process of life-place planning. In the future, the same kinds of executive skills as those required of corporate or agency CEOs are likely to be needed to manage the diverse participants in these delicate participatory processes. Likewise, legal and business skills will become increasingly important for coping with the various legal agreements, memoranda of understanding, or articles of 501 c-3 incorporation for nonprofit status that are necessary to life-place planning efforts.

A Suggested Bioregional Planning Process

Since no two bioregions and no two life-place planning efforts are identical, no singular process can be prescribed for all situations. However, a generalizable process is useful for projects just getting off (or "onto") the ground. Doug Aberley offers a number of steps for initiating such a bioregional process. They can be summarized as follows:

1. Define the boundaries of the bioregion as well as possible by mapping plant and animal communities, watersheds, physiographic regions, aboriginal territories, historic and current land use patterns, climate, soil, and special categories, such as "sacred spaces" and cognitive "homelands." Overlay this information to determine which bioregional boundaries are harder or softer than others.

2. Compile an extensive, detailed atlas of the natural and human elements over a long period of time, incorporating the wisdom and work of many people. Record this information in both map and narrative form.

3. Compile a history of the bioregion, both biophysical and cultural, paying attention to how the environment has been used to increase or decrease the health and well-being of people, plants, and animals. Expand the bioregional history to address the quantity and value of bioregional resources, including standard economic measures as well as ecological variables and values that were formerly "externalized."

4. Complete a survey of how the current structures of government and development are organized and operate in the bioregion. Document positive and negative effects of this existing system, identifying which influences are beyond the control of the region and how more local control could be incorporated.

5. Identify which laws, policies, and institutional forces are working against long-term bioregion health, and organize sustained, nonviolent resistance to those forces (making sure to engage simultaneously in step 6, below).

6. Spend equal time and effort evolving alternatives to degenerative forces, proposing new organizations, proposing new forms of bioregional education, introducing new public participation projects and actions, introducing new candidates and/or platforms for public office, and encouraging other creative and constructive actions.

7. Do an inventory of "success stories" that includes the contributions to local wisdom and effectively demonstrated stewardship practices made by all members of the community or bioregion, past and present. Make sure that the flow of information regarding this wisdom and success diffuses throughout the bioregional population.

8. Identify and aggregate the "bioregenerative patterns" that emerge from contributions of individuals and groups into a "pattern language" articulating an evolving vision for the life-place. Such a pattern language will incorporate many points of view, will constantly change, and will serve as a vocabulary to guide the future management of the life-place.

9. Involve all parties (who care enough to participate) in the ongoing creation of a bioregional vision, regardless of their point of view. Both vision and ongoing community participation are essential to the bioregional process. Allow enough time for the natural trust in the participatory process to ripen and mature into fruitful solutions.[18]

These recommended steps are useful both for those just becoming aware of their own life-places and for existing bioregional organizations, which can use the steps to clarify values or set goals.

Dissolving Boundaries, Emerging Boundaries

The convergence of various planning and geographical dimensions into a life-place or bioregion is likely to be a gradual, endogenous process. Because of the growing importance of environmental issues to regional planning, regions are increasingly identifying themselves with ecological attributes of the land's surface, such as water basins (the San Francisco Bay Area, the Northwest Coast, and the Sierra Nevada). Postindustrial locational criteria (such as where jobs are located) are being relaxed by the advent of computerized electronic communication, resulting in a lessening of the relationship between economic vitality and specific city centers. The decoupling of economic activity from structured space is well documented, and that decoupling is likely to increase, while problems relating to resources and ecosystems are likely to take on greater importance in public and individual life. In sum, the bioregional movement is witness and heir to the *dissolution* of some boundaries—former industrial geography, relevance of city centers, previous professional "territories"—and the *creation* of others based on natural features—watershed basins, similar vegetation, topography, or farming practices, for example. The life-place is a product of this unique boundary-dissolving/boundary-forming process.

Bioregional planning, like bioregions themselves, will be hierarchical. Small groups may combine into larger groups. Networks of smaller nongovernmental organizations may find they are more effective if they collaborate with their (bio)logical neighboring groups, as the Putah Creek Council, Upper Putah Creek Stewardship, Yolo Basin Foundation, Cache Creek Conservancy, and Blue Ridge–Berryessa Natural Area Conservation Partnership have in my own bioregion. Economies of scale will sort themselves out and reach an equilibrium, again most likely hierarchical.

Life-place planning requires a degree of interdisciplinary thinking that boggles the industrial-era mind. Everything is now connected—transit, housing, recreation, employment, economic development, environmental stewardship. Instead of abiding by formerly recognized systemic boundaries, planning procedures must now struggle to find the natural "breakpoints" between one natural region and another, while integrating formerly separate activities. While these boundaries will in part be scientifically determined, planners often forget that each of us constructs his or her own reality, sense of place, feeling of well-being, and cultural identity as a combination of responses to physical characteristics of the land, economic factors, social networks, and our complex internal cognitive and perceptual values, perceptions, and desires. Supposed "rational" methods of GIS, McHargian overlays, transit models, economic demand studies, and the like cannot fully grasp the critical qualitative meanings implicit in inhabiting a place, those personal values that lead us to save old-growth redwoods, to "daylight" (bring to the surface) urban streams, to protest additional development, and to protect endangered-species habitat. These variables are nearly impossible to quantify or to incorporate into predictive models. How would planners have predicted the explosion of volunteer watershed protection and conservation groups now functioning on the continent?

(In the bioregional context, there are no real lines between life-place planning, civic participation, education, and personal practice. All form a more comprehensive life-place culture based on awareness, concern, commitment, and action. Bioregional planners of the future will need an enormously broad set of knowledge and skills and will be best served by practical, general education pursued within the region where they will eventually work. The days when an "expert" was someone who lived more than thirty miles away may be numbered!)

Life-place planning is neither a precise science nor a unified body of theory nor a sophisticated art form nor a universally accepted procedure of any kind. Instead, it is an evolving trend, a convergence of practical activities toward emphasis on preserving and enhancing natural, local conditions. In a life-place, planning is merely one aspect embedded within a greater culture of permanence.

8 Building

MAKING BIOREGIONS WORK

Bioregional restoration is, first and foremost, a service we offer to nature and to each other. And at the same time, by giving us work to do in the landscape, it satisfies the first requirement of membership in the land community.

MICHAEL V. McGINNIS, FREEMAN HOUSE,
AND WILLIAM JORDAN, 1999

Propped next to my computer is perhaps the most intricate aerial photograph I have ever seen, in color, shot from an altitude of one hundred miles. It is a LANDSAT image of the entire Sacramento Valley bioregion taken in one pass. With eyes deliberately blurred, one could read it abstractly as a frame of dark green (upland mixed forest), with an outer mat of olive (foothill blue oaks) and an inner one of tan (terrace grasslands), containing a crazy quilt of minute rectangles of all possible greens, browns, yellows, and beiges (irrigated farmland), with swatches of gray-green (cities), threads of off-white (roads), and meanders and patches of near-black (rivers and reservoirs). To contemplate the photograph is to be barraged by various, not altogether consistent, thoughts: how much humans have changed this land; how wonderful it would be to return here from a trip to outer space; how the cities sprawl along the freeways; how compatible the colors are.

But the foremost impression is one of *pattern*. There is a spatial logic to the natural and built forms that make up this region, whether the region is currently "sustainable" or not. The logic that puts the life-place to work may be seen from a high altitude or experienced while traveling across the land's surface. Flat fertile lands are plowed, planted, and irrigated. Grasslands are grazed. Rivers and streams are harnessed. Towns and cities grow around existing nuclei. In spite of the current momentum of "development bashing" (and this book does its fair share), there is much to admire about human ingenuity and tenacity on the land. The overall pattern is organic, and in spite of the straight freeways, dammed rivers, and sprawling cities, there is an undeniable "nature" to the photograph. Humans have no choice but to alter the land, and to ascend in altitude and broaden the perspective is to see this alteration as increasingly organic and essential—to leave behind the particulars of individual opinion and see, instead, a species surviving, even thriving, on Planet Earth.

There are, of course, dimensions of this region that are more difficult to decipher literally from the satellite image, although some visual clues may exist. The Sacramento Valley is a classic city region in the best of Jane Jacobs's definition, with both primary and supporting metropolises embedded synergistically within the surrounding agricultural matrix. It is, as Robert Bailey, Hartwell Welsh, and others concur, an ecological region or bioregion— a life-place, even if some of its natural elements are mere palimpsests of former, stronger elements. Certainly, it is a nearly self-contained watershed, an area of self-similar climate, and a diverse but unique cultural territory. Also not represented by this grand aerial photograph is the multitude of ideas that have evolved for building the patterns of human intervention or modifying them slightly or substantially to ensure that life, in all of its manifest forms, might be perpetuated here for the indefinite future. If it were as easy to record a mosaic of all the emerging wisdom, forethought, and visionary prescription emanating from the region as it is to make one satellite photograph, there would be no reason for this book.

The point I wish to make is that the process of change implied by the notion of life-place is not necessarily revolutionary. It need not reinvent entire political realities, start from physically literal or figurative blank slates, annihilate old economic systems, or assume 180-degree turnabouts of human nature. Instead, a glance at the aerial photograph reminds us that humans are steeped in the logic of grounded patterns and accustomed to working pragmatically in a bioregional context, whether they realize it or not. The perspective gained from a bit of altitude tells us that the process of life-place realization is one of relatively minute adjustments in the organized ways we intervene on the land to restore our bioregions and make them work, coupled with a gradual, evolutionary adjustment in mind-set totally within the possible range of cultural adaptation.

A Whole-Life-Place Pattern

An overall, composite pattern for the Sacramento Valley (figures 8.1a–c) can be inferred from a triad of categories. First, from the creeks, sloughs, rivers, remnant wetlands, native oak woodlands, chaparral ridgelines, and flood bypasses, a framework for biodiversity may be coaxed into reality, building upon the vestiges of former corridors and linking the patches of habitat with a network of connective ecosystems. In this grand pattern, the

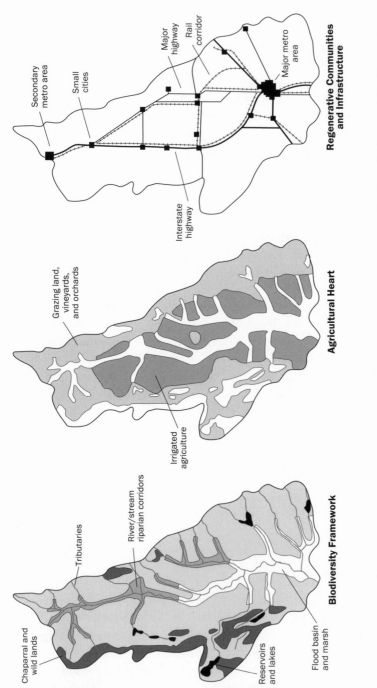

Figures 8.1a–c A generalized, "whole-life-place" pattern can be synthesized for the Sacramento Valley bioregion by examining three major components. *A: Biodiversity Framework:* The remnant natural riparian corridors, sloughs, wetlands, grasslands, chaparral, and woodlands form an armature for patterns preserving and enhancing biodiversity, wildlife habitats, open space, aesthetics, flood control, and water quality. *B: Agricultural Heart:* With some of the best alluvial soils in the world, the Sacramento Valley plain and its surrounding uplands suggest an array of patterns for sustaining the production of food and fiber as a major "purpose" for much of the land. *C: Regenerative Communities and Infrastructure:* When considered with respect to the two other components, the best patterns for developing human communities and providing infrastructure can be articulated. Based on original figures by Robert Thayer.

Labels in figure A (**Biodiversity Framework**): Chaparral and wild lands; Tributaries; River/stream riparian corridors; Reservoirs and lakes; Flood basin and marsh

Labels in figure B (**Agricultural Heart**): Grazing land, vineyards, and orchards; Irrigated agriculture

Labels in figure C (**Regenerative Communities and Infrastructure**): Secondary metro area; Small cities; Major highway; Rail corridor; Major metro area; Interstate highway capacity for biological productivity of the land as home to nonhuman, living neighbors gains parity with that of the land that we humans have expropriated for our own life needs. In this expanded circulatory system of water, soils, and vegetation, a migratory system for nonhuman life and a network of "nearby nature" capable of anchoring the human spirit may bind us more permanently to our food-producing matrix.

Second, the Sacramento Valley and its southern sibling, the San Joaquin Valley, combine to form one of the most unique landforms in North America, and together they contain some of the best agricultural soil on earth. In the landscape ecologist's terms, agriculture, for better or worse, has now become the valley's "matrix," or ground to which the figures of other landscapes now relate. In global terms, the once great grasslands of the valley, like most significant grasslands on earth, have succumbed to the plow. We cannot turn back; as long as there are people, there must be agriculture, especially here, in this life-place. Whether conservative or liberal, developer or preservationist, farmer or biologist, few would deny the necessity of maintaining the agricultural productivity of this bioregion.

Interwoven within this necessary agricultural and ecological fabric is the third major element of a whole-life-place pattern: regenerative human communities and infrastructure. Our built world, again to use the vocabulary of landscape ecology, consists of human patches of development linked by corridors through which people, water, energy, food, and material goods flow. This community-node and infrastructure-net pattern is our human lifeline to the earth, but it is not fixed. There is considerable potential for more compact towns and cities, placed in a more careful, respectful relation to agriculture, linked by more efficient transport, scaled in closer, less consumptive relation to sources of energy, water, and materials, and connected more affectionately to the agricultural, ecological, and recreational contexts by systems of nonmotorized trails and biodiverse watercourses. In short, our *human* network must be more delicately interwoven with the network of water and habitat upon which our companion species ultimately depend.

Like words, which evolve meaning in spatial, functional relationship to each other, regenerative life-place patterns grow and expand in relation, combining to increase the totality, complexity, resiliency, and longevity of life within them. These patterns are not necessarily new; most have been around for a while, awaiting a wise citizenry to rearrange them into an articulate whole. Neither are they formulas dictated from above; rather, they are manifestations of a life-place culture touching ground.

What follows is my attempt to articulate a bioregenerative framework of interconnected patterns emanating from the growing, collective wisdom of this life-place. In terms of a whole-life-place pattern, the Sacramento Valley bioregion weaves two kinds of "nets": one of natural habitats, of river, stream, and slough corridors, and the other of human communities, roads and rails, and other infrastructural connections. Each of these webs then weaves through the matrix of varied agricultural lands. By examining each of these components of the overall life-place mosaic in greater detail, we can identify an essential, spatial language. The beauty of a regenerative pattern approach, like any language, is that it may *expand* (new patterns may be added as they evolve from the collective wisdom, just as new words can enter any lexicon) and that patterns are *interconnected* (most do not fit cleanly into one category or scale but connect various scales and land uses, just as language gains meaning from connection and context). Furthermore, a life-place pattern language is highly dependent upon *place*, just as any dialect, involving as it does unique changes in meaning, reflects a particular, finite geography.

In the sections that follow, I offer and describe a "starter set" of twenty-four patterns for the Sacramento Valley, eight in each of the three major headings: "Biodiversity Framework," "Agricultural Heart," and "Regenerative Communities and Infrastructure." (These form only a rudimentary beginning, constrained by limited space in print. A fully articulated regenerative pattern language would be as rich and complex as any local dialect and would fill volumes.) For the sake of clarity, sample patterns under each of the three subsections have a parallel structure, or "syntax." They are presented in a uniform manner: a simple title (in capital letters); a problem statement (in bold type), with elaboration; a solution statement (in italics), with examples from the local life-place; and, where appropriate, theoretical progenitors, strategies for implementation, and interconnections with other patterns.[1]

Biodiversity Framework

The discussion of any life-place should begin with an enlightened awareness of origins and subsequent biodiversity (even though here agriculture is the dominant land use). In the Sacramento Valley, all of us must understand the physical and ecological processes that have created this place and how we humans have modified it. John McPhee has aptly labeled our valley an "earthen sea," describing both its present state and its origins. A former saltwater bay, the valley was forged as a structural basin bordered by

Sierra and Coast Range mountain-building activity, sealed off by tectonic upthrusts, and gradually filled up with sediments to a depth of thousands of vertical feet. The valley is a testament to the ability of floodwaters to deposit soil: without past floods, there would literally be no valley, no agriculture, and no unique biota. Now, the great farms and fields sit on one of the most dramatic deposits of alluvial sediment in the world. Across this matrix of world-class agricultural soils course the valley's major tributary streams. Clockwise from my home watershed, they are Putah, Cache, Stony, Thomes, Cottonwood, and Clear Creeks on the west; Sacramento, McCloud, and Pit Rivers at the northern apex; and Battle, Chico, Mill, Deer, and Butte Creeks and the Feather, Yuba, Bear, American, Cosumnes, and Mokelumne Rivers on the Sierra-born east side. These watercourses and a thousand minor sloughs and tributaries etch the valley with potential corridors for water, fish, wildlife, plant and animal migrations, soil deposition, gravel extraction, irrigation water "reclamation," and, often, the only visible "nature" on an otherwise unbroken agricultural horizon.[2]

Throughout the Sacramento Valley bioregion, habitat for other species is fragmented by human activity—by agriculture, which has taken over as the dominant landscape ecological matrix, and by countless small to vast urbanized or developed areas and multiple infrastructural corridors. The result is a highly fractured "natural" network no longer capable of providing adequate levels of ecosystem service, marked by rivers and streams that have been channelized, or with long sections devoid of riparian vegetation or adequate flow regimes, or impenetrable to anadromous fish; greatly reduced areas of native grassland; declining blue oak woodlands; immense invasions of yellow star thistle; minuscule proportions of once-vast seasonal wetlands or permanent marsh; little or no remaining floodplains; and falling water tables. In addition, very little accessible open space remains to ameliorate the pressures of urban life or to connect new human residents meaningfully to their natural—or even agricultural—surroundings.

Yet the skeletal pattern for a revitalized network of habitat for biodiversity and ecosystem function remains. Rivers, creeks, and minor sloughs can be restored, levees set back, wetlands reconstructed, oaks replanted, and remaining grasslands managed for increased native species and control of exotics. Time and time again, restoration efforts have been shown to make a positive difference. "If you build it, they will come!" has been proven by the return of waterfowl to flooded postharvest rice fields and of salmon to restored stream flows and clean spawning gravels. Agricultural lands play a critical role in this, providing forage and habitat for a diverse faunal population. But even more could be done; the whole-life-place pattern must be founded on biodiversity.

LIVING CORRIDORS

Streams, rivers, and sloughs are often the only slender remains of nonhuman "nature" in the valley, the rest of the land having been expropriated for agriculture, infrastructure, or development.

Ecological functions once spread broadly across the landscape are now squeezed into narrow corridors following rivers, streams, and sloughs. In many places where watercourses are diverted, impounded, channeled, or "undergrounded," these functions have been severely curtailed if not completely eliminated. As such, the remaining riparian network takes on importance far beyond its vestigial nature.

Protect what remains of natural river, stream, and slough corridors, and enhance their capacity to provide habitat for biodiversity, species mobility, water quality, erosion control, flood control, and amenity values for both private landowners and the public.

The pattern of riparian corridors and watercourses weaves the Sacramento Valley together at all scales, from the vast Sacramento Basin in its entirety to the smallest agricultural slough. To a great degree, river and creek basins, even artificial ones, are fractal in nature, repeating the same structure, function, and dynamic order across small to large land areas. To the greatest extent, all segments of water courses should be considered in terms of as many of the multiple functions as possible. Flood control, aquifer recharge, habitat connectivity, and aesthetic and recreational benefits accrue to water corridors at every scale.

The California Biodiversity Council, in its original memorandum of understanding on biodiversity, firmly established the direction of resolving local resource problems on a watershed basis. Of most critical importance would be the purchase of easements for ecological functions on either side of the narrow existing corridors, essentially widening them and increasing their functional capacity. Where riparian vegetation is narrow or nonexistent, the vegetated corridor can be widened; where sloughs are channelized, broader cross sections and bank profiles can be provided for accommodating riparian terraces and additional overstory and understory growth; where sloughs and streams have been straightened, the natural meanders in streams can be restored as profiles are modified without detracting from

Figure 8.2 While often mere vestiges of their previous form, remnant slough corridors such as Willow Slough, pictured here, are essential elements in conserving the nature of the valley bioregion. Photograph by Paul Robins; used by permission.

flood capacity. Habitat for numerous threatened or endangered species dependent upon riparian vegetation, such as Swainson's hawks and yellow-billed cuckoos, can be increased. Overstory shade can be increased on small streams to cool and protect spawning reaches, while native-grass filtering strips can buffer agricultural runoff from drainage sloughs (figure 8.3). In cases where small streams or sloughs have been "undergrounded" beneath urban development, there exists some potential for "daylighting" segments of these as land use changes evolve. The result of many of these small measures would add up to a significantly reconstituted network of environmental corridors. A minor portion of this revitalized network of habitat can be made available for public access by a growing local population starved for rehabilitory contact with "nature." Finally, an expanded network of environmental corridors built around existing riparian systems would serve as migratory routes for species moving from lowlands to foothills and vice versa.

A well-managed riparian corridor network can tie all land uses together, from wild lands, to agriculture, to towns, suburbs, and urban centers. Careful restoration and multistakeholder management of the bioregion's water

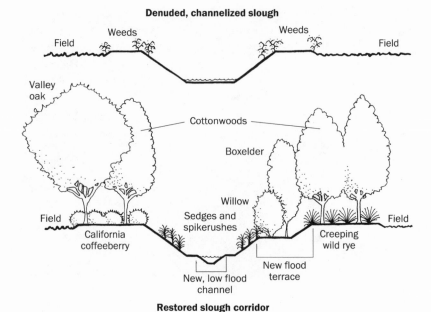

Figure 8.3 Small sloughs can be enhanced to add needed ecological function to the valley's agricultural and urbanized landscapes. Drawing by Robert Thayer.

circulation corridors is our common denominator and can perhaps do more to ensure the perpetuity of our life-place than any other pattern.

WHOLE WATERSHEDS

Often, people in the valley do not realize they are connected to the upper elevations through whole watersheds, and vice versa.

Downstream people may not know where their water comes from, and upstream people may not care what happens to their water once they have used it or even whether there is any water to flow downstream. Yet most water quality and quantity issues can only be considered in terms of whole drainage basins, or watersheds. As more issues surface in relation to water quality and quantity, it behooves valley residents to know about the totality of their dependence upon and relation to water.

Plan for and cooperatively manage whole watersheds, from headwaters to confluence or outflow.

Holistic watershed management and stewardship is one of the fastest grow-ing environmental fields, with interdisciplinary programs springing up at several American universities. The explosion of voluntary watershed groups and the recently redirected focus of the Environmental Protection Agency toward non-point-source pollution control by means of watersheds has made a strong case for integrated management on the whole-basin level. Most issues are watershed-wide. Anadromous fish habitat management ne-cessitates working on the entire watershed, from downstream outflow to up-watershed spawning habitat, and all potential impediments to migration in between. In the Sacramento River Basin, there are several basin-wide vol-unteer organizations. One notable example is the Spring Run–Chinook Salmon Work Group, which has focused its attention on collaborative pro-cesses for management of habitat for salmon, steelhead, and other anadro-mous fish. Tributary-based conservancies such as the Putah Creek Coun-cil and Battle Creek Conservancy have similarly achieved notable successes in resolving water supply issues for fish habitat. Some groups focus on im-proving small reaches: the Cache Creek Conservancy, for example, aims to restore a sixteen-mile former gravel-mined creek section. As time goes on, networking and cooperation among these groups will be more advantageous to the successful achievement of the goals of individual participating groups.[3]

Likewise, control of noxious riparian weeds also necessitates a whole-watershed approach that begins upstream and controls downstream spread. Both *Tamarix* and *Arundo*, two non-natives that disperse readily through-out the watershed, choke out more ecologically beneficial natives. The only hope for controlling these pests is coordinated, cooperative effort.

Coordinating the management of whole watersheds is necessarily a mul-tiscaled activity that cuts across all land and water uses. Groups as diverse as ranchers, fishers, loggers, hunters, ecologists, hydrologists, farmers, recre-ationists, and water managers now sit at the same tables together—making integrated watershed management very different from the old one-resource-at-a-time approach. "One" cannot manage a watershed, only "many" can, and the "many" required to manage whole watersheds must talk to each other, see through each other's eyes, meet in real time and space, share com-mon goals, build trust, and mutually undertake the work of keeping the wa-tershed functioning. It is hard—but necessary—work, the kind that is likely to build rather than destroy community.

One of the best ways to aid the work of watershed management at all scales is to put teeth in the statewide policy. Building on the memorandum of understanding on biodiversity, the state could earmark for watershed

Figure 8.4 Contractors apply heavy machinery to eradicate the invasive weed *Arundo donax* from the lands of the Cache Creek Nature Preserve. Photograph by Jan Lowrey. Courtesy of Cache Creek Conservancy.

groups some funding now given to each separate resource agency. No new taxes would be required, and the money aimed at watershed management could serve multiple, rather than singular, environmental purposes.

FOOTHILL CONSERVATION AREAS

Above the valley floor, in the hill-country headwaters of the streams etching the bioregion, essential lands and environmental services are at risk.

In the uplands edging the Sacramento Valley, low-density development fragments cohesive wildlife habitats; overgrazing threatens water quality and erodes soil; low beef prices discourage adequate range management; forest clear-cutting above the bioregion's edges and water impoundment and diversion all threaten anadromous fish habitat. These problems are endemic to the mosaics of private and public uplands typical of the edges of the Sacramento Valley. Public and private sectors must join in counteracting the escalating impacts of single-purpose land management. Although many local organizations—such as the highly successful Middle Mountain Foundation, which has sought protection for the Sutter Buttes through private conservation strategies—are working to protect foothills, uplands, and upstream wild and natural lands, public-private partnerships are often the key.

Define joint private-public natural areas in the upland foothill zones, and manage them as "quilts" of conservation.

In the upper watersheds of Putah Creek and Cache Creek in Lake, Napa, Yolo, and Colusa Counties, a remarkable effort of this sort is under way, coordinating forces to bring forth a multidimensional suite of linked conservation measures. The Blue Ridge–Berryessa Natural Area Conservation Partnership (BRBNACP), as described in its vision statement,

> is a voluntary group of private landowners, public land managers and regional inhabitants dedicated to the conservation, preservation and management of over 500,000 acres of natural, wild, agricultural and recreational lands located in the upper Cache and Putah Creek watersheds in Northern California. . . . Through a volunteer, inclusive, participatory process, BRBNACP seeks to enhance the level of local input and to generate and retain local revenues to protect natural and cultural values, while promoting an ecologically compatible level of public use and fully respecting private property rights.[4]

Of critical importance here is the effort to approach "conservation" and "stewardship" from multiple directions. The composition of the BRBNACP is instructive just in its basic makeup: partners include a large mining company, two federal agencies, two state agencies, several county parks departments, three land trusts, a major university, many private ranchers, vintners, landowners, hunting clubs, a nonprofit wilderness coalition, an organization of private resort owners, and numerous private citizens. Because the conservation partners recognize that there is "something for everyone" in the vast five-hundred-thousand-acre territory, entrenched attitudes have been minimized and a flexible dialogue has prevailed.

Implementing multipartner conservation in the foothills is likely to lead to diverse strategies for different partners applied in synergistic fashion. Conservation easements might be established for private lands, while memoranda of understanding and joint powers agreements could bind state, local, and federal agency management of public domains. New structural administrative arrangements are possible, such as special funding districts jointly supported by federal, state, local, and nonprofit sources. The resultant mosaic, while differing in each ownership patch, would remain viable as a whole to achieve mutually determined conservation goals.

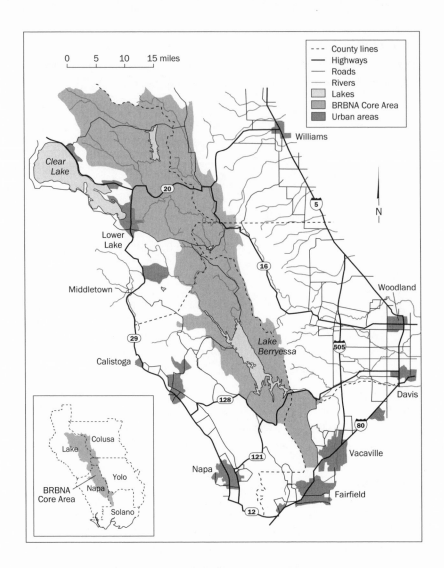

Figure 8.5 The Blue Ridge–Berryessa Natural Area (BRBNA) is a voluntary partnership of private and public landowners who cooperate to share information aiding the conservation, restoration, and responsible stewardship of over five hundred thousand acres of land straddling five counties in the upper Putah and Cache Creek basins of the interior Coast Range of California. Map based on original by Jacob Mann and Robert Thayer.

NEW FLOODWAYS

The Sacramento Valley bioregion was formed by flooding, yet we often pretend flooding doesn't—or somehow shouldn't—happen.

Farming and urban development in this valley are both presumptions of control over the very processes that placed the rich alluvial soils here in the first place. The accepted method of flood control is to build narrow levees and channelize the stream and slough corridors, forcing the water off any particular parcel as fast as possible (figure 8.6a). Early plowing and "bedding up" of individual agricultural fields sheds rainwater from the fields as fast as possible to allow farmers the earliest possible date by which to bring farm machinery onto the field. This only adds considerable volume and speed to the hydrographic curve; downstream farmers adjacent to sloughs are then placed at greater risk of flooding.

Give rivers, streams, and sloughs "room to roam" by restructuring levees and flood bypasses and by designating and compensating the owners of areas to be flooded ahead of time.

Several opportunities exist for returning the floodplain functions to rivers, streams, creeks, and sloughs. One is to expand the width between protective levees, giving more room for the rivers and streams to meander. Another alternative is to provide off-channel bypass corridors in locations parallel to the main channel. Both options emulate natural flooding patterns of streams (figures 8.6b–c). A third strategy suggests that certain farm fields be designated each storm season as flood overflow areas, where flows from overtopped streams would be purposely directed each winter. Owners of these lands would be compensated by funds normally spent on engineered structures, large-scale impoundments, and after-the-flood disaster relief measures. A fourth, peripherally related strategy would be to provide many small upstream/foothill stock/wildlife ponds to absorb rain earlier in the hydrological profile of the watershed. Finally, an approach to planning and designing the urbanized landscape that favors infiltration rather than hardened surfaces at all scales can lessen both floodwater quantity and quality problems. It is likely that a combination of all of these measures would be more cost-effective in managing floodwater than building large new reservoirs or raising downstream levees.

Because the natural morphology of a river or creek adapts to its own flooding regimes, strategies that allow as much infiltration of water as possible and as much off- or in-channel storage as possible at *all scales simultaneously* are necessary. Of the hierarchy of land uses, many (parks,

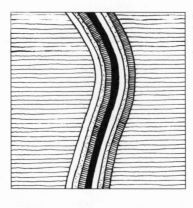

Channeled river
with "straitjacket"
levees...no safe
floodplain

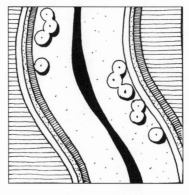

Levees set back
to create
in-channel
flood plain

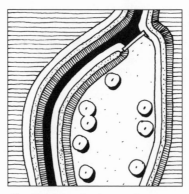

Off-channel
flood bypass

New floodways for rivers and streams

Figures 8.6a–c Many valley streams and rivers have been "straitjacketed" by levees *(A)*, disconnecting them from the ecological and flood control benefits of their former floodplains. Some of these functions can be returned by setting levees back from the channel *(B)* or creating off-channel flood bypasses *(C)*. Drawings by Robert Thayer.

wildlife habitat areas, seasonal playing fields, pasture, rice paddies, fallow fields, partially prepared row and field crop areas, temporary parking lots) can accept periodic flooding. The job of giving rivers and streams room to roam is therefore a comprehensive spatial challenge yielding a more dynamic form of land management.

RESTORED BASIN MOSAIC

Engineered flood bypasses in the valley (like Yolo and Sutter) don't provide the full range of ecosystem services once offered by river flood basins.

Given that the original floodplain is long gone, the Sutter and Yolo Bypasses do a credible job of accommodating overflow from the Sacramento River and its tributaries. However, agriculture within the bypasses is curtailed by seasonal restrictions, since the land is often under floodwater. Also, because of the flood engineers' fixation on eliminating "roughness" (i.e., vegetation that could cause friction and reduce the flow of floodwater), the large bypass levees as currently configured do not fulfill many of the ecological functions once provided by the river's erstwhile floodplain.

Collaboratively design downstream flood bypasses to include multiple functions once associated with original floodplains, including flood management, farming, wildlife habitat and forage, fish rearing, hunting, recreation, wildlife viewing, and education.

Despite the engineers' desires, a modest expansion of the "wetted perimeter" and cross-sectional area of flood bypasses would safely allow for some "roughening" of the profile with desirable marsh, seasonal wetland, and riparian plants, which would return much of the ecological functions characteristic of original floodplains. Plans such as these are actively being pursued in the new Yolo Basin Wetlands and in the North Delta Wildlife Refuge being proposed by the U.S. Fish and Wildlife Service, just west and southwest, respectively, of Sacramento. In each instance, a revised mosaic of land uses is proposed, guided in large part by an understanding of soil types and of the "virgin waterscape" of the Sacramento Basin—the predevelopment extent of permanent and seasonal marshes. In the Yolo Bypass and proposed North Delta Wildlife Refuge, year-round agriculture might continue on former grassland uplands, while original seasonal wetland areas could be a combination of seasonal agriculture and habitat. Former year-round marshes might be determined and partly restored to core permanent wetlands. By earmarking a percentage of lands to be kept under agricultural easements

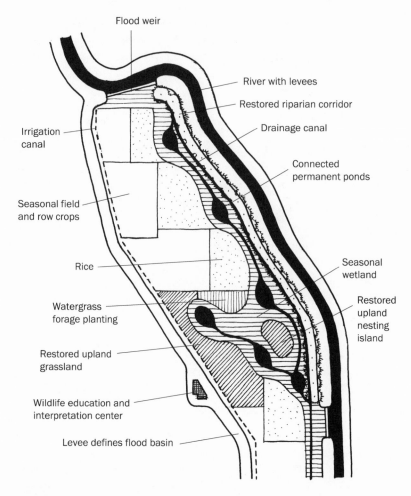

Flood weir

River with levees

Restored riparian corridor

Irrigation canal

Drainage canal

Connected permanent ponds

Seasonal field and row crops

Rice

Seasonal wetland

Watergrass forage planting

Restored upland nesting island

Restored upland grassland

Wildlife education and interpretation center

Levee defines flood basin

Figure 8.7 A complex mosaic of landscape covers and land uses can be established to return multiple functions to intentionally restored flood basins. Drawing by Robert Thayer.

or conservation easements or to be developed for passive recreation or education, a balanced mosaic of land uses might re-emerge in the engineered flood zones of the valley's creeks and streams (figure 8.7).[5]

DAYLIGHTED STREAMS

Valley streams and sloughs have often been straightened, channelized, and placed in underground pipes, leaving them devoid of ecological function.

The Sacramento Valley is one of the most disturbed watersheds on the continent. Most streams have been expropriated for water supply, and many have been engineered to deliver irrigation or remove runoff water. Hydrological criteria for these altered streams are often aimed only at speed and efficiency, to the great detriment of ecological function.

Where possible, bring channelized and undergrounded streams back to the surface and restore their natural meander and cross-section profiles in accordance with basin area and expected flow volumes.

Every watershed or basin, no matter how large or small, serves a drainage area, the configuration of which determines optimal meander frequencies and cross-sectional profiles. Even if only in short reaches, therefore, the return of a functional morphology to stream corridors provides a basis for the natural healing of riparian zones. Channel-forming flows can now be determined for any watercourse, whereupon the relative meander frequency and the cross-sectional flow at bank-full (one- to two-year flood) conditions can also be derived. Streams that regain their ecologically functional form will more easily reestablish the riparian vegetation conditions that come naturally to them, often with no additional planting being necessary, fostering overstory canopy trees and understory shrubs and providing shaded surfaces to keep the water cool and provide fish habitat.

NEARBY NATURE

Most natural ecosystems, such as free-flowing streams, riparian forests, grasslands, seasonal wetland, and marshland, have long since been eliminated from the valley, causing residents to look elsewhere for experiences in natural settings.

A rapidly increasing urban population needs some direct contact with agriculture and access to natural areas if it is to value either one. Yet because valley land has been predominantly private property in the "business" of agriculture, there is considerable resistance to the needs of a growing, nonfarming public for nature-based recreation. The existing network of river, stream, and slough corridors is therefore a framework for providing opportunities for contact between the public and the realms of nature and agriculture.

Restore the representative ecosystems endemic to the Sacramento Valley lifeplace, and give the public access to a portion of each restored ecosystem.

In the rush to restore our bioregional ecosystems, we in the Sacramento Valley region have often forgotten the human factor: we need to see and experience the return of nature to our life-place. As the critical ecosystems of the Sacramento Valley bioregion—its upland woods, grasslands, seasonal wetlands, permanent marsh, and riparian areas—are slowly identified, recognized, and restored, at least a portion of these should be made accessible to the public. Ideally, these sites should also be reachable by means other than cars and be within two to five miles of most towns, suburbs, or cities. Only by being allowed to access and know firsthand the importance, benefits, and delights of habitat and agriculture will the public support actions that help preserve these critical land uses and build lasting emotional and civic bonds with this region. Without such access, the public will care less, and the perpetuity of both habitat and agriculture will be placed at risk. In the lower Sacramento Valley, the Cosumnes River Preserve, the Davis Wetlands, and the Vic Fazio Yolo Basin Wetlands all allow limited public access, a strategy that has no doubt fostered an increased sense of local stewardship.

BIOREGIONAL WILDERNESS

Sacramento Valley residents tend to believe that "wilderness" and wildlands are found only in other, adjacent bioregions and not in theirs.

Too often, living in the Sacramento Valley means succumbing to the common California myth that the Central Valley is some sort of "void," without wildlands, designated wilderness areas, or large territories where "charismatic megafauna" such as mountain lion, black bear, elk, or eagles might be found. Too often the valley is assumed to be an inadequate and incomplete biological habitat, lacking large areas capable of serving as biodiversity reserves that could be connected to expedite the migration, recolonization, and cross-fertilization necessary for species perpetuation. For scientific and/or spiritual purposes, in other words, "wild" is thought to reside elsewhere than here.

Identify and protect the existing and potential wildlands in the midst of and toward the edges of the Sacramento Valley bioregion.

The myth that there are no wildlands in the Sacramento Valley bioregion is just that: a myth. Several significant wild areas exist, some under private management and some in the public domain. The Sutter Buttes, long a "labor of love" for the private Middle Mountain Foundation, is not only the "wild center" and spiritual heart of the bioregion but a significantly large

Figure 8.8 The Cache Creek Wilderness Study Area is representative of several nearby, yet often overlooked, wildlands at the fringes of the Sacramento Valley bioregion. Photograph by Jim Rose; used by permission.

and rich repository of biodiversity as well. Along the western edge of the valley are three major wildlands: the highly remote and federally designated Yolla Bolly–Middle Eel Wilderness, administered by the U.S. Forest Service, graces the conspicuous ridges west of Corning; Snow Mountain, another USFS wilderness, borders the valley some forty-five miles south of the Yolla Bollys; and still further south along the valley's edge lies the Blue Ridge– Berryessa Natural Area (BRBNA). BRBNA includes the Bureau of Land Management's Wilderness Study Areas of Cache Creek/Rocky Creek and Cedar Roughs. These are exceptionally wild and remote areas despite being within one hundred miles of both Sacramento and the San Francisco Bay. The Ishi Wilderness, named after the last truly wild indigenous resident of North America, due north of Chico and due west of Red Bluff, includes low-elevation volcanic oak woodland and chaparral.

When these wild places are considered in relation to smaller wildland areas along the Sacramento River and large potential marshland habitat reserves in the north delta, we see that both the habitat needs of animals and the spiritual needs of humans can be accommodated. Nothing says we must wait for "federal designation" before we identify and preserve the wild territories in our own bioregion. The wild beauty and utility of the Sacramento Valley life-place lie in protecting and connecting these wild reserves, both physically and in our hearts and dreams.

Agricultural Heart

In the Sacramento Valley, most of the best soils have been dedicated to production of food and fiber for well over a century. This dominant pattern is vital to the long-term well-being of the region, and its effect extends beyond fuzzy bioregional boundaries to all continental and global consumers dependent upon the food surpluses we export. Agriculture is our most logical land use and is important far beyond the 10 percent or so of the region's total measurable economic activity ascribable to agriculture. Farming—including orcharding and grazing—is the glue that holds the bioregion together; agriculture, by virtual unanimity of opinion, is the heart of our life-place.

However, because of the ways local food production is driven by global food distribution and conception, the agriculture practiced within this vast territory takes its toll on the surrounding biodiversity and ecosystem functions. Thin profit margins also place the future of agriculture at risk. Sprawling urbanization and continually expanding transit, water, and power corridors threaten both the agricultural heart and the ecosystemic framework.

In the next thirty years, Sacramento Valley residents will have to wrestle with the proper relationship between farming, ecosystem functions, and urban development. Images of Orange County and Silicon Valley—formerly two of the most productive agricultural regions of the state—loom like flashing yellow warning lights in our collective consciousness.

In this bioregion, however, the public understands and supports the critical role of agriculture and the need to preserve agricultural productivity in perpetuity. Unlike the agriculture of some remote midwestern grain-belt farm regions, California agriculture is blessed with an enormous and growing market for its products in its own backyard. In addition, there is expanding popular demand for more sustainable, lower-input agronomic methods and environmentally friendly farm practices and some indication that consumers will pay a premium for such products. Alternative agricultural production, distribution, and marketing are emerging with the expansion of certified organic farms, community-supported agricultural establishments, and direct-to-consumer farmers' markets. Many of these alternative agricultural establishments help reduce the size of the "food-shed" of any particular community. What is needed are the proper practices and mechanisms to prevent the further erosion of agricultural productivity by uncontrolled urbanization and to increase the regenerative capacity of the agriculture that does take place here.

Intertwined with these two basic goals is the need for farming and non-farming publics to *communicate.* As things stand, the nonfarming majority and the farming minority could hardly have less mutual awareness and understanding than they do today; any increase in communication between the two can only benefit the bioregion. Additionally, some means must be found to remunerate farmers for providing the various land service functions we now expect them to provide for "free" out of the thin profit margins on the sale of their commodities. Most important, they must be left with both land and water in perpetuity; lose one (or both), and the food stops growing.

FARMLAND PRESERVATION

Some of the best farmland in the world exists in the Sacramento Valley, yet portions of it are being rapidly consumed by development.

A recent study projected the population of the entire Central Valley (i.e., the Sacramento and San Joaquin Valleys) to grow by eight million people in the next four decades. If that occurs, by 2040, the Central Valley could lose more than one million acres of farmland to development (figure 8.9).[6]

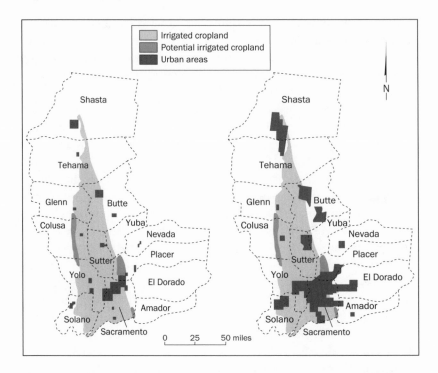

Figure 8.9 Urban expansion on irrigated cropland in the Sacramento Valley of California. *Left:* 1993 urbanization. *Right:* projected expansion by 2040, assuming current land use trends. Based on original cartography by Rudolph Platzek for the American Farmland Trust.

The prospect of seeing so much land removed from biological production is unthinkable to a majority of current valley residents, yet little legal framework or adequate regional planning policy exists to curtail development on prime agricultural soil. Federal and state governments seem incapable and unwilling to take steps to counter the slow loss of agricultural land uses to urban development. County governments, most strapped for budget money and lacking regional police power, have only limited effectiveness. Clearly, this is the single most critical problem facing the Sacramento Valley bioregion at this time. While the newly formed Great Valley Center is directing a considerable amount of effort toward this problem, it has only limited power to bring about a solution.

Identify and preserve in perpetuity the best farmlands in the valley, and mitigate the loss of agricultural land by preserving a great deal more of it than is developed.

It is not hard to identify the best farmlands, only hard to preserve them. A simple ingredient is the only thing lacking: *resolve.* A truly bioregional solution seems to be the only viable alternative. What is needed is a strategic agricultural reserve incorporating the most productive farmlands to be protected outright from development. Outside the reserve, a multicounty agricultural mitigation ordinance framework, involving transfers of development rights between cities and counties, is needed as well. Developers displacing critical agricultural land would be required to set aside conservation easements on prime agricultural land at a ratio of at least five acres preserved for one acre developed. Transfers of development rights and geographic restrictions on where mitigation must take place with respect to development would tighten loopholes in the system and offer equitable distribution of the benefits of development versus preservation.

Obviously, urban development and agricultural land preservation are two sides of the same coin. By means of compact development, the potential growth in the Sacramento Valley might consume less than half the acreage it would with the continuation of "sprawl" development, yielding a considerable advantage to prime farmlands. Although at present, "development" is seen as the "positive" and inevitable apogee of land use, built on "negative space," or farmland, this perception must change—and it will, but only if the value placed on farmland is, in itself, collectively held and ultimately positive.

BIOREGIONAL WATER

The Sacramento River Basin is already the principal source of origin for the largest irrigation project in the Western world. Further transfers of water, either temporary or permanent, may reduce the Sacramento Valley bioregion's ability to support agricultural uses and environmental values.

Through the Central Valley (federal) and State Water Project aqueducts, Sacramento River Basin water is expropriated to regions far beyond its boundaries, serving some thirty million people and irrigating millions of acres of farmland. Thirty-three million acre-feet of water fall annually on the basin as rain; about fifteen million of that either infiltrates, evaporates, or transpires from plants; the rest—eighteen million acre-feet—runs off the land's surface. Of that runoff, six million acre-feet are used in local agriculture, another six million are exported southward, and one million are designated for urban and industrial uses within the basin. This leaves about five million acre-feet for "environmental" water to keep all rivers and streams and their dependent biotic communities "alive."[7]

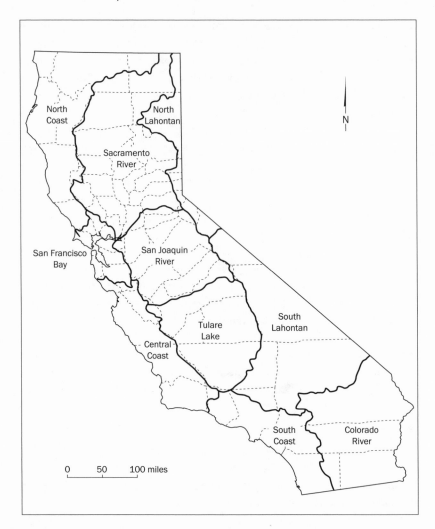

Figure 8.10 Hydrologic regions of California. Water transfers between agriculture and other uses should be restricted to those within, not between, regions. Map based on original cartography by the California Resources Agency, *California Water Plan Update* (Sacramento, Calif.: Department of Water Resources, October 1994).

Confounding this equation are water transfers. A water transfer is a temporary exchange of a water right between a user with excess water and a user in need of water. Water transfers have the potential to reduce not only in-stream uses of water but also the viability of agriculture and ag-related economies. Currently, there are few legal means of protecting environmental or agricultural flows from the potentially negative effects of water transfers. These negative effects include reduced farm-related employment and economic benefits due to fields left fallow for lack of water; lower groundwater levels and quality when groundwater is pumped to free surface water for transfer; and damage to wetlands or fisheries because of reduced instream flows.

Give environmental and in-stream uses the same legal standing as urban, industrial, and agricultural water uses, and limit future water transfers between any parties or uses to only those within the generally assumed hydrologic boundaries of the bioregion.

California manages the state's water quality by hydrologic regions, each of which is home to a Regional Water Quality Control Board office. These hydrologic regions are defined by major river and stream basins and are roughly coincidental with the California Biodiversity Council's designation of the state's bioregions (figure 8.10). Future water transfers should be constrained within each of these major regions, one of which is the Sacramento River hydrologic basin. Limiting water transfers to this "life-place" scale allows flexibility for a particular life-place to meet its various water needs without exceeding its carrying capacity or impoverishing either its agricultural or environmental base. Trusts could be established for the various uses (urban, agricultural, and environmental) within each bioregion or life-place, and temporary transfers of water could be exchanged, sold, or donated to and from each.

LIFE-PLACE "FOODSHED"

The average supermarket food item has traveled excessively—nearly 1,300 miles before it reaches the local consumer—yet the Sacramento Valley generates nearly two billion dollars in agricultural production, mostly for consumption in other regions, states, or countries.[8]

If one were to draw a hypothetical circle defining the existing "foodshed" of California, it would be three thousand miles across, roughly the east-west extent of the coterminous United States. In contrast, the foodshed of a typical farmers' market is on the order of five hundred miles across, and covers roughly one thirty-sixth of the area of the California foodshed. For this reason, considerable energy is "embodied" in the typical supermarket food item when we factor in the oil-derived pesticides, fertilizers, and fuel for cultivating and harvesting machines and all the processing, packaging, and transporting of the food from field to table. The ratio of these energy inputs (translated into calories) to the energy output from the food itself is astronomical: often on the order of ten to one.

To develop agriculture originally, humans had to receive more caloric energy from the food than they expended to grow it. Farm animals, then later wind and water power, and most recently fossil fuel have provided the increasing energy inputs to obtain the calories needed for survival. How sustainable is this?

Consider the life-place as a foodshed, and support local consumption of locally produced foods.

The simplest solution to the problem of this pattern is a two-word sentence: *Eat locally.* We who reside in the Sacramento Valley bioregion are blessed with over 250 different crops we can easily grow here; why should we be eating imported foods? While the current market-driven cash crop agriculture will remain, it is also possible and desirable to develop a strong local "foodshed" by means of community-supported farms, local farmers' markets, local marketing networks, and community food security organizations that ensure that food is available for the most disadvantaged sectors of the community. We should pay the slight increase in cost for the food grown locally and consider the surcharge a local charity donation or, better yet, an investment in the long-term viability of the life-place. Nationwide, the organic, localized food sector of agriculture is growing at 20 percent per year.[9] Here in the Sacramento Valley we have a chance to exceed that figure. This is one of the most logical life-places in the world in which to nurture and support the local foodshed.

A bioregion like the Sacramento Valley (less than two hundred miles in its greatest dimension) is an ideal scale for conceptualizing and actualizing self-reliance in food. At this scale, direct marketing is possible. The expanding population of the valley, while a danger to agricultural production if not placed off prime agricultural land, constitutes, moreover, a growing market for locally produced food. With some of the best soil and climate in the world, there is no limit to the integration of life-place, land use, and identity possible by joining inhabitation with food production and consumption.

Many strategies for implementation are already in place. Many communities already sponsor farmers' markets, with coordinated times to allow farmers to make the circuits. Community-supported farms have been established as willing local markets have been identified. Extending this status quo, truck farms and organic vegetable and fruit production leases might be implemented on publicly owned open-space lands as a productive alter-

Figure 8.11 The Davis Farmers' Market is not only a manifestation of a reasonably scaled and potentially sustainable foodshed but a keystone of the community. Photograph by Randii MacNear.

native to sterile landscape maintenance. Community gardens could be established on long-vacant lots unlikely to be developed. Citizens can form (some already have formed) cooperative food markets and neighborhood buying groups. Finally, agriculture can be celebrated and emphasized through deliberate landscape design and maintenance all the way from the country into the heart of the city.

EXPANDED "FARMING" ROLE

Farmers provide many land services expected by the nonfarming public without being paid for them.

Although there are certainly some farm subsidies, for the most part farmers must pay for all necessary stewardship of the lands under their management from the slim profit margins they receive from crop or commodity sales (on the order of 2 to 3 percent on their capital investments). We, the nonfarming public, expect farmers to provide clean air, clean water, aesthetic scenery, open space, wildlife habitat, aquifer recharge, and flood control, yet we pay them only for providing a food or fiber commodity.

Find ways to pay farmers for the ecological, cultural, and stewardship services they provide.

There is not now and never has been such a thing as a totally "free" market for agriculture in the United States. Many agricultural commodities have always been protected by tariffs or supported directly or indirectly by subsidies in some form or other. Instead of paying farmers not to grow certain crops, why not pay them to provide other services urban dwellers expect them to provide? Farmers and rural landowners should be allocated funds to restore riparian streams and sloughs, provide filter strips to protect soil from eroding into drainage sloughs, hold winter stormwater on rice fields to provide waterfowl habitat, build irrigation tailwater ponds, and engage in other beneficial management practices.

Farmers are at least in part correct when they claim to be the "original" environmentalists. They have a tradition of dynamically managing land under multiple uses and inputs for a variety of tangible outputs. One of the most organized and energetic land managers I know, Jan Lowrey, is a lifelong farmer and rancher who has recently taken on the role of executive director of the Cache Creek Conservancy. Thousands of farmers like Jan would be glad to apply their considerable skill and experience at multigoal, multimethod land management if the general public saw fit to pay them for it.

NATURAL BEEF

The average American eats nearly one hundred pounds of beef per year, yet contemporary beef production consumes resources and affects the environment disproportionately to its value as a food.[10]

Most of the environmental impact of beef production can be traced to the considerable irrigation, fertilizer, pesticides, and herbicides required by the field corn, alfalfa, and other crops that cattle consume, and most of the water pollution comes from nitrogen concentrations from feedlots, where cattle are kept in close quarters. Most of this process results not in lean muscle mass but only in added "fat," which the doctors tell us is not particularly healthy for us in the first place.

Form regional "natural" beef cooperatives that provide premium products to local and regional markets.

There is no reason to abandon beef production altogether; not only is the meat very popular, but it is also one of the only ways to generate protein from land not particularly suitable for row or field crops. By minimizing the extraneous, fat-producing, resource-wasting steps in the delivery of beef to the table, however, a product that is healthier to human individuals and to the environment might be guaranteed. Feedlots could be eliminated, and countless acres of land and acre-feet of water that now grow field corn and other supplemental grains could be redirected toward crops producing more efficient and nutritious carbohydrate calories. Beef fed substantially on natural grasses contains more beneficial omega-3 fatty acids and less cholesterol. An evolution in the public taste for beef might coincide with new marketing regimes and new recipes for diffusing the leaner product into the market. Prices would be higher as well, but experience from other American market segments suggests that people will likely pay for beef that is raised locally, organically, from cattle that are not fattened, fed with hormones, or forced to live in cramped, water-polluting quarters. We could turn for lessons to countries such as Argentina, which has been consuming range-fed beef for several centuries. In the foothill cattle country of the Sacramento Basin, premium "natural" or grass-fed beef cooperatives might be restructured to market their products directly to the bioregion's own consumers, led by gourmet positioning in local, upscale restaurants. The Gamble Ranch in the BRBNA has already achieved considerable success in this endeavor and sells Argentine-style grass-fed Black Angus beef.[11]

"Natural beef" ranches could also double as ecotourist destinations. Ranchers Scott and Hank Stone, adjacent to the BRBNA region, sponsor income-producing agricultural tours called "Combines, Bovines, and Fine Wines," featuring their beef cattle operations, their lowland crops, and a local winery in the Dunnigan Hills. In the nearby Bear Valley ranching district of BRBNA, a world-class wildflower habitat has prompted the acquisition of conservation easements for ranches in the highly scenic valley by the American Land Conservancy. This opens a potent opportunity for a natural beef marketing project in combination with overall tourism and environmental education in the entire BRBNA.

COVER CROPS

Most local crops are grown as monocultures, and fields typically remain bare, exposed to sun and wind, much of the year.

For many months of the year, fields in this region lie bare, soil exposed to wind and rain, with furrows prepped for spring planting. This practice aggravates wind-borne soil erosion, exacerbates flooding, and makes weeds more problematic. Row crops planted are nearly always monocultures. Even

Figure 8.12 Cover crops like this legume interplanted between orchard rows exemplify a new direction away from monocultures and toward multiple-goal, sustainable agriculture. Photograph by Robert Thayer.

vineyard and orchard crops, with permanent plantings, expose bare soil for most of the year. The spatial and temporal pattern subjects the crop to infestations of pests, since little or no habitat for beneficial insects exists, and bare soil is an open invitation for invasive weeds. How many of my fellow nonfarmers have, like me, pondered the fate of the airborne agricultural soils blown horizontally during our frequent, strong north winds? Is it presumed that what is removed from one field and sent southward is replaced by airborne soil brought in on the next north wind from the fields of northerly neighbors? Or is there a net loss of soil in this flat, windy valley as aeolian processes deliver topsoil into the ditch and drain system? According to some soil scientists, most of this region is not considered a high soil erosion zone, but particulate air quality during north winds might indicate otherwise.

Plant compatible cover crops in the times and spaces between major cash crops.

The Yolo County Resource Conservation District (YCRCD) reports that when tomato fields are planted in the off-season with a combination cover crop of peas and vetch, a 40 to 70 percent reduction in winter stormwater runoff volume can be attained, with increased infiltration and concurrent control of wind- and water-borne soil erosion. Furthermore, the YCRCD has found increased yields in the subsequent year's tomato crop, with better soil tilth and beneficial effects for preventing tomato root diseases due to increased microbial activity in the soil.[12]

In many of the local orchards and vineyards in this bioregion, growers know that interplanting with cover crops (figure 8.12) checks weed growth, increases water percolation and absorption, generates and retains important soil nutrients, metabolizes undesirable chemicals, cools tree and vine roots, prevents soil erosion, reduces pollution of tailwater canals, and harbors beneficial insects that prey on crop pests. Cover crops have many applications beyond vineyards and orchards: corn can be interplanted with legumes to the mutual benefit of both.

TAILWATER PONDS

In the Sacramento Valley bioregion, considerable soil is lost and water pollution generated by irrigation tailwater running off cultivated fields.

Typical agricultural irrigation applications in the region generate excess water that runs off irrigated fields by means of "tail" or "toe" ditches. Often, when this irrigation tailwater returns to canals, it is heavily laden with nitrates, phosphorus, other undesirable chemicals, and particulate sediment. It is not uncommon for the soil lost in runoff from crop fields in this region to weigh more than the harvested crop itself. Without deliberate action, this soil loss moves down the "synthetic" watershed of irrigated and drained fields, clogging storm drains, creek channels, and settling basins and ultimately requiring costly excavation.

Capture irrigation tailwater in two-stage tailwater ponds, the first to capture sediment and the second to provide wildlife habitat, water recycling, aquifer recharge, and a buffer for nitrates and chemicals.

John Anderson of the YCRCD has championed tailwater ponds (figure 8.13a–b) for years, having installed several on his own fields. Anderson's ponds have rather straightforward, oblong first-stage ponds to enable access for heavy equipment to excavate deposited field soil for reapplication to the fields. Once sediment has been captured in the first-stage pond, water flows into a larger, more elaborate second-stage pond with irregular

Figures 8.13a–b *A, right:* Farmer John Anderson's two-stage tail-water pond traps sediment in the first, oblong pond, then returns the water to the second, habitat pond, shown at eye level in *B, below.* Tailwater ponds achieve multiple conservation functions for valley agricultural fields. Photographs by John Anderson.

boundaries and an island for nesting winter waterfowl. Upland native plants and shrubs are planted on the berms resulting from pond excavation, and native bunchgrasses cover the understory, while marsh reeds and sedges emerge at the pond edges. According to Anderson, one pond for each hundred acres of level fields is sufficient to provide the multiple benefits of tailwater ponds: increased soil reclamation, reduced erosion and sedimentation of ditches and drainage canals, recirculated water, additional wildlife habitat, and support for beneficial insects.

An additional benefit of tailwater ponds is purely aesthetic. Each field is "marked" by an obvious symbol of good stewardship, and the break in monotony from mechanized agriculture provided by the tailwater pond—often punctuated by wildlife—lends a dimension of delight to an otherwise featureless and bland landscape view.[13]

NATURAL EDGES

Cultivation of vast expanses of valley land has eliminated much of the diverse range of native grasses, forbs, insects, birds, fish, reptiles, amphibians, and small mammals.

Most farm operations need reasonably large fields (fifty to one hundred acres minimum) to be "clear" of obstruction to make operation of mechanized farm equipment pay for itself. Yet too often the same "clean farm" mentality applied to the fields is mistakenly and inefficiently applied to the leftover sloughs, canal edges, corners, and leftover fragments, as if these, too, were providing a cash crop. In fact, the "crop" that these leftover lands provide is habitat for biodiversity and ecological functions, for which the farmer is not directly paid. A completely different approach is called for in the management of nonfarmed fragments from that used within the crop field itself.

Manage leftover, narrow, and hard-to-farm land fragments as multipurpose conservation areas.

Since the "matrix" of land in the valley is now agricultural, it is up to the fringes of agriculture to provide those ecological services once provided by the extensive interior patches. On upland fringes, roadside verges, and strips between canals and roads, deep-rooted native bunchgrasses can be reestablished, providing habitat, anchoring soil, and preventing erosion; they will also require little in the way of maintenance dollars, chemicals, and expenditures. In canals and ditches, sedges and other native, water-adapted grasses

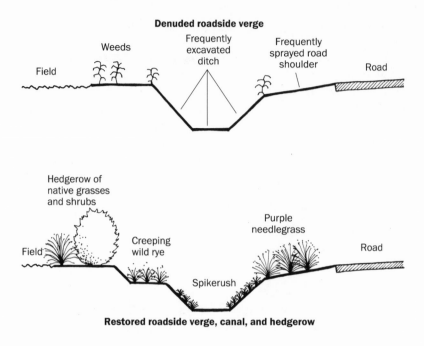

Figures 8.14a–b Typical "hard-to-farm" fragments, like roadside verges and irrigation ditches *(A, top),* can easily be modified to expand conservation values and reduce maintenance *(B, bottom).* Drawing by Robert Thayer.

can be established, and in upland areas, shrubs can be planted extensively, giving rise to wildlife habitat. Minor stream and slough corridors can be modified to reintroduce flood terraces and riparian trees, which will eventually shade out noxious ground-covering weeds that tend to choke the flow of water and require excessive maintenance (figures 8.14a–b).

Taken as a suite of landscape (or "farmscape") management strategies, these practices would go a very long way toward reducing farm inputs and expenditures and increasing the sustainability of regional farming. In addition, such natural farm edges would reverse a trend toward debilitation of the valley grassland/marshland/riparian ecosystems, win many friends for the farmers, and provide all with a more beautiful, logical place to live.

The management of nonfarmed edges and fragments as native habitat is a pattern reproducible at any scale, from the smallest field corner to the entire bioregion. In essence, the interlacing of naturally managed habitat with agricultural land represents the best stewardship possible in this place.

Regenerative Communities and Infrastructure

Unfortunately for our life-place, it is easier for humans to build cities on flat agricultural land than on any other kind of site. In the Sacramento Valley, grading land to provide pads for houses is hardly more difficult than plowing for crops. As urbanization expands outward, both agriculture and new development compete for the same "inexpensive" land, and development often wins this battle, since final-rotation "crops" of houses bring more profit than tomatoes, rice, almonds, or wheat. A seemingly endless supply of flat, buildable land capable of being wrested out of agricultural production has induced a low-density residential development pattern in the Central Valley averaging only about 4.5 persons per acre (compared to 5.7 persons per acre in coastal regions of the state). This resultant sprawl, from nearly all political perspectives, is unsustainable.[14]

However, as with attitudes toward agriculture and biodiversity, there is more agreement on *what* needs to be done in the way of urban development than one might expect; disagreement centers on *how.* As of this writing, dire predictions are being made as to the tens of millions of new human residents who are expected to move into the Central Valley in the next four decades. The growth issue in the valley is enframed within a triangle of possible options for any city or community: continued peripheral (or sprawled) growth, infill (or compact) growth, or no growth at all. Peripheral growth is constrained by increasing public and professional concern over loss of farmland and by escalating costs of providing infrastructure and city services far from city centers, yet is seen by the building industry as the path of least resistance. Infill, or compact growth that rebuilds on formerly developed sites, abandoned lands, and vacant city parcels, is widely accepted within professional planning and many local government circles as the best alternative. Yet this option is constrained by public fears that increased density will bring undesirable residents, added crime, and lower property values. The "no-growth" alternative for valley communities is simply constrained by the constitutional and legal framework of California and the United States, the strong predilection toward private property rights (i.e., the right to develop), and the need for any community to accept its "fair share" of regional growth. Each community or planning jurisdiction, therefore, must tailor its growth management approach within this policy triangle, with each extreme corner being a difficult political position to defend.

Fortunately, a number of patterns have emerged that respond to the need to control urbanization and its impact on agricultural heartlands, biodiversity frameworks, and resources. Together they paint a picture of possibility for the present and future populations of the valley.

COMPACT CITIES AND TOWNS

Low-density development on the edges of valley cities, towns, and suburbs consumes valuable farmland, increases traffic, reduces air quality, and creates more civic expense for infrastructure than it pays for.

While "sprawl" is a condition endemic to much of the American landscape, it is particularly acute in the Sacramento Valley bioregion, since cities and towns are often surrounded by flat, artificially "inexpensive" farmland with few other limitations to development. A mild climate eliminates the need for extensive foundations. Water, which often comes from the former agricultural use of the site, is normally adequate for the conversion to urban uses. One look at an air photo of the region will reveal the undifferentiated wedge of development between Interstate 80 and Route 50 northeast of Sacramento as characteristic of the potential for sprawl in this life-place. Much of the region has a gross density in its developed areas (counting commercial areas) of only three dwelling units per acre. A sprawled development pattern not only "eats up" the best farmland but also literally "stretches" infrastructure budgets beyond their limits, and the polluted air from resultant single-passenger auto traffic accumulates in the valley like water in a large bathtub, making Sacramento one of the worst air quality regions of the country.

Grow cities and towns inward and upward, not outward.

Steering this region into more compact, responsible land use while improving quality of life involves several strategies. Making prime farmland off limits to development with severe penalties and high mitigation ratios would be an essential step, with transfers of development rights accruing instead to parcels within developed areas or city boundaries. Urban growth boundaries, such as those now well known in Portland and required for all Oregon cities, should be established for most valley cities and towns. Townhouses, condominiums, and multistory apartment buildings can be attractively designed to augment single-family home markets, while single-family homes can be sited as two-story units with smaller "footprints" on the land. Creative zoning could allow increased development in low-density areas. A "cellular" approach to suburban renovation would create more spatially frequent neighborhood service centers, facilitating nonpowered and pedestrian circulation. Key to making increased density not only tolerable but desirable is a redoubled commitment to open-space corridors. Pedestrian spines connecting urban amenities to rural and wildland recreation venues become the "payoff" for allowing increased density. But the major change must come from residents themselves seeing the negative effects of continued sprawl on their own degraded quality of life.

A major factor preventing cities from becoming more dense is a mistaken assumption that density creates greater personal risk. In actuality, when auto ownership and travel are considered, dense cities are statistically much safer places than sprawled suburbs. Perceptions that density equals poverty and crime may be dispelled by comparison with statistics from the plentiful examples of higher-density, relatively crime-free neighborhoods.

INFILL DEVELOPMENT

"Edge" development on "new" land is always the path of least resistance for new urban growth in the valley, yet most towns, cities, and developed areas contain within their borders considerable undeveloped or underutilized space.

As villages grow into towns, and towns into cities, land uses and industries often change. Some lands remain vacant or become underutilized due to changes in industry, communication, transit, or technology. Former manufacturing industries fold and move elsewhere or overseas; agricultural processing plants consolidate or close; downtown businesses or shopping centers go bankrupt; transit shifts from barge, to rail, to truck, to air freight; telephone, power, equipment, and other service yards shrink; gas stations move to the freeway edges of town, often leaving columns of toxic pollution beneath their former sites. Yet zoning dominated by single uses and a false presumption that density equals crime prevent many of these sites from being developed.

Locate "new" development on "old" sites.

With rapid transformation of the "industrial" economy to the "information/service" economy, vast opportunities arise for converting former industrial and commercial lands into housing. In Sacramento, the rail yard of a former Southern Pacific railroad maintenance facility in the heart of downtown presents one such solution: build a complex, mixed-use neighborhood with apartments, attached housing, commercial, office, and recreation uses. Sites like this offer a natural "escape route" for residents to access both urban amenities and semiwild natural areas. Zoning that encourages "granny flats"—additional studio or one-bedroom apartments to be built as out-

Figure 8.15 The Crepeville Cafe building in Davis is an excellent example of mixed-use infill development. Apartments on the second and third floors offer housing above the ground-floor cafe. The site is located along major bike routes across from Central Park and the Farmers' Market. Photograph by Robert Thayer.

buildings or attached to garages—can add density to existing low-density suburbs. Second-story housing over street-level commercial districts, once the standard pattern for nineteenth-century America, can be resurrected for great benefit (figure 8.15).

The fear has always been that increased density only creates problems with transportation and land use, when in many instances, it resolves them. When residents have amenities closer to home, they walk more and drive less. Economies thrive on well-mixed land uses (including residential, commercial, and office space). In Taipei, one of the densest cities on earth, buildings are typically five to ten stories tall, with the ground floor dedicated to small commercial shops, the second floor reserved for offices, and the third floor and above for residential apartments. The vertical integration of Asian cities comes naturally to Asian cultures, whereas the western American illusion of "wide open spaces" works only when population is low. As population increases, new archetypes must be used to stimulate the public into accepting density.

NEW VILLAGE CENTERS

Shopping centers in the Sacramento Valley bioregion are too often single-story, single-purpose, sprawled, "out-of-style" environments devoid of character, vitality, or complexity.

As in many other regions, the cultural geography of auto-dominated shopping centers in the Sacramento Valley can be "read" chronologically and dated to the recent waves of development that have swept over the region. Most shopping centers have very low floor-area-to-asphalt ratios, contain few land uses other than shopping, and are not connected to other logical civic uses like parks, libraries, schools, and day care. Shopping centers almost always "aim" toward the freeway or commercial strip highway and turn their "backs" on adjacent neighborhoods. In addition, there is a "cultural ecological" hierarchy in which only a few centers in a particular region seem to be "in style" at any given time; centers built as recently as ten years ago drop from fashion and soon find themselves languishing in vacancy and misuse. While shopping centers have replaced some functions once provided by town centers (e.g., hangout places for teens), they are nowhere near as complex, diverse, flexible, or resilient as the traditional "Main Street" environment.

Redesign aging shopping centers as dense, vertically integrated, mixed-land-use centers containing commercial shops, offices, recreation, civic amenities, residential apartments, and townhouses.

The aging, semiforgotten, single-story suburban shopping center offers a prime opportunity to bring back into residential neighborhoods what was once provided by "Main Street." By building up two or more stories, placing parking partially underground or beneath commercial spaces, and offering diverse amenities, one can transform the moribund shopping mall into a vital village center for residential neighborhoods. With integrated housing, it can "aim" into the neighborhood with inviting and accessible pedestrian entrances, in addition to welcoming traffic from major arterial roads. With some creativity, new shopping villages can be linked with parks, day care centers, and community gardens. Like ecosystems, neighborhood shopping "villages" with a high degree of complexity and mixed use will be more resilient and lively than the land use monocultures they replace (figure 8.16).

Figure 8.16 Underutilized shopping centers offer potential for redevelopment as higher-density, multiuse village centers combining commercial, civic, and residential functions, as in this rendering by Eric Rowell. Courtesy of Randall Fleming, Community Design and Planning Services, U.C. Davis.

REGENERATIVE TRANSIT

Single-passenger automobile gridlock has begun to plague the Sacramento Valley, just as it has overwhelmed former agricultural regions like Orange County and Silicon Valley.

One does not have to look far to see the most obvious future consequence of the Sacramento Valley's over-reliance on the automobile: the dense traffic of the Los Angeles Basin and San Francisco Bay Area is what lies ahead for the Sacramento region if current trends continue. Once considered a backwater region of California, with ample room to grow and few traffic problems, the southern Sacramento Valley metropolitan area has become a nearly exclusive automobile domain. In terms of number of cars owned and automobile miles driven per capita, Sacramento ranks among the highest.

Provide multimodal bus-bicycle-rail transit, using fees extracted from the "real" costs of automobile sprawl.

If transportation modes were charged according to their actual costs and impacts, trucks would pay many times their current road taxes, and gasoline would be priced as it is in Europe: nearly three times as expensive as in the United States. "Subsidies" for nonauto transit, like bus and train systems, would not be necessary. One of the most sustainable transit systems in the Sacramento Valley bioregion is in Davis, and, in particular, on the U.C. Davis campus (figure 8.17), where a student-run bus company manages low-polluting, natural gas buses, and high parking fees discourage driving. Bicycles abound, and the transit and circulation system safely separates pedestrians from bicycles. A mild climate and flat topography make such a multimodal transit system possible. By extending Davis's model, the valley could fuel buses with some combination of biogas, solar electricity, and/or hydrogen. Buses and local trains could expand their accommodation for bicycles to make combined bus-rail-bike trips more feasible.

Sacramento can easily learn what eastern U.S. and European cities have known all along: when cities are dense and petroleum is accurately priced, other forms of regenerative transit become possible. Rail lines could be reclaimed for local travel between Redding and Sacramento, as has been done with Amtrak's Capitol Corridor route between Auburn and San Jose. Similarly underutilized rail lines between Sacramento, West Sacramento, Davis, and Woodland could be extended to Sacramento Airport to make a polygonal transit corridor that might guide future density and mixed land use development adjacent to rail corridors. These, in turn, could be linked to other areas by bicycle paths.

Figure 8.17 Combinations of bus, bicycle, and rail trips have great potential for serving the transit needs of the Sacramento Valley. Such multiuse modes are well established on the region's university campuses, Amtrak's Capitol Corridor route, and Sacramento's rapid transit system of bus and light-rail lines. Photograph by Robert Thayer.

RECYCLED WATER

Most reasonable water sources have already been exploited in the Sacramento Valley, yet population growth and development continue unchecked.

In a region dominated by agriculture, plagued by declining habitat quality, and threatened with an exploding human population, the need for additional water sources runs smack into its own obvious limits. There simply is not enough available "new" fresh water to supply the competing needs of these three groups of users. Too often, each party (farmers, environmental managers, and urban water interests) distrusts the other two, or two form an alliance against the remaining "other." While this three-way dance of alliance and avoidance of responsibility continues, the obvious fact is ignored: there is no more "new" water.

Reuse water in as many different ways, in as many different land uses, and at as many different scales as possible.

Fortunately, water is one of the most reusable resources on earth; it can be cleansed and reused many times and at many scales. Agriculture has only scratched the surface of recycling, using treated water from urban areas for certain crop applications. With careful monitoring and revision of arcane water laws, tertiary-treated sewage effluent can be reused for many agricultural, industrial, or commercial uses. New communities can be plumbed for "gray water recovery"; agricultural tailwater can be recaptured and reused or held for wildlife habitat; water-use "loops" in industry can be closed; and compatible industrial uses can be collocated so that one industry's wastewater becomes another's resource. Parking lots can store rainwater in underground tanks beneath the cars; roofs can gather rainwater into cisterns for dry-season storage. Constructed wetlands can treat or "polish" wastewater to a quality useful for agriculture or wildlife.

At the largest scale, recycling water in this bioregion might imply allowing winter rains to recharge underground aquifers overdrafted by summer irrigation; the floodplain of the Sacramento River itself, if managed properly, could serve as a "reservoir" to hold water. At smaller, household scales, gray water collected from sinks and showers using biodegradable soaps could be directed through simple sand filters and applied to vegetable gardens and landscape shrubbery.

The key to recycling water is largely one of education—learning that the hydrological cycle of nature can be emulated at many scales and applications in the humanized landscape.

PHOTOVOLTAIC ROOFS

The Sacramento Valley region is one of the sunniest in the country, yet we still rely primarily on nonrenewable fossil-fuel energy generated somewhere else.

Fossil fuel is the most potent drug of the developed world. The daunting task of facing up to the certain exhaustion of fossil fuel and the dependencies it causes is usually pushed far into the future, to be considered by a future generation. Yet ultimately the implicit entropy of a fossil-fuel-dependent culture must be confronted. Why not start now?

In the Sacramento Valley bioregion, most of our electrical production comes from fossil fuels (and most of that fossil fuel is from out of state), while our two most naturally abundant energy sources, agricultural biomass and ample solar energy, go largely untapped. In this life-place, hot summers are part of our very culture, with temperatures on many days exceeding 100 degrees Fahrenheit. The energy now embodied in the sunlight falling on the roofs and south walls of structures in the Sacramento Valley bioregion,

Figure 8.18 The best untapped source of clean, renewable energy for the Sacramento Valley is the rooftops of its buildings. Photovoltaic electric panels provide a majority of the electrical energy needed by this residential dwelling. Photograph courtesy of the Sacramento Municipal Utility District.

especially in summer, is mostly wasted on overheating interior space, which is then compensated for by traditional mechanical air-conditioning driven by fossil fuel or large hydroelectric power plants located elsewhere in the region or out of state.

Generate a significant portion of the region's power needs by capturing and converting sunlight via photovoltaic arrays integrated with structures and built surfaces.

Some estimates place the amount of solar energy harvestable by the built surfaces of the environment to be equivalent to the entire electrical demand of that environment. Parking lots, industrial and commercial building roofs, garages, and high-rise buildings may indeed be this region's electrical ace in the hole. Photovoltaic (PV) energy has an advantage tailor-made to this region: when temperatures are hottest, current from solar electric generation is greatest, so air conditioners run from PV power sources would show an exceptional source-to-end-use match. PV systems can be installed to add power to the grid when the sun shines, using the grid itself as a "storage" device. As one of the most advanced utilities in the nation, the Sacramento Municipal Utility District (SMUD) has pioneered cost-sharing programs for PV systems in its "PV Pioneers" program. Subsidies for the relatively high initial costs for PV installation are rising as SMUD recognizes the writing on the wall for future power in the region.[15]

As with water, sunlight-generated electrical power can cut across all scales and contextual applications, from tiny wristwatches to immense, factory-sized power plants. PV will achieve the best possible role in this region, however, when the hard surfaces of existing buildings and parking lots are converted to PV arrays that serve a dual purpose as both walls or roofs *and* power plants. Building-integrated PV is the architectural technology of the future, and its application in this bioregion should be preeminent in North America. A time may evolve when the integration of electrical production and local architecture will be looked upon as the best civic aesthetic possible.

NATURAL DRAINAGE

Paving the land has "hardened" the land cover, rendered it more impervious, and deprived the soil of water and the watercourses of their original ecological functions.

When urban development is built in natural floodplains, and when a high percentage of that developed land area is converted from porous, vegetated soil to impervious paving, more stormwater runs off the land and less percolates into the soil. This increases the severity of flooding, in terms of both the amount of floodwater and the rapidity with which that floodwater builds up. Often, rainwater falling on roofs never passes over permeable soil at all, dropping instead from hard roof, to gutter, to buried lateral, to storm sewer, to concrete-lined ditch, to river or bay. As a consequence of its hardened pathway, the runoff gathers pollutants en route, offers little in the way of aesthetics or habitat value, can never recharge the groundwater, and, perhaps most important, drops away from the conscious consideration of humans: out of sight, out of mind.

Build permeable pathways into the course of rainwater runoff, and link these "natural drainage" ways together at multiple scales.

Rainwater, when falling, collecting, and moving across developed areas, needs permeable landscape surfaces to percolate into soil and serve its typical eco-

Figure 8.19 Natural or "open" drainage systems, such as that shown here, in the author's neighborhood of Village Homes, return many ecological functions to the residential landscape. Photograph by Robert Thayer.

logical functions. At all scales, the path of stormwater should be softened to enable water to sink into the soil. In Village Homes, the community where I live, a "natural," open-drainage swale deliberately designed for water infiltration, aesthetics, and habitat value lies a mere sixteen feet from my office. The community has become world renowned for its environmental features, one of which is the storm drain system (figure 8.19), all of which is aboveground, designed to emulate a small, natural watershed. Rainwater, if not percolating into the ground close to the downspout, has ample chance to infiltrate the soil before an emergency overflow (very rarely needed) might take it into a traditional storm sewer. The natural drainage system of Village Homes works better than the city storm sewer system, which, when occasionally clogged, backs water up into *our* neighborhood in its search for an exit.

The drainage system in my seventy-acre neighborhood is analogous to the 360,000-acre Putah Creek watershed or the 26,500-square-mile Sacramento Hydrologic Basin: when rain falls, most of it should infiltrate the soil first, not run immediately off the surface of the land. When water is retained and allowed to enter the soil profile, flooding is reduced, trees need less artificial irrigation, soil structure is maintained, wells stay charged, base-level flow in adjacent creeks is more stable over time, erosion is prevented, water quality is improved, fisheries are benefited, and the resultant landscape is ecologically more resilient and visually more attractive.[16]

URBAN-TO-NATURE PATHWAYS

Residents of the typical valley community are forced to use automobiles to reach both urban amenities and nature-based recreation.

Conversion of farmland to the supposedly "higher" economic use of housing in the valley has perpetuated low-density and single-purpose land uses, often separated by considerable distance and linked only by multiple-lane arterial roadways. Much of the most recent housing development has lured residents from other regions by the potential of "more house for the money," but it is a false economy. Often what is gained in floorplan space per dollar is lost in the quality of surrounding community life.

Link residential areas to urban amenities and natural ecosystems through accessible, nonmotorized corridors.

Most of us need both urban amenities and contact with nature. We shop, buy groceries, mail packages, drop children off at day care, get haircuts, see doctors, work in offices, warehouses, or factories, worship in churches and synagogues, see movies, go to libraries, drink coffee, or attend school or college. We also watch birds, walk the dog, go for hikes, ride bicycles, have picnics, play sports, camp out occasionally, or just look at clouds by day or stars and moon at night. There would be no earthly reason for these activities to require us to get into an automobile if our communities were planned and built in sensitive relationship to the scale and rhythm of our lives. Placement of a spectrum of these typical land uses along a nonmotorized, pedestrian spine or corridor is an ideal way to serve a multitude of residents without requiring any of them to drive. On a scale of a mile or so, such a pedestrian/bicycle link, free of cars, could lead from the most urban shopping/office/civic center through various residential densities to agriculture, habitat, and wildland open space. Boulder's greenway system is nearly ideal in achieving this goal. In the Sacramento Valley bioregion, the American River Parkway and Bidwell Park in Chico achieve a similar integration. Where no "natural" river or creek exists, however, it is still possible to create corridors of open space connecting natural to urban amenities through a mixture of land uses.

My own neighborhood of Village Homes links two office buildings, a restaurant, apartments, a day care center, a swimming pool, community gardens, playing fields, a vineyard, several orchards, and a dance studio with a well-designed landscaped pathway system. Nothing sets the mind at ease like walking between the necessary functions and geographically distributed joys of life!

Evolution of a Bioregenerative Pattern Language

The patterns just described form a minimal vocabulary with which to suggest a far richer language of life-place structure, function, and restoration. In reality, a near infinite variety of patterns is emerging in response to the challenge of living in this region. These patterns, which connect across scales and across functions, have emerged from necessity and the minds of many individuals. If we do nothing to regenerate our life-place, it will be unsustainable and ultimately lifeless, but by implementing the bioregional urge to become regrounded, we bond ourselves to each other and to the larger community of life.

Here, in the Sacramento Valley, the patterns we need are becoming clear. We must build upon them to live here in a permanent way. It is the collective work we must do.

9 Learning

SPREADING LOCAL WISDOM

All education is environmental education. By what is included or excluded, students are taught they are part of or apart from the natural world. To teach economics, for example, without reference to the laws of thermodynamics or ecology is to teach a fundamentally important ecological lesson: that physics and ecology have nothing to do with the economy. It just happens to be dead wrong.

DAVID ORR, 1994

If you can't find the truth right where you are, where else do you expect to find it?

DOGEN ZENJI, circa 1250

Steve Chainey is lecturing to the class. He has no podium, no slides, no projector or screen, no microphone. Instead, his feet nearly touch the water's edge, and his arms gesture at the gravel bank and young riparian vegetation behind him. The university students listen attentively, standing beside the lower reach of Cache Creek, which for decades has been mined for the aggregate needed to build the roads, foundations, driveways, sidewalks, and concrete walls of the growing cities of the lower Sacramento Valley. Chainey is a restoration ecologist working for a preeminent local environmental consulting firm. He speaks clearly and directly, and his bearded, bespectacled appearance, exceptional delivery, and complete mastery of his subject could make him appear a professor, although this lecture is about as close to the campus as he wants to be. Chainey asks the students why, amid this wreckage of a creek channel, diverted and heavily mined for miles upstream and down, the creek water pooling in front of the class should be so crystal clear. Students take stabs at the answer, most missing the mark. With considerable gesturing, 360-degree pointing, and commentary, Chainey explains that this section of the creek is a "gaining reach," where water enters the stream from beneath the surrounding land due to the hydrological "pooling" of groundwater by the Plainfield Ridge, an underground geological formation that acts as a subsurface dam to back up the groundwater and force it to flow by gravity into the creek. It is October, and there has been no rain for months, yet the water is brilliantly clear, and fish slowly fin in the pools with obvious vigor. Chainey explains that in spite of the decimation of the creek by gravel extraction, there is great potential for restoration here because of these hydrological conditions, and he enumerates the various trees and shrubs that can be encouraged to recolonize this reach with very little extra effort: sandbar willow, Fremont cottonwood, and, higher up on the terraces, valley oak and black walnut. After the impromptu lecture, students can be heard commenting on their newfound truths as they ascend the creek bank back to the waiting university vans.

Bioregions have no walls—only transition zones where one moves from experienced and known territory into lands that clearly feel like another place. Yet one can never know one's bioregion too deeply or too well. Within any particular life-place lies a laboratory so well equipped as to keep countless students of all ages and persuasions busy learning for lifetimes. Yet in the age of the computer and the Internet, it is remarkable how little we rely on this real-world laboratory to teach our students; here-and-now learning has been displaced by "distance" learning, the educational buzzword for the new, presumably electronic, millennium.

But out among the minds of children and adults alike there is fertile ground for the cultivation of real-time, real-place educational experience. In response to today's widening web of "data," students of all ages respond increasingly well to immersion in the wisdom of lessons that they learn by looking deeply around them into the realities of place. Places change, too, so staying put and looking deeply is never boring, for the flow of life gathers, moves, and disperses across particular territories; one must only be mindful of the pace of things. In this manner, each life-place presents a learning stream with countless tributaries. Yet somehow in the course of human evolution, contemporary education seems to have lost its place.

The Current Place of Education

In his book *Earth in Mind*, David Orr asks some rather fundamental questions about education: What are we educating people to be? Successful consumers? Competitive workers? Happy and compassionate people? Should the goal of education be mastery of subject matter? Or should it be the mastery of one's whole person? How could the earth have been so vandalized— not by ignorant people but by those who have been highly educated? Why does education seem to teach abstraction rather than consciousness? Why does it separate mind from body? Why are we taught not to believe sensation and experience? Is it constructive, advisable, or necessary to break education down into "disciplines" when human experience is totally integrated? What should be its central narrative? *Where* should education take place?[1]

Most readers of this book are probably well educated via traditional means: elementary school, secondary school, college. Some perhaps have teaching credentials, and others have graduate or professional degrees. The typical educational "highway" from K through Ph.D. is for the most part unchallenged in its orientation and content.

At the elementary, junior high, and high school levels, a couple of familiar, entrenched attitudes toward education have been staked out and vigorously defended. One group, the Religious Right, decries the lack of moral and ethical education, demanding a return to "fundamental values," school prayer, and the purging of certain literature deemed immoral or anti-Christian. Another group, the Technologists, continually lobbies for more scientific technology, more computers in the classrooms, and more computerization of the curriculum, emphasizing the need to stay ahead of the competition in preparing students for a technology-driven future. Ironically, both of these groups are symptomatic of the loss of a unifying narrative for education. For one, education's purpose is to reinforce the correct God with a capital G. For the other, it is to promulgate the surrogate god Technology, which now dominates the ambient culture.

Neil Postman has written of the necessity of "gods" in education. By the term *god*, he wishes neither to exclude nor to particularly emphasize religious gods; instead, he suggests that without a unifying, shared narrative that interprets the past, explains the present, and reveals a possible future, education has no purpose. In Postman's view, the "purpose of a narrative is to give meaning to the world, not to describe it scientifically.... Does it provide people with a sense of personal identity, a sense of community life, a basis for moral conduct, explanations of that which cannot be known?"[2] Postman acknowledges that all such "gods" or defining narratives are imperfect, perhaps even dangerous. But we cannot do without them, for we are the "god-making" species:

> The point is that, call them what you will, we are unceasing in creating histories and futures for ourselves through the medium of narrative. Without a narrative, life has no meaning. Without meaning, learning has no purpose. Without a purpose, schools are houses of detention, not attention.[3]

Judging from the degree to which many students today are "tuned out," Postman's last point is well taken. We have tried and ultimately rejected many educational "gods" before: The ancient "God" of the Old and New Testaments was displaced by Science gods in the secular narratives of Descartes, Bacon, Galileo, Kepler, and Newton. Science gods eventually begot the modern god of rapidly progressing Technology, which, in turn has given birth to an even newer god: Global Corporatism. Now commerce is instantaneous and ubiquitous, worldwide mergers occur at a bewildering speed, formerly "public" radio is loaded with commercials, and trade barriers, tariffs, and environmental protection laws dissolve entirely. Versions of all the above-mentioned gods now vie for influence over the direction of education.

Educational Myths

From a slightly different perspective, David Orr looks deeply into today's educational context and finds six operative narratives, or "myths," that we seem to be accepting without question: (1) that ignorance is a solvable problem (rather than an inescapable part of the human condition); (2) that with enough knowledge and technology, we can "manage Planet Earth"; (3) that knowledge—and, by implication, human goodness—is always increasing; (4) that we can adequately restore what we have dismantled; (5) that the purpose for education is to give students upward mobility and material success; and (6) that our culture represents the pinnacle of human achievement.[4]

Orr's argument is particularly unsettling to many of us who sense that something fundamental is missing in our culture. "This is not the happy world that any number of feckless advertisers and politicians describe," writes Orr. "The fact is we live in a disintegrating culture," and our educational systems are both symptom and cause of this.[5] We have needlessly subdivided and disciplinarily partitioned our educational institutions, yet in doing so we have made of them agents of global, technical, economic, and cultural homogenization. Meanwhile, our educational culture does not emphasize those characteristics we consider the most noble in the human spirit: altruism, compassion, gentleness, caring, or generosity. It downplays vision, aesthetics, imagination, and spiritual sensitivity. And most importantly to the message of this book, our educational culture almost totally ignores the very context in which we find ourselves. Byrd Schas states:

> Instead of learning about the physical places where they live, children are taught to be constantly looking toward an abstract, unlocated future. They are instructed to use computer technology in order to hook into worldwide electronic webs, but without bioregional reference points, this only widens the gap between them and their actual locations.[6]

An Alternative Education

Let us consider for a moment a radical educational alternative that would reverse this entire picture—one that would emphasize civic responsibility and community instead of private gain; provide psychological satisfaction and peace of mind instead of consumer-driven craving; foster artistic, moral, and humanitarian values as being equal in importance with the explorations of science and the applications of technology; resurrect, rather than erode, the "Commons"; build identity and recognize community through advancement of local commerce and business; allow time enough to think, digest information, consider alternatives, and act responsibly; teach connections between things and phenomena rather than differences; and engender knowledge, affection, and care of the local place rather than ignorance and condescension.

The notion of life-place turns many of the unwritten assumptions of contemporary education upside down, and what follows is one of the most critical points of this book: what is needed is a holistic, cross-disciplinary view of the world as it is spatially partitioned into ecological regions, where human and environmental problems are more naturally scaled and reasonably solved, where a person's education is more realistically matched to the integrative, yet spatially contained ways in which humans have evolved to experience the world in the first place.

Kirkpatrick Sale suggests, with his concept of bioregions, that it might be easier to provide renewable energy for one million people than for 250 million or six billion.[7] But the problem of providing renewable energy, if we are to continue Sale's argument, is not merely an "engineering" problem but one involving total integration of most contemporary "disciplines." To solve it, we must ask multiple questions: For what purpose is the energy used? Who is affected? What traditions does it support or destroy? Which species will be harmed? How are other resources affected? What are the geographical limits and potentials of a particular type of energy? Who has final say over energy decisions? Humans do not go through life serially dividing their mental faculties into disciplinary chunks as if perceiving only "the economy" in this moment, only "the physical environment" in the next moment, only "the aesthetic environment" in the next, only "culture" in the next, and so forth. Instead, humans perceive the world as a continuum of integrated phenomena within the spaces they know and inhabit.

A life-place-based educational paradigm makes two fundamentally radical assumptions. First, it assumes that education is for the *whole person*, throughout his or her whole life cycle, and that education aims at integration over the *whole life-place*. It therefore dissolves typical disciplinary boundaries. Second, the bioregional educational paradigm assumes that humans can address the problems of the world only in spatial units that are humanly scaled and in proportion to the way humans evolved and the way we experience the world: with our bodies, our senses, and our immediate needs for air to breathe, water to drink, food to eat, resources to utilize, and other humans to be near. To allow the mind to grow, develop, and integrate perception, cognition, emotion, and action across the many dimensions and complexities of life within finite regions of land is to bring education home where it belongs.

Whole-Life-Place Learning

Of the three essential questions "Who am I?" "Where am I?" and "What am I supposed to do?" contemporary education fundamentally ignores the second one, with the consequence that the answer, by default, is "nowhere." An educational emphasis based on the life-place concept, however, can integrate these three existential questions and provide a solid grounding for the development of whole human beings within an emplaced community of other beings, human and nonhuman.

How might we learn a life-place, or teach our children, as Alan Durning calls it, the "practice of permanence"? The first step is to acknowledge that education takes *place*, quite literally. In the lower grades, classes are more apt to relate students to their immediate surroundings in a meaningful way. Learning skills and lesson plans are frequently tied to whole-body, multi-modal activities and often rely on direct experience and frequent field trips. Countless elementary schools currently engage their students in stewardship activities, tree planting, gardening activities, restoration, connections to the local community, and the like. My wife, Lacey, a third-grade teacher, prepares nearly all her lesson plans to cut across disciplines, involving simultaneous reading, comprehension, art, and science. Many focus on the local environment, whether built or natural. But somehow, as students move upward in grade level, this place-centered, multimodal, interdisciplinary orientation weakens, then disappears altogether, as older students are prepared for disciplinary specialization.

In a life-place-based educational system, this attachment to natural region and local community would begin at the earliest age, even before kindergarten, and would continue *throughout* higher education. A number of dimensions would characterize whole-life-place learning. First, it

Figure 9.1 Elementary school children participate in the Yolo Basin Foundation's "Discover the Flyway" program. Photograph by Robert Thayer.

would focus on developing the whole person, for the whole lifetime, within a context of the whole life-place, with no artificial distinctions constructed between "self" and "other" or between "individual," "community," and "place." Instead, life-place learning would reinforce connections between individuals and the community and between the community and the bioregion.

Second, a spatial, geographical awareness of the uniqueness, potentials, and limitations of the region would serve as the foundation for nearly every other activity. This spatial focus would hone students' often weak geographic skills to a fine edge, making spatial, geographic knowledge as central to one's education as reading or writing. This could be done by frequent direct exposure to the nature of the place and by excursions to or lengthy experiences in the more remote extremities of the bioregion. The youngest students would understand that they lived in an arid, grassy lowland, a forested upland, a coastal plain, or a mountainous region and would apprehend the unique physical and biological character and potential of the place.

Third, a life-place learning approach would be experientially based, with repeated exposure to direct experiences in the community and region in real time. A common buzzword in education these days is "distance learning": remote lessons delivered via the Internet by absentee instructors or, even

more extreme, by auto-tutorial "droids." Life-place learning directly coun-
ters such trends by emphasizing "*nearby* learning," featuring real human
beings, real places, real problems, real issues, and real solutions. At least half
of the learning activities in a life-place-based education system should be
directed toward real experience, community and regional connections, and
apprenticeship, to counterbalance abstract, "book/Web" learning.

Fourth, life-place learning would emulate the same multidimensional,
integrated ways humans naturally perceive the world. Connections between
phenomena, between past and present, between nature and culture, between
sciences, arts, and humanities, and between global generalizations and local
manifestations would receive at least as much emphasis as conventional education now gives to disciplinary fragmentation and differentiation. The world
seems to be "dis-integrating" or disconnected to so many of us because we
have been taught primarily to discriminate between things, not understand
their interconnections.

A life-place educational system would fully utilize the local natural region and its various communities as the primary laboratory for learning.
This has several implications. For one, a particular bioregion might pro-
mote an entire system of outdoor sites that could function as venues for
various educational opportunities. These might include arboreta, parks,
recreation areas, wilderness areas, wetlands, farms, ranches, factories, community facilities—and sewage treatment plants, power plants, dams, and
reservoirs. The antiquated concept of a "classroom" could be expanded to
include this kind of "necklace" of quasi-public or community sites. Furthermore, the bioregion could itself serve as a case study in virtually any
realm of education, from mathematics to dance, ecology, economics, history,
writing, planning, design, or agriculture. The great advantage to the scale
of the bioregion is that nearly every dimension of the human condition can
be demonstrated and thoroughly studied within fifty or so miles. Bioregions,
or life-places, are to a great extent the ideally scaled microcosms of the world
by which to offer students exposure to 90 percent of what might be typically expected in a more "conventional" educational delivery system.

With the dominant political, technical, and economic momentum pushing the world toward global corporatism and homogeneous culture, educational systems would of course be remiss if they pretended globalism was
not occurring. We have little danger of that happening, however, since globalism is happening *to* us whether we like it, or have asked for it, or not. What
would certainly be remiss would be if educational systems pretended
(through deliberate omission or mere oversight) that established community values, local economic and social durability, civic democracy, and re-

gional environmental quality were no longer important things to teach. The critical question is whether school districts and communities can find the fortitude and resources to give the kind of emphasis to the local life-place that it so desperately needs if it is to resist the negative implications of the global "network society." The best strategy is to presume that the future of education will be a balancing act between locality and globality, with locality needing every advocate, every dollar, and every individual time commitment that it can muster.

A fundamental principle of life-place learning is, as David Orr says, that "all education is environmental education."[8] Inquiry-based education could venture forth from a basic assumption that the ability of future generations to live in the same life-place would be ensured. Monitoring, questioning, and continual debating would characterize the learning activities, with the understanding that there are few, if any, absolute, irrefutable answers to most regional problems and conditions. All pedagogical approaches, methods, and conclusions would be open-ended, with all points of view on major issues represented, either by role playing or by actual representation. In other words, students would model the real world, yet do so within an assumed framework of civic negotiation, community participation, compromise, and consensus rather than a blind defense of entrenched positions, adversarial relations, and ultimate conflict.

Life-place learning would not shirk the responsibility of teaching right and wrong. Although the outcomes of such educational experiences might be arguable, ethics, morals, community responsibilities, peaceful negotiations, trust, and respect for different views and backgrounds would all be deliberately and realistically *taught*, rather than assumed to be communicated to students outside of "formal" education or elsewhere in their lives. An educational delivery system based in place would necessarily reflect the diversity of opinions and beliefs of individuals about that place.

To reinforce the theme of citizenship within a natural life-place, each school campus or major educational group could adopt a specific chunk of the bioregional landscape or territory to clean up, manage, preserve, or restore, much along the lines of the increasingly popular "Adopt-a-Watershed" curricula. Instead of being treated merely as a burden passed down from class to class, the stewardship and maintenance of such places could be thoroughly intertwined with inquiry-based, place-based curricula. Areas maintained and nurtured by this means could become the pride of each student/ teacher group, and management strategies and stewardship values could be inculcated as a dominant goal of the educational structure. The theme of "Taking Care" would spill over from the territory or landscape to other realms, such as family, elderly, children, or pets, reinforcing the idea that one is responsible for the welfare of more than just oneself.

An innovative idea linking students' understanding of the natural region to the practical dimensions of economics would be the establishment of a local currency within the school (or school district, or region itself). By establishing and modeling a local currency within an educational context, students would learn a basic understanding of the value of work, goods, and services and would see firsthand how economic exchange value operates and how it has the potential to reinforce a sense of community and security. Connections between local currency and environmental stability would be reinforced by formally comparing the operation of local currencies with national currencies.

In a similar fashion, students might build a life-place educational project around the concept of *energetics,* studying and comparing the energy produced within the region versus the energy consumed as a baseline index of local sustainability. Establishing a BTU or caloric "accounting system" would further tie energy into industries like agriculture and transportation and would reveal surpluses or shortages. This kind of ecological balancing or "eco-footprint" analysis could form the basis for a wide range of related learning activities and would allow the cross-disciplinary learning of physics, economics, and ecology. Studying regional consumption versus production or harvesting of other resources, like water, would be beneficial to students as well as government officials, business leaders, and citizens.

At all points in this kind of K–12 life-place education, local manifestations and approaches that attempted to integrate the whole learning experience would be continually discussed in relationship to and compared with the global/intellectual/disciplinary canon so that the increasingly global developments in technology, culture, economics, and politics would be perpetually examined and learned in proportion and relation to how they affected the local community and the bioregion. It is likely that this dynamic tension between globalization and local life-place would remain a fundamental characteristic of education into the foreseeable future.

Local Lessons

Let us examine an example of how a condition of the local bioregion might serve as a foundation for integrated life-place learning. In the Cache Creek watershed of Sacramento Valley, mercury in the water is becoming an issue of increasing concern. Mercury, when dissolved as methyl mercury in water, is toxic when taken up by living organisms and accumulated in muscle tissue in substantial quantities. The upper Cache Creek watershed drains an area with many former mercury or "quicksilver" mines, which provided the needed mercury to allow gold mined from the Sierra to be processed during the California Gold Rush. In addition, the thermal hot springs characterizing the severe, crustal-seismic-volcanic nature of the interior Coast Range origins of Cache Creek produce some natural mercury, irrespective of mining activity. Since Cache Creek winter runoff eventually flows into the Sacramento–San Joaquin Delta, recent attempts to restore the declining fish populations and ecosystem functions of the delta have identified Cache Creek as perhaps the worst tributary for mercury runoff in the entire Sacramento drainage basin (perhaps one of the worst in North America!). Furthermore, since mercury is accumulating in the tissues of warm-water fishes commonly caught and eaten by downstream and Sacramento–San Joaquin Delta residents (particularly poorer folk who need the fish for protein or recent immigrants whose culture predisposes them toward certain fish species most prone to mercury accumulation), the mercury issue affecting Cache Creek is a stem-to-stern watershed problem.

This situation is an educational opportunity, not merely an environmental crisis. Students of all ages could sample water at all points on Cache Creek and, using fairly simple indicators, could measure mercury in the water at different times of the year. They could learn basic chemistry from analysis of these water samples. They could likewise learn the local geology by studying how mercury comes to the surface and gets into the water. By studying the mercury mines in the upper watershed, they could learn something of California history—who settled the quicksilver mining districts, why mercury was needed, and how gold influenced the California economy. Students could determine how much gold they or their family possessed (and, therefore, how much they shared in the "responsibility" for the problem). Students could learn geometry by calculating how much water would run off from a particular tributary in a specific rainstorm. They could formulate questions about biology—"How does mercury affect living organisms?" "How much mercury is too much?"—and in the process they could learn about the aquatic life in Cache Creek and something of the nature of fish in general. The students could research the demography of various people downstream who consume the fish, learning about their culture and eating habits. And finally, students could familiarize themselves with various governmental regulations affecting water quality and could observe how local partnerships and volunteer organizations have come together to grapple with and ultimately resolve the mercury problem. In this fashion, a watershed would serve as the local educational delivery system for an entire range of subject matter, while grounding local students in a detailed understanding of the place where they live.

Consider another example of potential life-place learning: the art exhibit assembled by Heath Schenker, "Picturing California's Other Landscape: The Great Central Valley," that was mentioned in chapter 5. Schenker's exhibit reveals the many ways the interior, agricultural Sacramento and San Joaquin Valleys of California have been represented in art and visual media during the past several centuries. Let us propose that this topic be used as a foundation for integrated, place-based learning. Students could begin by studying the origins and culture of the first peoples to inhabit the valley, their design motifs and early artifacts. They could visit museums to record primary art and design patterns directly into their sketchbooks. They could read Greg Sarris's book *Mabel McKay: Weaving the Dream*, about a local Pomo basket weaver, and could visit the Sacramento Indian museum to see her works. Students could study original drawings, photos, lithographs, and other images of the recorded history of the precontact settlement of the Sacramento Valley, and they could examine early fruit box labels to determine what qualities of the region these were intended to communicate. Students could research the history and visual traditions of various waves of immigrants to the region, from the French trappers discovering Cache Creek, to the Spanish missionaries, to the early Anglo pioneers, to the Japanese and Chinese immigrants, and then produce their own creative interpretations of the valley and its watershed through the various visual "filters" of these successive peoples. Students could study the avant-garde exhibits of local high-art galleries and visit Sacramento's Crocker Art Museum and could then compare the vernacular expressions of various county fair art shows with the art of modern galleries and museums. Using inexpensive cameras, students could take photographs of the region and produce collages communicating the visual character and visual history of the valley. They could also create original advertising or public relations motifs for real or hypothetical local businesses or nonprofit organizations. And they might conclude their study by producing an original work of art interpreting the nature and culture of the valley, its watersheds, or communities. Through such a comprehensive focus on visual imagery, the region's history, geography, art, and culture could be fused and brought to life.[9]

In Winters, a small progressive town in our life-place, the fifth-grade curriculum is being structured around the Putah-Cache Creek watershed as part of a statewide movement embracing over twenty-two thousand K–12 students. Adopt-a-Watershed (AAW) is a community-school learning experi-

Figure 9.2 Basket weavers demonstrate native use of basketry materials to a mixed-age audience at Cache Creek Nature Preserve. Courtesy of Cache Creek Conservancy. Photograph by Steve Yeater; used by permission.

ence encouraging stewardship and weaving education with community, business, and government participation. By focusing on integrated sciences, AAW helps students identify local natural resource problems, monitor environmental conditions, work toward solutions, apply concepts, and engage in restoration activities. Early-grade curricular units feature tangible attributes of watersheds and simple activities, while upper-grade units incorporate study of ecosystems, physics, hydrology, chemistry, and water quality. Adopt-a-Watershed is funded and managed in part by the California Resources Agency and as a result is occasionally criticized by radical groups as being too "top down." However, the concept is being used successfully by many schools in California, and the general format is easily expandable to include more grassroots input and additional curricular focus on the watershed as a framework for the study of social sciences, arts, and humanities.[10]

Other life-place learning examples might include a thematic focus on food production, including multimodal explorations and projects aimed at experiencing regional agriculture, farmers' markets, and the local "foodshed." Students might also conduct a regionwide study of transportation, including everything from walking and cycling to bus, train, auto, truck, air, and water travel. Integrative life-place projects like these would be targeted at the level of sophistication and learning expected of a particular grade/developmental level; while all students would engage in sensory experiential learning, the complexity of the realm to be studied would increase with age and educational development. Real-time, real-place, integrated, inquiry-based learning begins in kindergarten and continues through completion of high school. However, this type of learning approach is also highly appropriate for university study. Integrated, problem-oriented, multidisciplinary, real projects already form the basis of studio education in collegiate schools of planning, architecture, and landscape architecture; there is no reason why the approach so commonly found in these environmental design disciplines could not be extended to other subjects.

Majoring in Place

With its emphasis on early experiential and multimodal learning, primary education may be the easiest venue for establishing a life-place learning structure. A more difficult venue is found in higher education. Many critics now suggest that we have established precisely the wrong priorities with our higher education system. Wes Jackson argues that the "universities now only offer one serious major: upward mobility. Little attention is paid to educating the young to return home, or to go some other place and dig in."[11]

University students change majors on the average of three times within their four-to six-year undergraduate education. In essence, they are strongly encouraged to choose a "career" or primary occupation first and then to base their decision to locate or "settle" on a mixture of primarily economic (and secondarily recreational) criteria. Combined with their professors' career- (not place-) driven choices regarding employment and the general condescension of academia toward "local" (as opposed to "worldly") affairs, this makes for a higher-education system almost totally alien to the idea of permanent inhabitation and emotional investment in the welfare of distinct and particular *places*.

Suppose for a moment that, instead, colleges could offer students the possibility of "majoring in place": of becoming intimate with a life-place in which to develop into full human beings and participating members of a community of all life forms. What if educational institutions offered students the flexibility to adjust their disciplinary (or better, *cross*-disciplinary) focus to fit the needs of a particular community, region, or ecosystem as a first priority, rather than adjusting their job location to meet their narrow specialization? Imagine attending an institution of education whose stated goals emphasized making the best life-place culture possible within the limits and potentials of the region occupied by that institution? What if they officially endorsed the idea that living permanently within a region necessitates a respectful, flexible, broad understanding of the physical, biological, economic, and cultural character of the place and structured curricular opportunities accordingly? Might we be able to combine the best of "global" academic knowledge with the evolving, broadly integrated wisdom of the place itself?

To restate one of David Orr's themes, the earth has been vandalized not by the poorly educated but by the extremely well "educated." Billions of hours of research, countless empirical studies, and millions of degrees, theses, and dissertations have contributed to the foundations of knowledge with which we now pollute the air, erode the soil, pave over arable land, exterminate species, overfish the oceans, mine rainforests, kill each other in wars, and concentrate wealth in the accounts of the few. A generous interpretation, of course, would presume that these are unintentional by-products of our system of higher education. A more critical view would ask how such a sophisticated educational system producing so much so-called knowledge could possibly allow such outcomes to occur.

My argument is simple: the presumption that we can understand the world or teach our young people to solve the world's global problems before we understand and solve our own regional problems is seriously flawed. As educators, we must of course deal with the phenomenon of globalization because it is "happening to us" whether we like it or not. But the effects of globalism are experienced locally, and any solution that does not acknowledge or involve local regions is no solution whatsoever. The educational system of the future will, out of necessity, bring the regional and local scale of the world (where it is most easily understood and cared for) into parity with the global scale. The educational system of the future must also place the humanities, design and fine arts, and natural, physical, and social sciences on an equal footing. Finally, the educational system of the future must acknowledge that true wisdom is integrated and tested knowledge, not fragmented, unrelated information.

A number of people, including Lewis Mumford, Daniel Kemmis, and Jane Jacobs, have argued that the city, together with its naturally bounded region, is the locus of democracy, the basic unit of economy, and the only cradle of true citizenship and genuine community. What if we were to build upon this notion of city-bioregions with semispecific natural boundaries and use this spatial structure to deliver applied general education in colleges and universities throughout the continent? Most watershed regions of the United States have university campuses, some of which are land grant institutions whose original charters provide education to the local community in exchange for the grants of land on which they are located. What if these campuses were to offer a truly multidisciplinary liberal education major focusing on the local life-place—that physically bounded, regional community of animals, plants, and humans in which the campus is placed? Such curricula might be labeled "Sacramento Valley Studies" at U.C. Davis, "Willamette Valley Studies" at Oregon State University, "San Francisco Bay Area Studies" at Berkeley, or "Great Basin Studies" at Utah State.

The focus of each local bioregional studies major would be to prepare students with a general education for responsible participation and community citizenship as inhabitants of the particular life-place. Subjects would include courses with practical, theoretical, historical, cultural, scientific, or aesthetic orientations. As in the elementary and secondary educational venue, for each college course in a bioregional studies focus, the life-place would be the laboratory of study. Students might compare and integrate the "global knowledge" of any particular subject, or hopefully, several subjects, with the local wisdom. Art could be taught comparatively by examining the local genre represented at galleries and county fairs in relation to the "high art" of the global avant-garde. Local farmers could teach soil management techniques in relation to global knowledge of the world's major soil types. Government classes could require participation or direct attendance of students in local governmental affairs; students might compare classical political theories to the actual manifestations of the local city council or county board of supervisors. History could be actively learned by direct research at historical societies, county courthouses, and museums, or by oral interviews, again with a comparative eye toward national or world historic events. The strict lines between outreach, research, and education and between the arts, the humanities, and the social, physical, and natural sciences could be deliberately blurred.

Every good elementary school teacher knows that education is best learned by integrating subjects, teaching students to ask good questions, and relating global to local phenomena. Education pioneer Ernest Boyer embodied many of these concepts in his notion of the "basic school" as a true "community for learning."[12] But why should such an elementary educational integration with local realities peter out in high school and become absent entirely from higher education?

Occasionally, opportunities arise. One semester I found myself offering a studio course to university students of landscape architecture aimed at teaching the systems that form our everyday landscapes: physical, biological, climatic, and sociocultural. Concurrently, my wife, Lacey, was teaching environmental themes to her third graders. Together, we came up with a brainstorm: have the landscape architecture college students each prepare a ten-minute, hands-on lesson for the third graders on how landscapes and related natural and social processes operate, using multidisciplinary, participatory, multimodal experiences. The college students would be evaluated on how well they conveyed the information about local landscape processes to the third graders. The results were inspiring. Landscape architecture students taught forest competition by crowding third graders together in a small space as "trees" competing for light and soil; third graders poured "rainwater" on model watersheds in sandboxes that landscape architecture students had constructed to demonstrate erosion and sediment deposition; school students, guided by college students, made soil by grinding rocks with their hands and adding organic matter they had blended up in a mixer. At the end of the two-hour session, Lacey and I just stared at each other across the room with tears in our eyes.

A Life-Place Curriculum

My colleague Joyce Gutstein, always a constructive critic, reminds me that higher education is nearly always a time of increased mobility and "migration" for students, something that is unlikely to change and must be incorporated into any life-place-based educational strategy. However, the ability to "major in place," or to immerse oneself in the complexities and emotional rewards of learning about a specific place, need not compel students to remain in the vicinity of campus permanently upon graduation. One of the advantages of life-place studies would be to offer students a taste of what it means to attach to a place, thereby allowing them to "reinhabit" another region of their choice elsewhere in the future. If local, integrated, bioregion studies majors were to be established, however, it is likely that the percentage of students choosing to remain within the region upon graduation might increase, with positive benefits accruing to both former students and the place itself.

What kinds of curricula might a college or university offer to encourage a student to remain as a participating and dedicated inhabitant of the particular home life-place? For starters, a life-place major would be simultaneously both *general* and *applied*. It would teach a wide, connected set of theories, philosophies, and skills by immersing students in the locality while encouraging them to inquire into the sources of local knowledge. Students would explore how local realities are influenced by global phenomena and how worldly academic theories are modified and utilized in local practice. Foundations of the life-place major would include continuing dialogues between global knowledge and local wisdom, between philosophical structures and practical applications, and between on-site, "real-time-and-place learning" and the evolving electronic-encyclopedic library/Web. The study of geography, a subject in varying stages of health or decline within contemporary educational hierarchies, would be revitalized as a framework within which to examine global-local life-place interactions.

Within a life-place curriculum would be a wide variety of topics, each of which would connect global principles and local manifestations. Consider the following partial list of curricular topics or course offerings:

1. *Mapping, spatial analysis, and regional geography:* Students would study the local bioregion from a hierarchical physiographic perspective, learning mapping skills, studying geographic principles, and gradually focusing closer and closer on the home place.

2. *Regional geology and climate:* Through the extensive examination of the geology of the region, students would learn about the forces that caused the land to become the way it is, seeing their life-place as a manifestation of larger tectonic forces and geological processes and learning how it interacts with macroclimatic factors to manifest a unique local climate.

3. *Bioregional flora and fauna:* By means of extensive field trips and on-site learning experiences, students would come to know the plants, mammals, reptiles, amphibians, insects, birds, soil organisms, and resultant associations that make up the nature of the bioregion.

4. *Life-place history, legends, and stories:* Students would gather an "applied" historic education through a combination of reading and discussion of classical history, direct investigation of local sources such as historical societies and county museums, oral interviews, storytelling, and review of all major cultural "tributaries" to a particular life-place.

5. *Life-place arts:* By similar means comparing worldly "high art" history to local vernacular artistic expression, students would interpret the particular life-place through original works of painting, performance, film, sculpture, photography, music, and various creative media.

6. *Life-place literature:* To uncover the literature of the life-place, students would compare various known literary traditions to the production of local poetry, fiction, and essays, completing original works of their own and commenting on how the region is expressed in the written and spoken word.

7. *Life-place languages:* The study of various linguistic "tributaries" that grew from or migrated into the region would form the basis for learning the multilingual nature of a particular life-place.

8. *Community structure, organization, and change:* By examining the specific human communities and civic institutions within a life-place, students would learn how to connect historical, political, and cultural axioms to the particulars of living in place as a community.

9. *Regenerative economic development:* By direct apprenticeship, participation, study, and discussion, students would learn the economic foundations of the particular region and would engage in direct experiences aimed at strengthening the local economy and ensuring a sustainable foundation for regional development.

10. *Hydrology and watershed analysis:* By means of direct experience, students would learn the basic hydrology of the life-place—how water falls upon, is collected by, is transported through, and is utilized within the bioregion to make human and nonhuman life possible.

11. *Water resource management:* Building upon a foundation of watershed knowledge, students could engage in various educational experiences related to allocation of water resources, assessment of water quality, irrigation, flood management, or water reuse and recycling.

12. *Landscape ecology and restoration:* Students would study the dynamic spatial patterns and distributions of species within the life-place, learning to identify, protect, and restore the critical habitats, corridors, and networks upon which the ecological integrity of the region depends.

13. *Regenerative resource management:* Depending upon which resources (e.g., timber, fish) have been traditionally harvested within a particular life-place, students would conduct in-depth studies of the ways in which those resources have been utilized in the past and the most regenerative means by which they could be utilized in the future.

14. *Sustainable agriculture:* Using a foundational method of analyzing a "foodshed," students would study the ability of the local region to provide sustainably for the food needs of its residents, looking at both changes to existing agronomic systems and impacts of farming on surrounding and integral cultural and natural systems.

15. *Ethics and civic responsibilities:* In this course, students would continually debate and discuss the various rights and responsibilities of citizenship and the local laws as actualized in the local life-place.

16. *Conflict resolution and participatory problem solving:* This applied course would teach the fundamentals of group participation, dispute resolution, negotiation, and consensus building, using both hypothetical and real cases from the life-place itself.

17. *Local recreation planning and tourism:* Students would explore and help develop the ability of the immediately surrounding life-place to satisfy local recreational and leisure demands.

18. *The university campus as a bioregional resource:* At each particular "bioregional" campus, students would staff administratively sanctioned outreach centers in order to fulfill the obligations of education to be directly tied to the needs of the local life-place.

In addition, the curriculum would offer practical internships with regional environmental and community organizations, or field courses in which students live for a semester in the heart of the city or at rural or remote field stations within the bioregion.

Each institution would tailor its curriculum to the needs of the specific ecological region. Some courses might require team teaching—especially those with controversy as their central content, such as local planning goals and local economic development. The ethics course would be one continuous debate, but one that would be highly educational for the students and would prepare them well for the true business of citizenship to follow.

Such a curriculum would offer a general, fully interdisciplinary liberal education. Anthropology, for example, might be taught using the river basin as a metaphor, exploring the various "cultural" tributaries that make up the sense of an emplaced community. Art could be taught from the local perspective as a nexus of vernacular, place-based, imported, and high-art influences. Literature would compare local writers and poets with national and international figures. One of my favorite concepts is a multidisciplinary course in integrated watershed studies, looking at a broad, multidisciplinary perspective grounded in both nature and culture.

What are the chances of the universities taking on such a curriculum? Currently slim, but rapidly improving. Disciplinary pressure to explore narrow, focal subjects under assumptions of globalization has always prevailed over multiviewpoint, integrative exploration of place-tested truth (the kind required by the real world). However, the story of an effort in which I have participated for the past eight years on my home campus bears telling.

It is just after noon on a Wednesday in 1997, and I arrive at the square table in the small meeting room in the thirty-year-old "Temporary Building 101" where the weekly meeting of our "Putah-Cache Bioregion Project" takes place. English professor and de facto spark plug of the group, David Robertson wears a loud shirt, straw hat, and broad grin—he is obviously in his usual good spirits. Peter Moyle, the fish biologist, joins us from via the back door, still dressed in his field jacket. At the table are several other coconspirators in this mild-mannered plan to refocus a bit of academic-based energy toward the watersheds of Putah and Cache Creeks, the "backyard" of the campus. Amy Boyer, creative writer and recent master's degree recipient, holds in her hand the latest offprint of the project's Web page (figure 9.3) and talks to Laurie Glover, a brilliant and energized English instructor who has established a bioregionally focused writing class on campus. Joyce Gutstein, Ph.D., a transplanted New Yorker and associate director of the Public Service Research Program (PRSP), in whose space we are now meeting, pulls her chair from her office and takes her place at the table, still talking to Carmia Feldman, a graduate student who is helping her prepare a million-dollar educational grant proposal to the National Science Foundation on regionally based science education. Jake Mann, a graduate of the landscape architecture program and my assistant, watches quietly as we chatter away. Finally Dennis Pendleton, Joyce's colleague and the director of PSRP, emerges apologetically from his office, the "nerve center" of many campus outreach projects relating to local environmental issues.

For several years this core group of individuals has had the good fortune of aiming our collective energies toward increasing the university's awareness and participation in affairs affecting the two major local creek watersheds. Our informal rule of thumb has been to focus on a reasonably defined chunk of physical territory while deliberately blurring usually sacrosanct intellectual boundaries between academic territories: a three-dimensional boxlike diagram I drew on the easel at one meeting erased the normal lines between teaching, education, and outreach on one dimension; between sciences, arts, and humanities on another; and between children, college students, and adults on a third. The holism emergent from our many collabo-

Figure 9.3 "Are You Here?": Opening images from the University of California, Davis, Putah-Cache Bioregion Project Web site, http://wdsroot.ucdavis.edu/clients/pcbr/. Cartography by Jacob Mann; Web page design by Amy Boyer; photograph by Robert Thayer.

rative efforts is at times extremely heady, and on certain occasions, I leave the meetings elated, in delighted disbelief that something so different and so important is actually occurring in the halls of academe.

Our actual accomplishments read nothing like the perfunctory "results" of so many other funded research projects, yet collectively the tangible and many other seemingly intangible results accumulate to a critical mass. We have organized a guided tour of the watersheds, introducing the geology, hydrology, archaeology, history, ecology, popular culture, and aesthetics of the region. We have monitored the biological condition of Putah and Cache Creeks, categorizing the fish populations, with humanities students working alongside biology majors in seining the stream during fish counts. We have placed members of our core group on nearly every local grassroots watershed organization: Cache Creek Stakeholders, Putah Creek Council, Yolo Basin Foundation, Upper Putah Creek Stewardship, and the Blue Ridge–Berryessa Natural Area Conservation Partnership, to name a few. For several years running, we have administered an Artists and Writers in Bioregional Residence program, accepting applications and awarding stipends to writers, poets, photographers, sculptors, and painters from the watershed region, to support works derived from the nature and culture of the place. We have published several editions of *Putah and Cache*, a brief but elegant folio of writing and photography inspired by the local area. We have prepared conceptual plans for a "Pacific Flyway Center," a prototypical educational and research center to be located at the new Yolo Basin Wetlands. We have aimed at least six different university courses toward cross-disciplinary examination of the local watersheds, placing English majors, landscape architects, ecologists, poets, fisheries biologists, education majors, community development specialists, and geography students shoulder to shoulder, enticing them to think nontraditionally about the place itself. We have offered graduate courses on the emerging theory and literature of the bioregional movement. Laurie Glover's writing sequence, structured around the local watershed region, has culminated in a student-written guidebook of local educational and recreational opportunities. As another by-product of her initiative, a student Bioregion Club has been born. David Robertson is producing a series of monographs accompanied by his original interpretive photographs of the entire Putah Creek and Cache Creek watersheds. Finally, the entire group is coauthoring an eclectic but comprehensive guidebook to the local region, which attaches original chapters of fiction, poetry, and expository sections on geology, archaeology, ecology, history, and popular culture to a point-by-point itinerary of the two-hundred-mile Putah and Cache tour.

To some of our colleagues on campus, this eclectic effort may seem unfamiliar, even frivolous. But collectively, our efforts have galvanized considerable local knowledge, awareness, and feeling toward the region occupied by the campus, as well as a palpable momentum of interest, concern, and action. Pivotal to our work has been our presumption that wisdom does not solely exist on campus to be disseminated to the masses by some presumed educational elite; real knowledge and stewardship of place also reside *outside* academic walls and are worthy of bringing *into* the academy. Farmers, native Americans, local land managers, and working professionals, overcoming their initial nervousness at being asked to speak on campus as "experts," have enriched our group enormously by sharing their knowledge and experience.

To me, in retrospect, the sum total of this activity has been nothing short of revolutionary. My participation in the Putah-Cache Bioregion Project quite literally changed my life and allowed me to elevate my understanding of what it means to be an "educator" within the total bioregional context.[13]

Conclusions about Life-Place Learning

When one deeply explores a local place, one finds strong connections between personal inhabitation and the larger patterns of existence; the local life-place becomes a bright illustration not only of the uniqueness of a region but of the universality of existing as a human being on a living earth. Having studied and practiced many of the ideas embodied in this chapter for nearly a decade, I am led to the following observations:

- *People are hungry for knowledge about the places where they live,* especially knowledge that will help them understand and feel connected to the place. These people are highly receptive learners for those willing and able to teach them.

- *Life-place education is by nature multimodal and multidisciplinary,* and people learn best when artificial boundaries are transcended.

- *Precise "bioregional" boundaries are irrelevant;* people seem to sense what is unique about their own regions and about where these end and "other" regions begin.

- *Life-place education is appropriate for both genders, any age, and those of any background,* and often a mixture of ages, genders, and experiences heightens the learning.

- *A life-place setting can be likened to a spatial network* wherein the actual sites for educational experience form a kind of necklace of beads or a net of knots—representing places from arboreta to dams, historic buildings, local libraries, sewage treatment and power plants, factories, mines, halfway houses, council chambers, Indian reservations, wildlife preserves, restoration projects, schoolyards, and university campuses.

- *In a world of global specialists, there is great need for local generalists.* People who have specialized all their lives often thirst for generalizable knowledge of how to live better "in place."

- *People of considerably different backgrounds and opinions can share feelings of belonging, identification, and caring for specific natural places.* In the process of learning about a life-place, many can find new common ground with people with whose political opinions they might otherwise or previously have disagreed.

- *Life-place learning processes expose different political and social groups to one another* and thus permit these groups' false caricatures of one another to dissolve, leaving a more honest, "clean" understanding of different positions without the degree of paranoia usually caused by a lack of actual interaction with "others."

And, perhaps most important:

· *There is no end to the depth and sophistication of wisdom and knowledge one may learn about a specific life-place.* Most of us have been brought up to believe that true wisdom resides "out in the world" and that local phenomena are somehow finite, second- ary, and less important.

Nothing could be farther from the truth.

10 Acting

TAKING PERSONAL RESPONSIBILITY

The transformation of our culture and our society would have to happen at a number of levels. If it occurred only in the minds of individuals, it would be powerless. If it came only from the initiative of the state, it would be tyrannical. Personal transformation among large numbers is essential, and it must not only be a transformation of consciousness, but must also involve individual action.

ROBERT BELLAH ET AL., 1985

It is a clear day in March 1996, and I can see the Blue Ridge to the west, the Sierra to the east, and the Sutter Buttes to the north. The rain-soaked farm fields glisten an alternating brown-and-silver corduroy, enframed by mint-green annual grasses. Escaped almond trees shoot spurts of pink-tinged pop-corn flowers skyward from the ditches, and the black walnut buds yearn to burst. Workers are preparing the strawberry beds on the corner northwest of town, burning holes in the plastic mulch to insert the starts, anticipating the onslaught of suburbanites flocking to the small roadside sales shed. At the farmers' market, Satsuma mandarin season is just about over, and as-paragus is next. Rainfall has caught up to, even passed, the normal to date. Waterfowl in the local habitat ponds are enacting their mating rituals, as if anticipating a bountiful year. The golden eagle has been seen soaring again above Deganawidah-Quetzalcoatl University, the Native American college out along Road 29.

I'm riding my bicycle home from campus, past the university research fields. For some reason, I am thinking kinesthetically about life-place cul-ture and wondering how one might communicate this complex notion word-lessly via body or hand gestures. Life-place culture, I think, is not a concept to be grasped hard by a tightly clenched fist; rather, it must be held lightly and balanced in the palm of an open hand. It also requires the joining of many hands—the active engagement of student hands raised in question, of clasped hands around shovels, of cradled hands around new seedlings, of hands shaking in agreement, of hands patting people on the back, of hands raised in celebration.

A life-place is action centered; one must *live* it. As Jacob Bronowski said,

"We have to understand that the world can only be grasped by action, not by contemplation."[1] This personal engagement is what most crisply differentiates the life-place notion from other ecological planning strategies or concepts. It is not enough to rely on a team of experts to determine where development should occur, which energy source to utilize, when development should be approved, or what regulatory policies should be established to protect biodiversity. To engage in a life-place practice is to accept the realities of a place, yet also to accept the personal responsibility to become part of the solution. The actions that follow individual life-place practice, of course, will aggregate to the collective—few single individuals will find the power to make change on their own, yet their individual actions are essential to the combined effort toward realizing a life-place. As the saying goes, "If you want government off your back, try shouldering some responsibility." To make the fundamental change needed to turn the momentum of unsustainable development and degenerative land management around, each individual will need to make a commitment to the place.

How might one live bioregionally, or practice "reinhabitation"? There are undoubtedly as many different paths as there are individuals. Often the steps one takes toward a life-place practice begin to accrue unselfconsciously. Prior to my being introduced to the idea of "bioregionalism" (much less fully understanding it or studying it), I found I was *doing* many of the things that I have now come to consider as "reinhabitory." I was riding a bicycle to work and living in an extremely energy-efficient house. I was buying more food from local sources like the Davis Farmers' Market. I had subscribed to a local community-supported organic farm. I had thoroughly explored—and sampled the products of—the regional wineries and breweries. I began to shop more in the downtown area of Davis, paying the 10 percent extra cost over the "big-box" discount store price for the positive feeling of keeping my economic support local. I started giving more money to local charities than to the big international funds. I became involved with local environmental and political issues (as I grew more suspicious of and disengaged from state and national politics). I let my cable TV subscription expire. I volunteered in local schools. Most important, I joined several local environmental initiatives and organizations, and I took a sabbatical internship at the Yolo County Resource Conservation District. I began volunteering for creek cleanups in the local watershed and trail-building workshops in the local Bureau of Land Management (BLM) wildlands.

As I observed my own community and regional behaviors changing, I discovered that I had become, in fundamental ways, a different person. Bioregional perspectives are meaningless unless directly experienced and backed by personal commitment and action. Each individual's understanding of the region and its various communities, both natural and human, and his or her actions to sustain it are bound to be vastly different; one person's idea of sustenance is apt to appear to another as exploitation. What the bioregional view asks, however, is not a specific political or environmental correctness but a long-term commitment to *be involved with a natural place and its communities.* This is perhaps the ultimate bioregional hypothesis: *People who resolve to live in a place indefinitely with deep commitment, no matter what their politics or philosophical views may be, are the key to that place's future.*

Individual commitment, then, is more fundamental to a life-place practice than political position. When commitment to a life-place is *practiced* by many inhabitants, the life-place literally "comes alive."

Steps Toward a Life-Place Practice

For a great many people, the idea of inhabiting a life-place is a new concept, or at least a notion hovering at the fringes of their contemporary realities. The *awareness* of one's residency within a territory that is *alive* may represent a significant initial breakthrough in consciousness. I have listened to conservative rice farmers comment on their responsibilities toward migratory waterfowl; I have heard corporate growers reiterate the importance of reduced pesticides and herbicides to the welfare of their migrant farm laborers; I have read the writings of a retired engineering-college dean who has turned his full effort and attention toward the region's wildlife, writing an informative and accessible book on the subject. It is surprisingly easy to tell which people have become aware that they reside within a living framework and which have not.

This step of *awareness* may be followed by subsequent steps in a life-place practice: *acceptance* of the imperfections, inconsistencies, and peculiarities of a life-place; *education* about all aspects of the life-place; *engagement* in the civic processes of the life-place; and, ultimately, *actualization,* or acting in ways that, for the individual, seem to dissolve boundaries between self and place and provide a heightened sense of personal meaning and embeddedness within a natural community. This is, in essence, a manifestation of E. O. Wilson's idea of *biophilia,* with the added suggestion that such an affection may best take root in a specific place.[2] Let us look at these processes of life-place practice more closely.

AWARENESS

Awareness is the stage where information reaches our consciousness and takes root. Simplistically, it is the raw material upon which humans build their cognitive realities. To be simply aware does not necessitate deep comprehension, positive or negative attitude, acceptance, or action, but only awakening to the existence of something. This is no small step, however.

Only the most die-hard reductionist academics and scientists still argue against the notion of a holistic life-world and in favor of an atomized collection of individual organisms and separable phenomena; opinion on the street is swinging back toward holism after a few centuries' break. Yet we have lived at the height of this reductionism, and the single-purpose character of our built environments still embodies our fragmented thinking, overwhelming and insulating us from the enveloping matrix of life. So an awareness that the world is *basically alive*, rather than basically dead, is no small change and can lead to fundamental changes in the way in which we envision or pattern the world. In short, awareness of our existence within a life region (rather than a sterile political one) literally changes the mental maps we carry around with us.

ACCEPTANCE

Much of life, especially when we are younger, is spent in transition between adolescence and adulthood, between education and career, between one place and another or one job and another. In the process of evolving as whole human beings, we seek places to locate, often motivated by idealized visions of future geographies. It is, no doubt, a process similar to selecting a mate: we hope to find someplace closely resembling our ideals. But, just as in the process of partnering, we become attached to and hold close to the heart the positive attributes and learn to accept those that might be less than truly ideal. Then the heart's capacity for affection enlarges. Sociologists tell us that dwelling on the irritating habits of a partner or spouse is often an indication of a fundamental dissatisfaction with the relationship, or with one's own self. The same goes for regions of dwelling. But the acceptance and transcendence of minor deviations from some presumed perfect condition is an indication of psychological (or, in the case of a life-place, sociological) health. Healthy regions and communities tolerate diversity.

Regions have endemic personalities and peculiarities to the extent that those unfamiliar with a particular region may wonder what keeps its residents attached. This cross-regional skepticism is demonstrated by attitudes toward natural hazards. A Midwesterner, repeatedly exposed to tornadoes, wonders how Californians tolerate earthquakes, while Californians can't imagine how East Coast or Gulf residents can stand hurricane after hurricane. Similarly, there are times when I curse the twenty or so days when the temperature in my region exceeds 100 degrees Fahrenheit. Yet I now take this phenomenon decreasingly as an irritation and increasingly as a marker of where I am. When the cool delta breeze finally kicks in, dropping the evening temperatures into the sixties, the sweetness of life is palpable.

EDUCATION

We are typically expected to study the world broadly and a particular discipline deeply, yet there is nothing to prevent the mind from doing the precise opposite: learning a very great deal about a specific life-place on earth. In *PrairyErth*, his patiently thorough study of Chase County, Kansas, author William Least Heat-Moon gave us the important analogy of a *deep map*, which is really an acknowledgment of the vastness of the mind's capacity for knowledge about a place.[3] People who begin to reverse the expected educational behavior are surprised that the container of wisdom about a specific natural territory actually has no bottom and that it can be explored, studied, compared, contrasted, investigated, tested, synthesized, imagined, sung, painted, photographed, danced, and dreamed indefinitely.

For one participant in David's and my watershed tour, this discovery was a galvanizing and life-affirming experience. Hope (not her real name) was a woman whom life had obviously bumped around a bit, and she clearly was neither wealthy, young, socially skilled, nor in perfect health. After the first Putah-Cache tour, however, she was overjoyed, and she showed up to attend the next tour with a sheath of photocopied archival materials she had combed from various county libraries. Upon skimming her material (which she insisted that I take for my files) I knew immediately that it was deep, substantive historical data that my own twenty-five years of exposure in the place had not yet revealed. What was most important, however, was not the information I received but the transformation that we both underwent in the process.

ENGAGEMENT

Sociologist Robert Bellah, in his wonderful book *Habits of the Heart*, articulates with great insight the complex American relationship between in-

Figure 10.1 Volunteers at "Restoria," a well-loved site of revegetation activity along Putah Creek, pause for a group portrait by participant-photographer David Robertson. The place-name is appropriate; more than the landscape is being restored here. Used by permission.

dividualism and social commitment. He reminds us that in spite of our culture's overemphasis on the mythology of the individual (our "first language"), America is actually a land where the individual is *expected* to get involved—hence Bellah's suggestion that we articulate a "second language" of commitment, civic participation, and social action. From the observations of Alexis de Tocqueville on the benefits of civic participation in the New England township to the emerging participatory frameworks of ecosystem management, the thread of collective, voluntary social action runs strongly through American society. Even the resistance identities referred to by Manuel Castells in response to the rise of the global network society are avenues of social engagement whereby the individual, through action, becomes an effective social subject. As we have seen, bioregional groups, watershed conservancies, and the like have offered Americans new opportunities to exercise their traditional social construction of an individual identity, even as the excesses of globalism have tended to strip away opportunities for such social construction.[4]

In this fashion, to practice life-place culture is to become a participant in a civil society. It just so happens that these days some of the very best examples of civil societies are, in the truest of American tradition, those forming around stewardship of natural regions.

ACTUALIZATION

When awareness, acceptance, education, and engagement occur within the context of a life-place, individuals often experience a heightened degree of self-actualization. In an age when work, social discourse, market exchange, and even routine daily communications are all highly mediated, often virtual and even globalized, to *act* tangibly and locally is one of the clearest paths to an individual identity. The action itself, whether it is speaking at a public hearing, planting a tree, or helping in a soup kitchen, completes the palette of human possibilities. Actions may be highly symbolic: to plant a tree may be to plant oneself. Moreover, when local volunteers revegetate an eroded stream bank, both the concrete and the symbolic levels of personal and social meaning can be said to be congruent; actor, action, and implication form a philosophically unified whole.

Creative Life-Place Practice

The collective result of singular life-place practices is life-place *culture*. Because it is built from so many individual practices, no distinct theory or prediction of where a particular bioregional culture will lead is possible. For that reason, life-place practice may disappoint those people who are fixated upon specific visions of the future. However, inherent in the notion of a life-place practice are the elements of *trust* and *faith*—that individuals who are engaged in a local place will *take good care of it*.

Yet faith and trust—concepts inadequately dealt with by the modern, scientifically oriented academic institution—are only two of many components of life-place culture. A third underappreciated ingredient is *creativity*—the intentional individual and collective process of envisioning the future. Even though no one person's specific vision of the future is likely to be realized in detail, the *act of envisioning a future* is an essential ingredient in life-place culture and a necessary function of the individual actor in a bioregional context. Creative intuition, once nearly banished from science, may at last become part of the scientific effort, while science itself may be an indispensable instrument for the cultural creativity necessary to create and perpetuate the life-region. It is precisely a *lack* of creativity that has allowed the physical world to degenerate while a virtual one takes its place. One might argue that for a true life-place to emerge, it must be created by the broadest possible constituency, not left to the supposed "experts."

BOUNDARIES AND NO BOUNDARIES

Life-place practice represents a shift in the epistemology of humans in relation to the earth. It is a concept that transcends dualisms: it is both internal and external, created and existential, cultural and natural. It dissolves intellectual and disciplinary boundaries while at the same time recognizing that finite regions form the best framework for addressing environmental problems. It offers individuals a means of social identity through awareness, acceptance, education, engagement, and actualization rooted in place. In doing so, it resolves the three existential questions: "Who am I?" "Where am I?" and "What am I supposed to do?"

Life-place practice might be misinterpreted as a fringe activity were it not for the fact that thousands, if not millions, of people are already doing it. Joining a nonprofit organization dedicated to increasing local awareness and sustaining life in a watershed, coastal zone, or forest is hardly the stuff of New Age esoterica, just as participating on the local planning commission does not necessarily imply radical rejection of the entirety of government. Life-place practice is becoming quietly ubiquitous, as more people awaken to the inevitable realization that they share a living world with other people and other species. Furthermore, there is nothing peculiar about the *forms* this practice takes: going to meetings, visiting libraries, taking hikes, imagining solutions, speaking out, writing grant proposals, making maps and plans, teaching others, and most important, communicating face to face with neighbors. For all of its supposed threats to existing academic, social, and economic institutions, the bioregional concept is actually a sheep in wolf's clothing.

Throw My Ashes in Putah Creek

. . . we cannot attain awakening for ourselves.
We can only participate in the awakening of life.
STEPHEN BATCHELOR, 1997

Monday, August 31, 1998, 8 A.M.: Rumsey Canyon is on fire. Where Cache Creek emerges from its notch in the steep and rugged Blue Ridge before turning south into pastoral Capay Valley, the entire left flank up Glascock Mountain is either charred or burning.

1 p.m.: One-hundred-five-degree heat and dead, smoky air from the fire to the northeast. It is the first day of classes for the Davis Joint Unified School System. Lacey Thayer and her teaching partner, Heather Roemer, help their new fourth graders mop up after coming in dripping sweat from hot asphalt recess.

5 p.m.: Neal Thayer, age fifteen, plays his junior-varsity soccer game in the bright, motionless heat. Clouds of insects swarm against the afternoon sun, framed by sprinklers watering the next soccer field west. I watch the game listlessly, sweating, buzzed by flies, imagining the scene creating the tan smear in the sky toward the northwestern region of the Cache Creek watershed I know very well. Is Rayhouse Road burning? Is the southern Blue Ridge in flames? What about the new BLM trail I helped to build? Will the fire burn the entire region where, in approximately four weeks, I will lead a class of landscape architecture students in a bioregional planning exercise?

Tuesday, September 1, 1998, 4:30 a.m.: I awaken after a restless sleep in a solar house not equipped with air-conditioning and turn on the whole-house exhaust fan as the temperature finally drops below seventy degrees. I must go to the fire today; a part of me is burning.

10 a.m.: Interstate 5, north of Woodland, aims northwest at the fire. A long, thin, brownish-gray haze obscures the normally visible Blue Ridge as I drive north. Not a branch, leaf, or stalk moves; the still trees seem to suffer in the bright sunlight. I pass fields of ripening feed corn, leaves turning a crisp tan on ten-foot stalks. The roadside verge is dry, save the weeds closest to the pavement, which entraps a tiny ration of moisture on their behalf. Plowed brown fields simmer in the late morning light, having yielded their first crop of the season. Stacks of tawny hay bales capture the essence of this heat, and the spilled roadside tomatoes from the cannery trucks speeding around curves bring the familiar, sweet tomato-rot smell of this region in August and September. A field of ripe, umber-colored safflower awaits harvest, looking coarse, scratchy, and thistlelike. Browns, tans, beiges, yellows, oranges, and reds seem to yell out from the landscape, drowning out the greens, which somehow, today, seem gray and powerless.

A procession of agricultural landscapes passes me as I head north: stacks of empty almond crates in a utility yard; across the freeway another displaying partly rusted, used farm machinery. A pistachio orchard here, a walnut orchard there, then an almond orchard, all framed by the ubiquitous exotic weed, yellow star thistle, that has invaded the valley, its flower heads wearing thorny crowns like little miniature statues of botanical liberty. Rice and grain silos of every size, shape, and degree of upkeep punctuate the frontage roads. Countless big rigs move north and south in the slow lanes. Black walnut trees accompany the invasive star thistle in the occasional highway cloverleaf. A rail line parallels the interstate, bordered by leaning telephone poles, while irrigation tailwater ditches provide the best and only bird habitat for miles. I see from the speeding car window what is, remarkably, a rather tidy farmstead, with deep-red-painted barns, trim lawn, and functional, spacious equipment yard. It is a rarity in the predominant visual jumble of disconnected outbuildings, dilapidated barns, derelict farm machinery, and patchwork absentee landownership.

In this cluttered landscape grows an impressive array of crops: fields of tomatoes, spotlessly uniform soybean fields, submerged rice fields in every stage of growth, and the ubiquitous fields of alfalfa: young, mature, cut, raked, piled, baled, or stacked. Off to the west come the gold Dunnigan Hills, and a dark green vineyard gives away the region's newly granted status as a prime wine grape appellation. Caterpillar tractors pulling various plows throw towers of dust high into the heated air. One treaded, tanklike tractor drags a long land plane designed to smooth even the most minuscule bump or ripple into a uniform, laser-level surface for furrow irrigation. Giant power lines march unimpeded yet barely noticed across an agricultural mosaic into the foothills. A tiny church with a blunt, pyramidal steeple marks a bend in the freeway occupied by the small community of Zamora, and across the freeway, a row of grain hopper cars on a siding awaits filling at the gray rice silos.

I am in familiar country—home enough for me to look past the motley collection of buildings, machinery, wires, ditches, and silos to the richly productive fields—and feel hungry. I'm no farmer, but I'm no fool either. Want a pizza? Tomatoes and wheat at the ready. Need a snack? Try some toasted almonds. Got the urge for a burger? Black Angus cattle grazing in the low foothill pasture just beyond. Feel like Chinese food tonight? Plenty of rice and soy sauce. Dessert? Apricot crisp, strawberry shortcake, pistachio ice cream, pears flambé—it's all right out the car window. To live here is to connect the taste buds to the land and to temper the mind's political conclusions with the pangs of an empty stomach.

But as I drive toward the smoke on the northwestern horizon—now looming taller and darker—I wonder why we nonfarmers try to plow straight through our lives and landscapes, as if neither obstacle nor circumstance could give us pause. The land-dependent farmers and ranchers of this region are seasoned gamblers, accustomed to keeping one eye on the land and sky and the other on the commodity markets, trusting in their gut or their neighbor on when and what to plant and whether to "hold" or "fold." Such people position themselves well with respect to life, leaning neither too far forward nor too far back on their heels. They learn from their own mistakes, read the land and the numbers, and don't expect perfection. If we were to stop and learn philosophy from them, we would realize that with firm roots in a piece of territory, living things can bend with wind and circumstance—even recover from catastrophic fire, whether literal or figurative, by sprouting from the root crown, like the chamise presently being infernally reincarnated on Glascock Mountain. I turn off the freeway and head west on Sand Hill Road, led by the dark, towering smoke plume.

Fires bring out a natural human ambivalence that is both deep and atavistic. Rice farmers burn their fields to rid the soil of the rice blast fungus. Native Californians burned oak grasslands to encourage greater acorn crops. Fire is so essential to this bioregion's flora and to local weed control that to imagine the place without fire would be impossible. Yet we discuss wildfire as a "natural disaster," which is, upon closer examination, an oxymoron. "Disasters" imply violated human values, but for nature, it's business as usual.

12 noon: On the Sand Creek–Cache Creek saddle, just east of Blue Ridge: Helicopters hover over the burning brush, dumping five-hundred-gallon buckets of water from long tethers towed beneath. A twin-engine spotter plane lazily circles the fire, now covering about four thousand acres. California Division of Forestry (CDF) trucks crawl up makeshift dirt roads amidst the burnt chaparral, while bulldozers grind noisily at the hillsides. I have a front-row seat to watch this war being waged against the fire. I eat my sandwich and banana and take pictures conspicuously, hoping the CDF spotters in the choppers above will not consider me a prime arson suspect.

Soon I am joined by a pickup truck, out of which emerges Todd, a young farmer from Grimes, located eastward on the Sacramento River. He is a volunteer firefighter and has taken leave of his fields today to come watch the firefight. A graduate of Chico State University in crop science, he engages me in conversation, and we share brief background stories and comments about fire ecology, which land is affected by the burn, and the fatness of the deer that will result from the flush of new forage growth after the fire. We both feel our awkward attraction to the fire. "It's bad, but it's also good," he says. I agree.

Local inhabitants have witnessed several wildfires in the recent past: South Berryessa near Putah Creek in 1987, Bartlett Springs on the Upper Cache watershed in 1996, and now Glascock Mountain in 1998. Knobcone pine, gray pine, manzanita, and chamise are all fire adapted, requiring the heat of intense flame to activate seed germination. In this region, fire is life giving as well as life taking and is healthy in the long run. Chaparral burns at approximately twenty- to twenty-five-year intervals; at ten-year intervals, a chamise monoculture occurs. More frequent burning may destroy the seed bank of fire-adapted shrubs altogether and result in an annual grassland. This technique is deliberately employed by many ranchers to provide additional cattle forage, but it also decreases soil moisture, raises flooding risk, and increases erosion potential. Rarely is a chaparral shrub stand more than fifty years old before fire takes it. Layers of charcoal in the soil strata allow scientists to record burn frequencies, and a twenty-year fire frequency or so allows a mixed-species chaparral typical of natural conditions. Fires like the one I am watching now burn up to one thousand degrees Fahrenheit at the soil surface, hot enough to melt the aluminum beer cans I can see strewn about the edge of this clearing. The spent brass pistol cartridges lying in a pile on the ground ten feet away, on the other hand, might persist. As fire is to this place, firearms and beer seem to characterize the particular subculture of humans who frequent these hot, chaparral-covered hills.

To live here is to be adapted to intense heat, regardless of the organism. Like the knobcone pine, whose cones are glued shut with natural resins until fire opens them and disgorges their seeds, we human inhabitants have learned to withstand the twenty- to thirty-odd days per year of heat over one hundred degrees. Eventually, a cool south breeze always breaks these heat spells, awakening new seeds of possibility in our own lives. We're heat-adapted, too; our temperaments become insulated and crusty, only to flush with life at the appropriate climatic moments.

Today, however, the south breeze is nowhere to be found, nor any breeze from any other direction. The heat hovers intently like the CDF helicopters. After Todd leaves in his pickup, I remain sitting in the relative shade of the front seat of my open-doored car, finishing my lunch. As I am about to turn the ignition key, the hillside a half-mile in front of me bursts into flame, and gray pines go up like two-hundred-foot tiki torches. CDF, apparently, has set a "backfire" ("Fight fire with fire"). After gazing incredulously at these new flames, I realize that perhaps it is best for me to retreat. One should get only as close to a power object as one can stand. This fire is powerful, and I'm too close. I drive downhill past the staging area for helicopters and smoke jumpers, many of whom are casually eating lunch under shade awnings. They are in no hurry. Wildfires demand of humans a new perspective on time, and the best way to fight certain fires is via strategic waiting. They know what they're doing. Crossing the old Cache Creek bridge at Rumsey, I look back upstream at a most unusual scene. Foreground

Figure 10.2 Fire and water at Rumsey Bridge, Cache Creek.
Photograph by Robert Thayer.

water seems to emerge from background fire; the swirling gray smoke of burning chaparral in the distance shares a peculiar artistic turbulence with the rapids in Cache Creek as it flows under the bridge. Like swirls of smoke and water, life in this region moves on, although not always smoothly.

I turn my car southbound on Route 16, passing the Rumsey Grange Hall, which is now surrounded by red-and-green CDF vehicles as the command point for the firefight. The smoke plume recedes in my rearview mirror, and down the road out of sight of the fire, the region's business goes on as usual.

7 P.M.: The slow, southerly drift of the upstream fire fills the westward Blue Ridge with haze as the sun dips orange toward the horizon. Far down the watershed now, I take down the small canoe and double-bladed paddle from atop the car and, balancing the thirty-two-pound boat upside down on my head, make my way through star thistle and shrub willow to lower Putah Creek. In the waning light I see a float-tube fisherman and two men out for bass in the tiniest of electric-powered boats. We smile and acknowledge each other, none wishing to break pleasant silence or diligent concentration. The blades alternatively dip, pull, and return, splashing drops in the bow as I paddle westward, upstream, toward the illuminated skyline. Clumps of algae dot the smooth water surface, dragonflies dart about patrolling for mos-

quitoes, while scores of various other insects glow around their edges, back-lit by the sun.

Soon I'm paddling too fast. The residual heat of the day, the fire, and the ideas in my head push the blades too vigorously alongside the canoe, and although I came seeking water, greenery, and peace, I break into my ump-teenth sweat of this hot day. To the sides of the narrow creek corridor, how-ever, luxuriant growth offers a cooling diversion for my normally forward glance. Cottonwoods, willows, and foothill ash overhang the banks. Crickets hum in near unison, and a jay squawks, head bobbing, on a branch. The slow current against which I paddle now quickens, and I push the bow onto a small gravel-bar rapid, jumping hastily overboard to drag the lightweight craft into the laminar flow again, leaping in to push off upstream. In the quiet water, my rhythm returns, and the blades alternately dip and swing.

I am once again on a small pilgrimage of sorts to the particular spot on the creek—*my* spot—where I wrote my wedding vows in 1980, and where, figuratively, I began this book. In the past ten years, places—very small places—have taken on great meaning to me: the weedy irrigation ditch where I stop for water breaks on my frequent bike rides; the shrub-cornered common-area lawn outside our house where I exercise my dog; the tiny al-tar and black cushion where I briefly sit most mornings. This evening, how-ever, I aim for a place that has taken on additional significance.

To live half a century on earth, and half of that right here, is to realize the value of permanence within the context of impermanence. Since writing my vows that day, I have raised three children with Lacey. They pad-dled this stretch as school kids themselves during summer-day Camp Putah programs. If life is a stream, she and I have grabbed ahold of the bank for a time at this spot, to set down roots and plant seed. Eventually, our time will come, and we will float away and release our grasp on this world, like for-mer trees over a cut-bank creek or the charcoal dust of a once vigorous chamise plant in the smoldering chaparral beyond the headwaters. There is a Zen saying: "Die while alive and be completely dead. Then do whatever you will, all is good." It is the spot toward which I paddle that for me has begun to embody this necessary act of acceptance. To become completely alive in a place, perhaps we must decide that it is an acceptable place to die. Somehow, the thought of my eventual ashes at the bottom trophic level of this particular point in the stream is sufficient and fitting thanks for all the local almonds, corn, tomatoes, and fish I have consumed in twenty-five years. I am suddenly reminded of an amusing statistic: California, of all the polit-ically defined states, always sends the highest percentage of its deceased out of state for burial elsewhere, as if somehow, in the longest of runs, living

Figure 10.3

here didn't count. For far too many, California is a temporary island in the stream. I have seen my fill of islands. My special place, toward which I am now vigorously paddling, is a small peninsula jutting just far enough into the stream to create a quiet back eddy. Through droughts and floods in the past eighteen years, it has remained the same relative shape, anchored, iron-ically, by a non-native transplant, Bermuda grass, which, like me, has taken root here as well. There is nothing elaborate, striking, or pristine about this small place. Another reinhabitant, a young blue-gum eucalyptus whose genes evolved in a different hemisphere, has made the peninsula its home.

This evening I reach the designated place panting, violating every preconceived idea I hold of it and of myself, banging the paddle clumsily on the gunwales as I exit the boat. I pull the canoe up on the bank and use it as a stool, sitting on the bow to catch the breath and clear the mind. I have arrived here with too many thoughts: wildfires, creeks, life, death, love, regions, places, the joys and pains of writing this book. I respond by just sitting, breathing, and paying attention. The little rapid in the stream gurgles like a newborn baby. Just upstream from this bend in the creek and within plain sight is the Pedric Road bridge. A deteriorating fifty-five-gallon drum lies in several pieces just across the creek. Small freshwater clams, also relative newcomers to this region, from Japan, anchor to the shallow stream bottom. Although the evening is still very hot, I sense the cooling power of the enveloping vegetation and the cavitating water. A feeding carp breaks a wake in the still, shallow water downstream, and a double trailer truck full of tomatoes barrels across the bridge. Finches in the sandbar willow flit about, crickets hum incessantly, and the half-moon dances with the box elder branches. I hear the sound of a submersible pump pulling irrigation water to the vineyard nearby, while farther away a tractor with the slow, monotone pull of a plow groans at the setting sun. I contribute my own sound, a "kee-kee-kee" aimed at attracting a bird of prey, and I am rewarded by a gliding osprey who lights in the valley oak above me on the opposite creek bank.

I have been to this spot numerous times—in a canoe, on foot, and pedaling by on the gravel road above. I always nod or make some other deliberate gesture toward my spot, as if it were alive. On one occasion I even growled, "I'm not dead yet!" directly and defiantly at it as I stood out of the saddle and hammered my mountain bike past on the road, joyfully feeling the air rushing in and out of my lungs. The spot never answers, and just sits there, waiting patiently. Tonight in the still heat, a new gesture suggests itself to me. Stepping off the bank, I stand facing downstream in the foot-deep water, then sit, butt crunching the cool submerged gravel. Then, tipping backward, I lie down, and the shallow but cold water rushes around my neck and over my shoulder blades like boat wakes. A rush of exhilaration overcomes me as a long day's accumulated heat vanishes within several heartbeats.

In a mere moment, I get up, pull the canoe into the water, and push off downstream, my breath calming and steadying as I paddle with newfound slowness. The postsunset twilight is sweet on my eyes, and the air on my wet skin makes for a perfectly neutral thermal relationship: nothing gained, nothing lost. An unseen beaver slaps a tail warning, followed by a black-crowned night-heron who races past me, heading downstream. The current takes me effortlessly, and I float homeward.

Notes

PREFACE

1. Wes Jackson, *Becoming Native to This Place* (Lexington: University Press of Kentucky, 1995).

INTRODUCTION

1. I heartily credit Peter Berg of Planet Drum Foundation for coining the term *life-place* as a clearer alternative to *bioregion*. See Peter Berg, *Discovering Your Life-Place: A First Bioregional Workbook* (San Francisco: Planet Drum Foundation, 1995).

2. See Hartwell H. Welsh, Jr., "Bioregions: An Ecological and Evolutionary Perspective and a Proposal for California," *California Fish and Game* 80, no. 3 (1994): 97–124; James Hickman, ed., *The Jepson Manual: Higher Plants of California* (Berkeley: University of California Press, 1993); California Resources Agency, *Memorandum of Understanding: California's Coordinated Regional Strategy to Conserve Biological Diversity* (Sacramento: California Resources Agency, 1991); and Philip L. Fradkin, *The Seven States of California: A Natural and Human History* (New York: Henry Holt, 1995).

3. See Sierra Club, "Ecoregions," retrieved February 1, 2001, from www .sierraclub.org/ecoregions/.

4. See Judith Plant, "Revaluing Home: Feminism and Bioregionalism," in *Home! A Bioregional Reader*, ed. V. Andruss et al. (Philadelphia: New Society, 1990), 21–25.

CHAPTER 1. GROUNDING

1. See W. Köppen, *Grundriss der Klimakunde* (Berlin: Walter de Gruyter, 1931); L. R. Holdridge, *Life Zone Ecology*, 2d ed. (San José, Costa Rica: Tropical Research Center, 1967), 206; Frederick Clements and Victor Shelford, *Bioecology* (New York: John Wiley, 1939); Lee R. Dice, *The Biotic Provinces of North America* (Ann Arbor: University of Michigan Press, 1943); Miklos D. F. Udvardy, *A Classification of the Biogeographical Provinces of the World*, IUCN Occa-

sional Paper No. 18 (Morges, Switzerland: International Union for Conservation of Nature and Natural Resources, 1975); Raymond Dasmann, *Environmental Conservation* (New York: John Wiley, 1984); and Robert Bailey, *Ecosystem Geography* (New York: Springer, 1996).

2. See Patric Reuter, "Terroir: The Articulation of Viticultural Place" (master's thesis, University of California, Davis, 1999).

3. See John McPhee, *Assembling California* (New York: Noonday Press, 1993).

4. See American Farmland Trust, *Future Urban Growth in California's Central Valley: The Bottom Line for Agriculture and Taxpayers* (Washington, D.C.: American Farmland Trust, 1995).

5. S. W. Hardwick and D. G. Holtgrieve, *Valley for Dreams: Life and Landscape in the Sacramento Valley* (Lanham, Md.: Rowman and Littlefield, 1996).

6. See California Department of Finance, *Population Projections by Race/Ethnicity for California and Its Counties,* Report 93 P-1 (Sacramento: California Department of Finance, 1993). See also Paul Campbell, *Population Projections for States, by Age, Sex, Race, and Hispanic Origin: 1993 to 2020,* Current Population Reports, P25-1111 (Washington, D.C.: U.S. Bureau of the Census, 1994); Alvin Sokolow and Colin Laird, *Municipal Density and Farmland Protection: An Exploratory Study of Central Valley Patterns,* Research Paper No. 3, California Agriculture and Open Space Policy Series (Davis: University of California, Davis, Agricultural Issues Center, 1996); American Farmland Trust, *Future Urban Growth.*

7. H. O. Carter and C. F. Nuckton, eds., *California's Central Valley: Confluence of Change* (Davis: University of California, Davis, Agricultural Issues Center, 1990).

CHAPTER 2. LIVING

1. See California Resources Agency, *Memorandum of Understanding: California's Coordinated Regional Strategy to Conserve Biological Diversity* (Sacramento: California Resources Agency, 1991).

2. For the evolution of the community-continuum debate in plant biogeography, see Frederick Clements, *Plant Succession: An Analysis of the Development of Vegetation* (Washington, D.C.: Carnegie Institution, 1916); H. A. Gleason, "The Structure and Development of the Plant Association," *Bulletin of the Torrey Botanical Club,* no. 53 (1917): 7–26; Frederick Clements and Victor Shelford, *Bioecology* (New York: John Wiley, 1939); and especially Michael G. Barbour, "American Ecology and American Culture in the 1950s: Who Led Whom?" *Bulletin of the Ecological Society of America* 77, no. 1 (1996); and "Ecological Fragmentation in the Fifties," in *Uncommon Ground,* ed. William Cronon (New York: Norton, 1996).

3. John Sawyer and Todd Keeler-Wolf's *A Manual of California Vegetation* (Sacramento: California Native Plant Society, 1995) is the most thorough and authoritative treatment of California plant associations, or series, available.

4. See Hartwell H. Welsh, Jr., "Bioregions: An Ecological and Evolutionary

Perspective and a Proposal for California," *California Fish and Game* 80, no. 3 (1994): 97–124.

5. See Michael G. Barbour et al., *California's Changing Landscapes* (Sacramento: California Native Plant Society, 1993), for a general discussion of plant communities in California.

6. See John Muir, *The Mountains of California* (New York: Century, 1894).

7. See Alfred Kroeber, *The Patwin and Their Neighbors,* University of California Publications in American Archaeology and Ethnology, vol. 29 (Berkeley: University of California Press, 1932), for the most thorough research on Patwin ethnography and place names.

8. See John Game and Richards Lyon, *Fifty Wildflowers of Bear Valley, Colusa County* (San Francisco: American Land Conservancy, 1996), for the wildflowers of Bear Valley.

9. See Patti Johnson, "The Patwin," in *Handbook of North American Indians,* vol. 8, *California,* ed. Robert Heizer (Washington, D.C.: Smithsonian Institution, 1978), 350–60; and Chester King, "Protohistoric and Historic Archeology," in Heizer, *Handbook,* vol. 8, 58–79.

10. See Michael Marchetti and P. B. Moyle, "Effects of Flow Regime and Habitat Structure on Fish Assemblages in a Regulated California Stream," *Ecological Applications* 11 (2001): 530–39; and Peter B. Moyle, *Inland Fishes of California,* 2d ed. (Berkeley: University of California Press, 2002).

CHAPTER 3. REINHABITING

1. Daniel Kemmis, *Community and the Politics of Place* (Norman: University of Oklahoma Press, 1990).

2. Hazel Henderson, *The Politics of the Solar Age* (New York: Anchor Press, 1981), 25, quoted in Raymond Dasmann, *Environmental Conservation* (New York: John Wiley, 1984), 412.

3. Dasmann, *Environmental Conservation,* 412.

4. See Alfred Kroeber, *Area and Climax,* University of California Publications in American Archeology and Ethnology, vol. 37 (Berkeley: University of California Press, 1936).

5. See James Omernik and Robert Bailey, "Distinguishing between Watersheds and Ecoregions," *Journal of the American Water Resources Association* 33 (1997): 935–49, for a discussion of the differences between ecoregions and watersheds.

6. For Penutian language distribution, see Alfred Kroeber, *Handbook of the Indians of California* (1925; reprint, New York: Dover, 1976); for acorn distribution, see J. R. Griffin and W. D. Critchfield, *The Distribution of Forest Trees in California,* U.S. Forest Service Research Paper PSW 82 (Berkeley, Calif.: Pacific Southwest Forest and Range Experiment Station, 1972).

7. See J. J. Gibson, *The Ecological Approach to Visual Perception* (Boston: Houghton Mifflin, 1979).

8. See Neil Everenden, *The Social Construction of Nature* (Baltimore: Johns Hopkins University Press, 1992).

9. Manuel Castells, *The Rise of the Network Society,* vol. 1 of *The Information Age: Economy, Society and Culture* (Malden, Mass: Blackwell, 1996), and *The Power of Identity,* vol. 2 of *The Information Age: Economy, Society and Culture* (Malden, Mass.: Blackwell, 1997).

10. Castells, *Rise of the Network Society,* 378.

11. Castells, *Power of Identity,* 9.

12. Ibid., 360–61.

13. Ibid., 357.

14. See Joshua Karliner, *The Corporate Planet* (San Francisco: Sierra Club Books, 1997); William Greider, *One World, Ready or Not: The Manic Logic of Global Capitalism* (New York: Simon & Schuster, 1997); John Ralston Saul, *The Unconscious Civilization* (Concord, Ontario: Anansi, 1995).

15. See Kemmis, *Politics of Place;* also Daniel Kemmis, *The Good City and the Good Life* (Boston: Houghton Mifflin, 1995).

16. Daniel Kemmis, "A Democracy to Match Its Landscape," in *Reclaiming the Native Home of Hope: Community, Ecology, and the American West,* ed. Robert B. Keiter (Salt Lake City: University of Utah Press, 1998), 7.

17. Ibid.

18. Mark Nechodom, "Democracy, Ecology and the Politics of Place" (Ph.D. diss., University of California, Davis, 1998); Doug Aberley, "Interpreting Bioregionalism: A Story from Many Voices," in *Bioregionalism,* ed. Michael McGinnis (London: Routledge, 1999), 13–42; Michael V. McGinnis, ed., *Bioregionalism* (London: Routledge, 1999); and Timothy Duane, *Shaping the Sierra* (Berkeley: University of California Press, 1998), all address the relationship between social theory and grassroots action in ecosystem management and bioregionalism.

CHAPTER 4. FULFILLING

1. See Thomas Berry, *The Dream of the Earth* (San Francisco: Sierra Club Books, 1988), 166, 168.

2. See Robert Glotzbach, ed., *A Bridge to the Future: Proceedings of Shasta Bioregional Gathering IV* (Glen Ellen, Calif.: Regeneration Resources, 1995).

3. See Albert Elsasser, "Development of Regional Prehistoric Cultures," in *Handbook of North American Indians,* vol. 8, *California,* ed. Robert Heizer (Washington, D.C.: Smithsonian Institution, 1978), 37–57; Robert Heizer and Albert Elsasser, *The Natural World of the California Indians* (Berkeley: University of California Press, 1980); and Alfred Kroeber, *Handbook of the Indians of California* (1925; reprint, New York: Dover, 1976).

4. See Catherine Callaghan, "Lake Miwok," in *Handbook of North American Indians,* vol. 8, *California,* ed. Robert Heizer (Washington, D.C.: Smithsonian Institution, 1978), 264–73.

CHAPTER 5. IMAGINING

1. I am grateful to Heath Schenker for allowing me to paraphrase wisdom from the book that she edited, *Picturing California's Other Landscape: The Great*

Central Valley (Berkeley: Heyday Books, 1999). Readers interested in the art of the Central Valley are strongly directed toward this volume.

2. See David Robertson, "Photographing California's Other Landscape," in Schenker, *Picturing California's Other Landscape*, 117–55; and Stephen Johnson, Gerald Haslam, and Robert Dawson, *The Great Central Valley: California's Heartland* (Berkeley: University of California Press, 1993).

3. See Stan Yogi, ed., *Highway 99: A Literary Journey through California's Great Central Valley* (Berkeley, Calif.: Heyday Books, 1996).

4. Rachel Dilworth, "The Glory Hole," in *Putah and Cache 3*, ed. David Robertson (Davis: University of California, Davis, Putah-Cache Bioregion Project, 1998). Reprinted by permission of Rachel Dilworth.

5. Maria Melendez, Dan Leroy, Linda Book, Rob Thayer, Laurie Glover, and Amy Boyer, "Tule Fog Haiku," in *Putah and Cache 7*, ed. David Robertson (Davis: University of California, Davis, Putah-Cache Bioregion Project, 1999). Reprinted by permission of the authors.

6. See Lucy Lippard, *The Lure of the Local* (New York: New Press, 1997), 286–87.

7. See Ursula Le Guin, *Always Coming Home* (New York: Bantam, 1985).

8. Ibid., 428.

CHAPTER 6. TRADING

1. Quantities from the 1998 Annual Crop Reports compiled by the California County Agricultural Commissioners, retrieved January 2000 from www.nass.usda.gov/ca/bul/agcom/indexcac.htm.

2. See Herman Daly, *Beyond Growth* (Boston: Beacon Press, 1996), 48.

3. Ibid.; Herman Daly, "Free Trade: The Perils of Deregulation," in *The Case against the Global Economy*, ed. Jerry Mander and Edward Goldsmith (San Francisco: Sierra Club Books, 1996), 229–38; and Herman Daly and John Cobb, *For the Common Good* (Boston: Beacon Press, 1989).

4. John Naisbitt, *Global Paradox* (New York: Avon Books, 1994), 4.

5. Ibid., 20, 21.

6. Ibid., 20; Manuel Castells, *The Power of Identity*, vol. 2 of *The Information Age: Economy, Society and Culture* (Malden, Mass.: Blackwell, 1997), 8.

7. See Jane Jacobs, *Cities and the Wealth of Nations* (New York: Random House, 1984). This book remains the cornerstone of relocalized economics.

8. Ibid., 102.

9. Ibid., 161.

10. Paul Hawken, *The Ecology of Commerce* (New York: Harper, 1993), 197.

11. Ibid.; see also Daly, "Free Trade."

12. Thomas Power, *Lost Landscapes and Failed Economies: The Search for a Value of Place* (Washington, D.C.: Island Press, 1996), 233.

13. See Marc Reisner's *Cadillac Desert: The American West and Its Disappearing Water* (New York: Viking, 1986) and his *Overtapped Oasis: Reform or Revolution for Western Water* (Washington, D.C.: Island Press, 1990).

14. Daly, "Free Trade," 231.

15. Mago Yoshihira, "Global Monoculture and Its Impact on Communities" (M.S. thesis, University of California, Davis, 1996), 103 (based on 1993 data from the Japanese Ministry of Agriculture, Forestry, and Fishery).

16. See W. P. Hedden, *How Great Cities Are Fed* (Boston: D. C. Heath, 1929); Arthur Getz, "Urban Foodsheds," *Permaculture Activist* 7, no. 3 (1991): 26; and John Hendrickson, "The Foodshed: Heuristic Device and Sustainable Alternative to the Food System," paper presented at the Conference on Environment, Culture, and Food Equity, Association for the Study of Food and Society, Pennsylvania State University, State College, Pa., June 3–6, 1993.

17. See Joan Gussow, *Chicken Little, Tomato Sauce and Agriculture: Who Will Produce Tomorrow's Food?* (New York: Bootstrap Press, 1991); Jennifer Wilkins, "Seasonal and Local Diets: Consumers' Role in Achieving a Sustainable Food System," *Research in Rural Sociology and Development* 6 (1995): 149–66; and Gail Feenstra, "Local Food Systems and Sustainable Communities," *American Journal of Alternative Agriculture* 12, no. 1 (1997): 28–36.

18. Retrieved in January 2000 from California Energy Commission, "California Energy Facts," www.energy.ca.gov/html/calif_energy_facts.html.

19. From California Energy Commission data (ibid.) and my original quantitative analysis.

20. Retrieved January 26, 2000, from Public Citizen, "Critical Mass Energy and Environment Program," www.citizen.org/CMEP/RAGE/Nader%27scomen dereg.htm; see also www.citizen.org/CMEP/renewables/greenbuy.htm.

21. For the latest on rice-straw by-products, see www.arb.ca.gov/rice/rice fund.

22. See Vince Bielski, "Paper Panacea: Rice-Straw Paper May Mean More Clean Air in Sacramento," *Sacramento Bee*, June 1996.

23. Retrieved April 2002 from BizStats.com, "Estimated E-Commerce/Online Sales," www.bizstats.com/ecommerce.htm.

24. See Paul Glover, "Creating Ecological Economics with Local Currency," *Whole Earth Review*, Fall 1995, 24–25.

25. Ibid., 25.

CHAPTER 7. PLANNING

1. Per Råberg, "The Ecological Life Region," in *The Life Region: The Social and Cultural Ecology of Sustainable Development*, ed. Per Råberg (New York: Routledge, 1997), 92.

2. Ibid., 93.

3. For a good discussion of "sustainable" planning and design, see Judy Corbett and Michael Corbett, *Designing Sustainable Communities: Learning from Village Homes* (Washington, D.C.: Island Press, 2000).

4. See Timothy Duane, *Shaping the Sierra* (Berkeley: University of California Press, 1998).

5. California Resources Agency, *Memorandum of Understanding: Califor-*

nia's Coordinated Regional Strategy to Conserve Biological Diversity (Sacramento: California Resources Agency, 1991), 1.

6. See ibid., 1; and Mark Nechodom, "Democracy, Ecology and the Politics of Place" (Ph.D. diss., University of California, Davis, 1998).

7. Mark Luccarelli, *Lewis Mumford and the Ecological Region* (New York: Guilford Press, 1995), 26; see also Lewis Mumford, *The Myth of the Machine,* vol. 1, *Technics and Human Development* (New York: Harcourt, Brace and World, 1967); and Doug Aberley, "Interpreting Bioregionalism: A Story from Many Voices," in *Bioregionalism,* ed. Michael McGinnis (London: Routledge, 1999), 13–42.

8. Lewis Mumford, preface to *Design with Nature,* by Ian McHarg (Garden City, N.Y.: American Museum of Natural History, Natural History Press, 1969), viii.

9. See Ian McHarg, *Design with Nature* (Garden City, N.Y.: American Museum of Natural History, Natural History Press, 1969); and Frederick Steiner, *The Living Landscape: An Ecological Approach to Landscape Planning* (New York: McGraw Hill, 2000).

10. See Philip M. Lewis, Jr., *Tomorrow by Design* (New York: John Wiley, 1996).

11. See *Maps with Teeth* (video), dir. Peg Campbell, prod. Heather MacAndrew and David Springbett, Asterisk Productions, available from Bullfrog Films, P.O. Box 149, Oley, PA 19547, Tel: 610-779-8226, www.bullfrogfilms.com; Doug Aberley, ed., *Boundaries of Home: Mapping for Local Empowerment* (Philadelphia: New Society, 1993); and Doug Aberley, ed., *Futures by Design: The Practice of Ecological Planning* (Philadelphia: New Society, 1994).

12. See Christopher Alexander et al., *A Pattern Language* (New York: Oxford University Press, 1977), x.

13. See Joan H. Woodward's "Signature-Based Landscape Design," in *Ecological Design and Planning,* ed. J. Thompson, J. William, and Frederick Steiner (Washington, D.C.: Island Press, 1997), 201–25, and her *Waterstained Landscapes* (Baltimore: Johns Hopkins University Press, 2000).

14. See Urban Ecology, Inc., *Blueprint for a Sustainable Bay Area* (Oakland, Calif.: Urban Ecology, Inc., 1996).

15. See Owen Furuseth and Chris Cocklin, "An Institutional Framework for Sustainable Resource Management: The New Zealand Model," *Natural Resources Journal* 35 (1995): 243–73.

16. See Timothy Beatley and Kristy Manning, *The Ecology of Place* (Washington, D.C.: Island Press, 1997).

17. See Mathis Wackernagel and William Rees, *Our Ecological Footprint: Reducing Human Impact on the Earth* (Philadelphia: New Society, 1996).

18. See Doug Aberley, "Building a Bioregional, Sustainable Alternative," in *Home! A Bioregional Reader,* ed. V. Andruss, C. Plant, and E. Wright (Philadelphia: New Society, 1990) 159–60; and Aberley, *Boundaries of Home.* I have modified these steps somewhat.

CHAPTER 8. BUILDING

1. I am indebted to my assistant Jake Mann for his conceptual work on the patterns in this chapter.

2. See John McPhee, *Assembling California* (New York: Noonday Press, 1993).

3. See the Cache Creek Conservancy's Web site at www.cachecreekconser vancy.org.

4. Blue Ridge–Berryessa Natural Area Conservation Partnership, "Mission Statement," unpublished document, 2001, 1.

5. See the Yolo Basin Foundation's Web site at www.yolobasin.org.

6. American Farmland Trust, *Future Urban Growth in California's Central Valley: The Bottom Line for Agriculture and Taxpayers* (Washington, D.C.: American Farmland Trust, 1995).

7. W. L. Kahrl et al., California Water Atlas (Sacramento: California Department of Water Resources, 1979).

8. John Hendrickson, "The Foodshed: Heuristic Device and Sustainable Alternative to the Food System," paper presented at the Conference on Environment, Culture, and Food Equity, Association for the Study of Food and Society, Pennsylvania State University, State College, Pa., June 3–6, 1993; California Agricultural Commissioner's Office, *California Agricultural Commissioner's Annual Report* (Sacramento: California Agricultural Commission, 1998).

9. California Sustainable Agricultural Research and Education Program, personal communication, April 2001.

10. See Jeremy Rifkin, *Beyond Beef: The Rise and Fall of the Cattle Culture* (New York: Dutton, 1992), 1–5.

11. See the Gamble Ranch's Web site at www.napagrassfedbeef.com.

12. Gene Miyao and Paul Robins, *Influence of Fall-Planted Cover Crop on Rainfall Run-off in a Processing Tomato Production System* (Woodland, Calif.: Yolo County Resource Conservation District, 2001).

13. See the Yolo County Resource Conservation District's Web site for demonstration of several patterns in this chapter (www.yolorcd.ca.gov).

14. See Alvin Sokolow and Colin Laird, *Municipal Density and Farmland Protection: An Exploratory Study of Central Valley Patterns,* Research Paper No. 3, California Agriculture and Open Space Policy Series (Davis: University of California, Davis, Agricultural Issues Center, 1996).

15. See Sacramento Municipal Utility District, "Solar PV Pioneer Programs," retrieved February 2002 from www.smud.org/pv/.

16. See Robert L. Thayer, Jr., *Gray World, Green Heart: Technology, Nature and the Sustainable Landscape* (New York: John Wiley, 1994); Thomas Richman and Associates, *Start at the Source: Residential Site Planning and Design Guidance Manual for Stormwater Quality Protection* (Palo Alto, Calif.: Bay Area Stormwater Management Agencies Association, 1997); and Judy Corbett and Michael Corbett, *Designing Sustainable Communities: Learning from Village Homes* (Washington, D.C.: Island Press, 2000), for more information on natural drainage.

CHAPTER 9. LEARNING

1. See David W. Orr, *Earth in Mind: On Education, Environment, and the Human Prospect* (Washington, D.C.: Island Press, 1994).

2. Neil Postman, *Technopoly: The Surrender of Culture to Technology* (New York: Alfred A. Knopf, 1992), 7.

3. Ibid.

4. Orr, *Earth in Mind*, 8–12.

5. Ibid., 12.

6. See Byrd Schas, "Schools Can Construct the Path Back to Where We Are," *Raise the Stakes: Planet Drum Review* 26 (Spring 1996): 1.

7. See Kirkpatrick Sale, *Dwellers in the Land: The Bioregional Vision* (San Francisco: Sierra Club Books, 1985).

8. Orr, *Earth in Mind*, 12.

9. See Heath Schenker, ed., *Picturing California's Other Landscape: The Great Central Valley* (Berkeley, Calif.: Heyday Books, 1999); and Greg Sarris, *Mabel McKay: Weaving the Dream* (Berkeley: University of California Press, 1994).

10. See the Web site of Adopt-a-Watershed (www. adopt-a-watershed.org) for further information on AAW programs.

11. See Wes Jackson, *Becoming Native to This Place* (Lexington: University Press of Kentucky, 1995), 3.

12. See Ernest L. Boyer, *The Basic School: A Community for Learning* (Princeton, N.J.: Carnegie Foundation for the Advancement of Teaching, 1995).

13. See the Web site of U.C. Davis's Putah-Cache Bioregion Project at http://bioregion.ucdavis.edu.

CHAPTER 10. ACTING

1. Quoted in David Schiller, *The Little Zen Companion* (New York: Workman, 1994), 302.

2. See Edward O. Wilson, *Biophilia: The Human Bond with Other Species* (Cambridge, Mass.: Harvard University Press, 1984).

3. William Least Heat-Moon, *PrairyErth: A Deep Map* (Boston: Houghton-Mifflin, 1991).

4. See Robert N. Bellah et al., *Habits of the Heart: Individualism and Commitment in American Life* (New York: Harper & Row, 1985); Manuel Castells, *The Power of Identity*, vol. 2 of *The Information Age: Economy, Society and Culture* (Malden, Mass.: Blackwell, 1997).

General Bibliography

Abe, Masao. 1992. *A Study of Dogen: His Philosophy and Religion.* Edited by Steven Heine. Albany: State University of New York Press, 1992.

Aberley, Doug. "Building a Bioregional, Sustainable Alternative." In *Home! A Bioregional Reader,* edited by V. Andruss, C. Plant, J. Plant, and E. Wright, 159–60. Philadelphia: New Society, 1990.

———. "Interpreting Bioregionalism: A Story from Many Voices." In *Bioregionalism,* edited by Michael McGinnis, 13–42. London: Routledge, 1999.

———, ed. *Boundaries of Home: Mapping for Local Empowerment.* Philadelphia: New Society, 1993.

———, ed. *Futures by Design: The Practice of Ecological Planning.* Philadelphia: New Society, 1994.

Alexander, Christopher, S. Ishikawa, M. Silverstein, M. Jacobson, I. Fiksdahl-King, and S. Angel. *A Pattern Language.* New York: Oxford University Press, 1977.

Alexander, Donald. "Bioregionalism: Science or Sensibility?" *Environmental Ethics* 12, no. 2 (1990): 161–73.

American Farmland Trust. *Future Urban Growth in California's Central Valley: The Bottom Line for Agriculture and Taxpayers.* Washington, D.C.: American Farmland Trust, 1995.

Andruss, V., C. Plant, J. Plant, and E. Wright, eds. *Home! A Bioregional Reader.* Philadelphia: New Society, 1990.

Bailey, Robert G. 1976. *Ecoregions of the United States.* Ogden, Ut.: U.S. Forest Service, 1976. Map.

———. *Descriptions of the Ecoregions of the United States,* 2d ed. Misc. Pub. No. 1391. Ogden, Ut.: U.S. Forest Service, 1995.

———. *Ecosystem Geography.* New York: Springer, 1996.

———. *Ecoregions: The Ecosystem Geography of the Oceans and Continents.* New York: Springer, 1998.

Barbour, Michael G. "American Ecology and American Culture in the 1950s: Who Led Whom?" *Bulletin of the Ecological Society of America* 77, no. 1 (1996): 44–51.

———. "Ecological Fragmentation in the Fifties." In *Uncommon Ground,* edited by William Cronon, 233–55. New York: Norton, 1996.

Barbour, Michael G., B. Pavlik, F. Drysdale, and S. Lindstrom. *California's Changing Landscapes.* Sacramento: California Native Plant Society, 1993.

Batchelor, Stephen. *Buddhism without Beliefs: A Contemporary Guide to Awakening.* New York: Riverhead Books, 1997.

Beatley, Timothy. *Habitat Conservation Planning: Endangered Species and Urban Growth.* Austin: University of Texas Press, 1994.

Beatley, Timothy, and Kristy Manning. *The Ecology of Place.* Washington, D.C.: Island Press, 1997.

Bellah, Robert N., Richard Madsen, William M. Sullivan, Ann Swidler, and Steven M. Tipton. *Habits of the Heart: Individualism and Commitment in American Life.* New York: Harper & Row, 1985.

Berg, Peter. *Discovering Your Life-Place: A First Bioregional Workbook.* San Francisco: Planet Drum Foundation, 1995.

———, ed. *Reinhabiting a Separate Country: A Bioregional Anthology of Northern California.* San Francisco: Planet Drum Foundation, 1978.

Berg, Peter, and Raymond Dasmann. "Reinhabiting California." In *Home! A Bioregional Reader,* edited by V. Andruss, C. Plant, J. Plant, and E. Wright, 35–38. Philadelphia: New Society, 1990.

Berman, Daniel M., and John T. O'Connor. *Who Owns the Sun? People, Politics, and the Struggle for the Solar Economy.* White River Junction, Vt.: Chelsea Green, 1996.

Berry, Thomas. *The Dream of the Earth.* San Francisco: Sierra Club Books, 1988.

Berry, Wendell. *The Unsettling of America: Culture and Agriculture.* New York: Avon Books, 1977.

———. *Sex, Economy, Freedom, and Community: Eight Essays.* New York: Pantheon, 1993.

———. *Another Turn of the Crank.* Washington, D.C.: Counterpoint Press, 1995.

———. "Community in 17 Sensible Steps." *Utne Reader,* March–April 1995, 71.

Bielski, Vince. "Paper Panacea: Rice-Straw Paper May Mean More Clean Air in Sacramento." *Sacramento Bee,* June, 1996.

Borgmann, Albert. *Crossing the Postmodern Divide.* Chicago: University of Chicago Press, 1992.

Bowers, Chet. "The Role of Education and Ideology in the Transition from a Modern to a More Bioregionally-Oriented Culture." In *Bioregionalism,* edited by Michael V. McGinnis, 191–204. London: Routledge, 1999.

Boyer, Ernest L. *The Basic School: A Community for Learning.* Princeton, N.J.: Carnegie Foundation for the Advancement of Teaching, 1995.

Brave, Ralph. "Flatland: Does the Valley Get into Your Soul?" *Sacramento News and Review* 10, no. 5 (1998): 20–25.

California Department of Finance. *Population Projections by Race/Ethnicity for California and Its Counties.* Report 93 P-1. Sacramento: California Department of Finance, 1993.

California Resources Agency. *Memorandum of Understanding: California's Coordinated Regional Strategy to Conserve Biological Diversity.* Sacramento: California Resources Agency, September 1991.

———. *California Water Plan Update.* Sacramento, Calif.: Department of Water Resources, October 1994.

Callaghan, Catherine. "Lake Miwok." In *Handbook of North American Indians.* Vol. 8, *California,* edited by Robert Heizer, 264–73. Washington, D.C.: Smithsonian Institution, 1978.

Campbell, Paul. *Population Projections for States, by Age, Sex, Race, and Hispanic Origin: 1993 to 2020.* Current Population Reports, P25-1111. Washington, D.C.: U.S. Bureau of the Census, 1994.

Carter, H. O., and C. F. Nuckton, eds. *California's Central Valley: Confluence of Change.* Davis: University of California, Agricultural Issues Center, 1990.

Castells, Manuel. *The Rise of the Network Society.* Vol. 1 of *The Information Age: Economy, Society and Culture.* Malden, Mass: Blackwell, 1996.

———. *The Power of Identity.* Vol. 2 of *The Information Age: Economy, Society and Culture.* Malden, Mass.: Blackwell, 1997.

Clements, Frederick. *Plant Succession: An Analysis of the Development of Vegetation.* Washington, D.C.: Carnegie Institution, 1916.

Clements, Frederick, and Victor Shelford. *Bioecology.* New York: John Wiley, 1939.

Corbett, Judy, and Michael Corbett. *Designing Sustainable Communities: Learning from Village Homes.* Washington, D.C.: Island Press, 2000.

Daly, Herman. *Beyond Growth.* Boston: Beacon Press, 1996.

———. "Free Trade: The Perils of Deregulation." In *The Case against the Global Economy,* edited by Jerry Mander and Edward Goldsmith, 229–38. San Francisco: Sierra Club Books, 1996.

Daly, Herman, and John Cobb. *For the Common Good.* Boston: Beacon Press, 1989.

Dasmann, Raymond. *Environmental Conservation.* New York: John Wiley, 1984.

Dice, Lee R. *The Biotic Provinces of North America.* Ann Arbor: University of Michigan Press, 1943.

Dilek, Y., E. Moores, D. Elthin, and A. Nicholas. *Ophiolite and Oceanic Crust: New Insights from the Ocean Drilling Program.* Geological Society of America Special Paper 349. Boulder, Colo.: Geological Society of America, May 2001.

Dillon, Brian. *History and Prehistory of the Boggs Mountain Demonstration State Forest, Lake County, California.* California Department of Forestry and Fire Protection, Archaeological Report no. 15, vol. 1. Sacramento: California Department of Forestry and Fire Prevention, 1995.

Dilworth, Rachel. "The Glory Hole." In *Putah and Cache 3,* edited by David Robertson, unpaginated. Davis: University of California, Davis, Putah-Cache Bioregion Project, 1998.

Dodge, Jim. "Living by Life: Some Bioregional Theory and Practice." In *Home! A Bioregional Reader,* edited by V. Andruss, C. Plant, J. Plant, and E. Wright, 5–12. Philadelphia: New Society, 1990.

Duane, Timothy. "Managing the Sierra." *California Policy Choices* 8 (1993): 169–94.

———. *Shaping the Sierra.* Berkeley: University of California Press, 1998.

Durning, Alan. "Are We Happy Yet?" In *Ecopsychology: Restoring the Earth, Healing the Mind,* edited by T. Roszak, M. Gomes, and A. Kanner, 68–76. San Francisco: Sierra Club Books, 1995.

———. *This Place on Earth: The Practice of Permanence.* Seattle: Sasquatch Books, 1996.

Elsasser, Albert. "Development of Regional Prehistoric Cultures." In *Handbook of North American Indians.* Vol. 8, *California,* edited by Robert Heizer, 37–57. Washington, D.C.: Smithsonian Institution, 1978.

Everenden, Neil. *The Social Construction of Nature.* Baltimore: Johns Hopkins University Press, 1992.

Feenstra, Gail. "Local Food Systems and Sustainable Communities." *American Journal of Alternative Agriculture* 12, no. 1 (1997): 28–36.

Fisk, Pliny, III. "Bioregions and Biotechnologies: A New Planning Tool for Stable-State Economic Development." Working paper, Center for Maximum Potential Building Systems, Austin, Tex.

———. "Regional Planning and Sustainability: A Conceptual Model for Urban-Rural Linkage." Working paper, Center for Maximum Potential Building Systems, Austin, Tex.

Fleming, Randall. 1999. *Integrated Sustainable Design: Urban Village Development for the Central Valley.* Sustainable Communities Consortium Document, Community Design and Planning Services. University of California, Davis: Department of Environmental Design, 1999.

Forman, Richard T. T. *Land Mosaics.* Cambridge, England: Cambridge University Press, 1995.

Fradkin, Philip L. *The Seven States of California: A Natural and Human History.* New York: Henry Holt, 1995.

Frenkel, Stephen. "Old Theories in New Places? Environmental Determinism and Bioregionalism." *Professional Geographer* 46 (1994): 289–95.

Furuseth, Owen, and Chris Cocklin. "An Institutional Framework for Sustainable Resource Management: The New Zealand Model." *Natural Resources Journal* 35 (1995): 243–73.

Game, John, and Richards Lyon. *Fifty Wildflowers of Bear Valley, Colusa County.* San Francisco: American Land Conservancy, 1996.

Getz, Arthur. "Urban Foodsheds." *Permaculture Activist* 7, no. 3 (1991): 26–27.

Gibson, J. J. *The Ecological Approach to Visual Perception.* Boston: Houghton Mifflin, 1979.

Gleason, H. A. "The Structure and Development of the Plant Association." *Bulletin of the Torrey Botanical Club,* no. 53 (1917): 7–26.

Glendinning, Chellis. "Technology, Trauma, and the Wild." In *Ecopsychology: Restoring the Earth, Healing the Mind,* edited by T. Roszak, M. Gomes, and A. Kanner, 41–54. San Francisco: Sierra Club Books, 1995.

Glenn, Joshua. "Beardless in Barnesville: Getting Plain at the Second Luddite Congress." *Utne Reader* 76 (1996): 80–83.

Glotzbach, Robert, ed. *A Bridge to the Future: Proceedings of Shasta Bioregional Gathering IV.* Glen Ellen, Calif.: Regeneration Resources, 1995.

Glover, Paul. "Creating Ecological Economics with Local Currency." *Whole Earth Review,* Fall 1995, 24–25.

Godfrey, N. J., B. G. Beaudoin, and S. L. Klemperer. "Ophiolitic Basement to the Great Valley Forearc Basin, California, from Seismic and Gravity Data: Implications for Crustal Growth at the North American Continental Margin." *Geological Society of America Bulletin* 109 (1997): 1536–62.

Goldhaft, Judy. "History of Bioregionalism." In *A Bridge to the Future: Proceedings of Shasta Bioregional Gathering IV,* edited by Robert Glotzbach, 5–8. Glen Ellen, Calif.: Regeneration Resources, 1995.

Greider, William. *One World, Ready or Not: The Manic Logic of Global Capitalism.* New York: Simon & Schuster, 1997.

Griffin, J. R., and W. D. Critchfield. *The Distribution of Forest Trees in California.* U.S. Forest Service Research Paper PSW 82. Berkeley, Calif.: Pacific Southwest Forest and Range Experiment Station, 1972.

Groening, Gert, and Joachim Wolschke-Bulmahn. "Some Notes on the Mania for Native Plants in Germany." *Landscape Journal* 11, no. 2 (1992): 116–26.

Gussow, Joan. *Chicken Little, Tomato Sauce and Agriculture: Who Will Produce Tomorrow's Food?* New York: Bootstrap Press, 1991.

Halstead, Ted, and Clifford Cobb. "The Need for New Measurements of Progress." In *The Case against the Global Economy,* edited by Jerry Mander and Edward Goldsmith, 197–206. San Francisco: Sierra Club Books, 1996.

Hardison, O. B., Jr. *Disappearing through the Skylight: Culture and Technology in the Twentieth Century.* New York: Viking, 1989.

Hawken, Paul. *The Ecology of Commerce.* New York: Harper, 1993.

Heat-Moon, William Least. *PrairyErth: A Deep Map.* Boston: Houghton-Mifflin, 1991.

Hedden, W. P. *How Great Cities Are Fed.* Boston: D. C. Heath, 1929.

Heizer, Robert, ed. *Handbook of North American Indians.* Vol. 8, *California.* Washington, D.C.: Smithsonian Institution, 1978.

Heizer, Robert, and Albert Elsasser. *The Natural World of the California Indians.* Berkeley: University of California Press, 1980.

Henderson, Hazel. *The Politics of the Solar Age.* New York: Anchor Press, 1981.

Hendrickson, John. "The Foodshed: Heuristic Device and Sustainable Alternative to the Food System." Paper presented at the Conference on Environment, Culture, and Food Equity, Association for the Study of Food and Society, Pennsylvania State University, State College, Pa., June 3–6, 1993.

Hickman, James, ed. *The Jepson Manual: Higher Plants of California.* Berkeley: University of California Press, 1993.

Higgs, Eric. 1991. "A Quantity of Engaging Work to Be Done: Ecological Restoration and Morality in a Technological Culture." *Restoration and Management Notes* 9, no. 2 (1991): 97–104.

Holdridge, L. R. *Life Zone Ecology.* 2d ed. San José, Costa Rica: Tropical Research Center, 1967.

Holmes, Hannah. 1993. "Living Where You Live: Bioregionalists Reinvent 'Home.'" *Ms Magazine,* September/October 1993, 30–31.

Jackson, Wes. *Becoming Native to This Place.* Lexington: University Press of Kentucky, 1995.

Jacobs, Jane. *Cities and the Wealth of Nations.* New York: Random House, 1984.

Johnson, Patti. "The Patwin." In *Handbook of North American Indians.* Vol. 8, *California,* edited by Robert Heizer, 350–60. Washington, D.C.: Smithsonian Institution, 1978.

Johnson, Stephen, Gerald Haslam, and Robert Dawson. *The Great Central Valley: California's Heartland.* Berkeley: University of California Press, 1993.

Kahrl, W. L., et al. *California Water Atlas.* Sacramento: California Department of Water Resources, 1979.

Karliner, Joshua. *The Corporate Planet.* San Francisco: Sierra Club Books, 1997.

Kellert, Stephen R., and E. O. Wilson, eds. *The Biophilia Hypothesis.* Washington, D.C.: Island Press, 1993.

Kemmis, Daniel. *Community and the Politics of Place.* Norman: University of Oklahoma Press, 1990.

———. *The Good City and the Good Life.* Boston: Houghton Mifflin, 1995.

———. "A Democracy to Match Its Landscape." In *Reclaiming the Native Home of Hope: Community, Ecology, and the American West,* edited by Robert B. Keiter, 2–14. Salt Lake City: University of Utah Press, 1998.

King, Chester. "Protohistoric and Historic Archaeology." In *Handbook of North American Indians,* vol. 8, *California,* edited by Robert Heizer, 58–79. Washington, D.C.: Smithsonian Institution, 1978.

Köppen, W. *Grundriss der Klimakunde.* Berlin: Walter de Gruyter, 1931.

Kroeber, Alfred. *The Patwin and Their Neighbors.* University of California Publications in American Archaeology and Ethnology, vol. 29. Berkeley: University of California Press, 1932.

———. *Area and Climax.* University of California Publications in American Archaeology and Ethnology, vol. 37. Berkeley: University of California Press, 1936.

———. *Handbook of the Indians of California.* 1925. Reprint, New York: Dover, 1976.

Kroker, Arthur, and Weinstein, Michael A. *Data Trash: The Theory of the Virtual Class.* New York: St. Martin's Press, 1994.

Le Guin, Ursula. *Always Coming Home.* New York: Bantam, 1985.

Leopold, Aldo. *A Sand County Almanac.* New York: Oxford University Press, 1949.

Lewis, Martin W. *Green Delusions: An Environmentalist Critique of Radical Environmentalism.* Durham, N.C.: Duke University Press, 1992.

Lewis, Philip M., Jr. *Tomorrow by Design.* New York: John Wiley, 1996.

Lippard, Lucy. *The Lure of the Local.* New York: New Press, 1997.

Lipschutz, Ronnie D. *Global Civil Society and Global Environmental Gover-*

nance: *The Politics of Nature from Place to Planet*. Albany: State University of New York Press, 1996.

Luccarelli, Mark. *Lewis Mumford and the Ecological Region*. New York: Guilford Press, 1995.

Mander, Jerry, and Edward Goldsmith, eds. *The Case against the Global Economy*. San Francisco: Sierra Club Books, 1996.

Marchetti, Michael, and P. B. Moyle. "Effects of Flow Regime and Habitat Structure on Fish Assemblages in a Regulated California Stream." *Ecological Applications* 11 (2001): 530–39.

McGinnis, Michael V., ed. *Bioregionalism*. London: Routledge, 1999.

McGinnis, Michael V., Freeman House, and William Jordan. "Bioregional Restoration: Re-Establishing an Ecology of Shared Identity." In *Bioregionalism*, edited by Michael McGinnis, 205–22. London: Routledge, 1999.

McHarg, Ian. *Design with Nature*. Garden City, N.Y.: American Museum of Natural History, Natural History Press, 1969.

———. *A Quest for Life: An Autobiography*. New York: John Wiley, 1996.

McHarg, Ian, and Frederick R. Steiner. *To Heal the Earth: Selected Writings of Ian L. McHarg*. Washington, D.C.: Island Press, 1998.

McPhee, John. *Assembling California*. New York: Noonday Press, 1993.

McTaggart, W. Ronald. "Bioregionalism and Regional Geography: Place, People, and Networks." *Canadian Geographer* 37 (1993): 307–19.

Meadows, Donella, D. L. Meadows, and J. Randers. *Beyond the Limits*. Post Hills, Vt.: Chelsea, 1992.

Melendez, Maria, Dan Leroy, Linda Book, Rob Thayer, Laurie Glover, and Amy Boyer. "Tule Fog Haiku." In *Putah and Cache 7*, edited by David Robertson, unpaginated. Davis: University of California, Davis, Putah-Cache Bioregion Project, 1999.

Meriam, C. Hart. *Life Zones and Crop Zones of the United States*. Biological Survey Bulletin 10. Washington, D.C.: U.S. Department of Agriculture, 1898.

Meyrowitz, Joshua. *No Sense of Place: The Impact of Electronic Media on Social Behavior*. New York: Oxford University Press, 1985.

Miller, D., ed. *The Lewis Mumford Reader*. New York: Pantheon, 1986.

Miller, Kenton. *Balancing the Scales: Guidelines for Increasing Biodiversity's Chances through Bioregional Management*. Washington, D.C.: World Resources Institute, 1996.

Mills, Stephanie. *Whatever Happened to Ecology?* San Francisco: Sierra Club Books, 1985.

———. *In Service of the Wild*. Boston: Beacon Press, 1995.

Miyao, Gene, and Paul Robins. *Influence of Fall-Planted Cover Crop on Rainfall Run-off in a Processing Tomato Production System*. Woodland, Calif.: Yolo County Resource Conservation District, 2001.

Morris, Davis. "Free Trade: The Great Destroyer." In *The Case against the Global Economy*, edited by Jerry Mander and Edward Goldsmith, 218–28. San Francisco: Sierra Club Books, 1996.

Moyle, Peter B. *Inland Fishes of California.* 2d ed. Berkeley: University of California Press, 2002.

Muir, John. *The Mountains of California.* New York: Century, 1894.

Mumford, Lewis. *Values for Survival.* New York: Harcourt, Brace, 1946.

———. *The Myth of the Machine.* Vol. 1, *Technics and Human Development.* New York: Harcourt, Brace and World, 1967.

———. Preface to *Design with Nature,* by Ian McHarg. Garden City, N.Y.: American Museum of Natural History, Natural History Press, 1969.

Naess, Arne, and David Rothenberg. *Ecology, Community and Lifestyle.* Cambridge, England: Cambridge University Press, 1989.

Naisbitt, John. *Global Paradox.* New York: Avon Books, 1994.

Natural Resources Law Center. *The Watershed Source Book: Watershed-Based Solutions to Natural Resource Problems.* Boulder: University of Colorado School of Law, 1995.

Nechodom, Mark. "Democracy, Ecology and the Politics of Place." Ph.D. diss., University of California, Davis, 1998.

Norberg-Hodge, Helena. "Shifting Direction: From Global Dependence to Local Independence." In *The Case against the Global Economy,* edited by Jerry Mander and Edward Goldsmith, 393–406. San Francisco: Sierra Club Books, 1996.

Odum, Eugene P. *Fundamentals of Ecology.* 3d ed. Philadelphia: W. B. Saunders, 1971.

Omernik, James, and Robert Bailey. "Distinguishing between Watersheds and Ecoregions." *Journal of the American Water Resources Association* 33 (1997): 935–49.

Orr, David W. *Earth in Mind: On Education, Environment, and the Human Prospect.* Washington, D.C.: Island Press, 1994.

Parsons, James. "On 'Bioregionalism' and 'Watershed Consciousness.'" *Professional Geographer* 37, no. 1 (1985): 1–6.

Plant, Judith. "Revaluing Home: Feminism and Bioregionalism." In *Home! A Bioregional Reader,* edited by V. Andruss, C. Plant, J. Plant, and E. Wright, 21–25. Philadelphia: New Society, 1990.

Postman, Neil. *Technopoly: The Surrender of Culture to Technology.* New York: Alfred A. Knopf, 1992.

———. *The End of Education: Redefining the Value of School.* New York: Vintage, 1995.

Power, Thomas. *Lost Landscapes and Failed Economies: The Search for a Value of Place.* Washington, D.C.: Island Press, 1996.

Råberg, Per, ed. *The Life Region: The Social and Cultural Ecology of Sustainable Development.* New York: Routledge, 1997.

Reich, Robert. *The Work of Nations.* New York: Vintage, 1992.

Reiniger, Clair. "Bioregional Planning and Ecosystem Protection." In *Ecological Planning and Design,* edited by Frederick Steiner and William Thompson, 185–200. New York: John Wiley, 1997.

Reisner, Marc. *Cadillac Desert: The American West and Its Disappearing Water.* New York: Viking, 1986.

————. *Overtapped Oasis: Reform or Revolution for Western Water.* Washington, D.C.: Island Press, 1990.

Reuter, Patrick. "Terroir: The Articulation of Viticultural Place." Master's thesis, University of California, Davis, 1999.

Richman, Thomas, and Associates. *Start at the Source: Residential Site Planning and Design Guidance Manual for Stormwater Quality Protection.* Palo Alto, Calif.: Bay Area Stormwater Management Agencies Association, 1997.

Rifkin, Jeremy. *Beyond Beef: The Rise and Fall of the Cattle Culture.* New York: Dutton, 1992.

————. *The End of Work: The Decline of the Global Labor Force and the Dawn of the Post-Market Era.* New York: Tarcher/Putnam, 1995.

Robertson, David. "Bioregionalism in American Nature Writing." In *American Nature Writers,* edited by John Elder, 1013–24. New York: Scribners, 1996.

————. *Real Matter.* Salt Lake City: University of Utah Press, 1997.

————. "Photographing California's Other Landscape." In *Picturing California's Other Landscape: The Great Central Valley,* edited by Heath Schenker, 117–55. Berkeley, Calif.: Heyday Books, 1999.

Sacramento Municipal Utility District. "Solar PV Pioneer Programs." Retrieved February 2002 from www.smud.org/pv/.

Sale, Kirkpatrick. *Dwellers in the Land: The Bioregional Vision.* San Francisco: Sierra Club Books, 1985.

Sarris, Greg. *Mabel McKay: Weaving the Dream.* Berkeley: University of California Press, 1994.

Saul, John Ralston. *The Unconscious Civilization.* Concord, Ontario: Anansi, 1995.

Sawyer, John, and Todd Keeler-Wolf. *A Manual of California Vegetation.* Sacramento: California Native Plant Society, 1995.

Schas, Byrd. "Schools Can Construct the Path Back to Where We Are." *Raise the Stakes: Planet Drum Review,* no. 26, Spring 1996, 1.

Schenker, Heath, ed. *Picturing California's Other Landscape: The Great Central Valley.* Berkeley, Calif.: Heyday Books, 1999.

————. "Picturing California's Other Landscape." In *Picturing California's Other Landscape: The Great Central Valley,* edited by Heath Schenker, 15–89. Berkeley, Calif.: Heyday Books, 1999.

Schiller, David. *The Little Zen Companion.* New York: Workman, 1994.

Sierra Club. "Ecoregions." Retrieved February 1, 2001, from www.sierraclub.org/ecoregions/.

Silver, Michele. "The Ultimate Barter (It's about Time)." *Mother Earth News,* August/September 1993, 32–67.

Smith, Gregory. "Shaping Bioregional Schools." *Whole Earth Review,* Winter 1993, 70–74.

Snyder, Gary. *Turtle Island.* New York: New Directions, 1974.

————. *The Practice of the Wild.* San Francisco: North Point Press, 1990.

————. *A Place in Space.* Washington, D.C.: Counterpoint, 1995.

————. *The Gary Snyder Reader.* Washington, D.C.: Counterpoint, 1999.

Sokolow, Alvin, and Colin Laird. *Municipal Density and Farmland Protection: An Exploratory Study of Central Valley Patterns.* Research Paper No. 3, California Agriculture and Open Space Policy Series. Davis: University of California, Davis, Agricultural Issues Center, 1996.

Steiner, Frederick. *The Living Landscape: An Ecological Approach to Landscape Planning.* New York: McGraw Hill, 2000.

Stoll, Clifford. *Silicon Snake Oil: Second Thoughts on the Information Superhighway.* New York: Doubleday, 1995.

Thayer, Robert L., Jr. *Gray World, Green Heart: Technology, Nature and the Sustainable Landscape.* New York: John Wiley, 1994.

———. "Information Saturation and the Dilution of Place." In *Nature and Technology,* edited by Gina Crandall, 131–42. Proceedings, 1995. Council of Educators in Landscape Architecture Conference, Ames, Iowa, 1996.

Thomashow, Mitchell. "Toward a Cosmopolitan Bioregionalism." In *Bioregionalism,* edited by Michael McGinnis, 121–32. London: Routledge, 1999.

Thompson, J. William. "Commonsense Visionary." *Landscape Architecture* 86, no. 7 (1996): 66–71.

Thompson, J. William, and Frederick Steiner, eds. *Ecological Design and Planning.* Washington, D.C.: Island Press, 1997.

Udvardy, Miklos D. F. *Dynamic Zoogeography, with Special Reference to Land Animals.* New York: Van Nostrand Rinehold, 1969.

———. *A Classification of the Biogeographical Provinces of the World.* IUCN Occasional Paper No. 18. Morges, Switzerland: International Union for Conservation of Nature and Natural Resources, 1975.

U.S. Army Corps of Engineers. *Environmental Assessment, Yolo Basin Wetlands.* Sacramento, Calif: U.S. Army Corps of Engineers, Sacramento District, South Pacific Division, September 1995.

U.S. Department of Agriculture. *Agricultural Statistics, 2000.* Washington, D.C.: USDA. Table 7–72.

Urban Ecology, Inc. *Blueprint for a Sustainable Bay Area.* Oakland, Calif.: Urban Ecology, Inc., 1996.

Wackernagel, Mathis, and William Rees. *Our Ecological Footprint: Reducing Human Impact on the Earth.* Philadelphia: New Society, 1996.

Wallace, Alfred Russell. *The Geographical Distribution of Animals.* London: Macmillan, 1876.

Welsh, Hartwell H., Jr. "Bioregions: An Ecological and Evolutionary Perspective and a Proposal for California." *California Fish and Game* 80, no. 3 (1994): 97–124.

Wilkins, Jennifer. "Seasonal and Local Diets: Consumers' Role in Achieving a Sustainable Food System." *Research in Rural Sociology and Development* 6 (1995): 149–66.

Williams, Daniel R. "Mapping Place Meanings for Ecosystem Management." Technical report submitted to the Interior Columbia River Basin Ecosystem Management Project, U.S. Forest Service, Walla Walla, Wash., 1995.

Wilson, Edward O. *Biophilia: The Human Bond with Other Species*. Cambridge, Mass.: Harvard University Press, 1984.

Woodward, Joan H. "Signature-Based Landscape Design." In *Ecological Design and Planning*, edited by J. Thompson, J. William, and Frederick Steiner, 201-25. Washington, D.C.: Island Press, 1997.

————. *Waterstained Landscapes*. Baltimore: Johns Hopkins University Press, 2000.

Wright, Robert. *Three Scientists and Their Gods*. New York: Harper & Row, 1988.

Yaffee, Steven, Ali Phillips, Irene Frentz, Paul Hareby, Sussanne Maleki, and Barbara Thorpe. *Ecosystem Management in the United States*. Washington, D.C.: Island Press, 1996.

Yogi, Stan, ed. *Highway 99: A Literary Journey through California's Great Central Valley*. Berkeley, Calif.: Heyday Books, 1996.

Yoshihira, Mago. "Global Monoculture and Its Impact on Communities." M.S. thesis, University of California, Davis, 1996.

Index

Page numbers in italics indicate figures and tables.

Text: 10/13 Aldus
Display: Franklin Gothic
Cartographer: Bill Nelson
Compositor: Integrated Composition Systems
Printer and Binder: Edwards Brothers, Inc.